DOTTIR

DOTTIR

My Journey to Becoming a Two-Time
CROSSFIT GAMES CHAMPION

KATRIN DAVIDSDOTTIR

with RORY McKERNAN

ST. MARTIN'S
PRESS
NEW YORK

First published in the United States by St. Martin's Press,
an imprint of St. Martin's Publishing Group

DOTTIR. Copyright © 2019 by Katrin Davidsdottir. Foreword copyright © 2019
by Ben Bergeron. All rights reserved. Printed in the United States of America.
For information, address St. Martin's Publishing Group, 120 Broadway,
New York, NY 10271.

www.stmartins.com

The Library of Congress Cataloging-in-Publication Data is available upon request.

ISBN 978-1-250-14264-1 (hardcover)
ISBN 978-1-250-14265-8 (ebook)

Our books may be purchased in bulk for promotional, educational, or business
use. Please contact your local bookseller or the Macmillan Corporate and
Premium Sales Department at 1-800-221-7945, extension 5442, or by email at
MacmillanSpecialMarkets@macmillan.com.

First Edition: August 2019

10 9 8 7 6 5 4 3 2 1

Think to the sky,
Keep your feet on the ground,
And your heart in the right place.
Remember: Light up the day with the rays of appreciation.

These words were written by my grandmother,
Hervör Jónasdóttir, to whom this book is dedicated. I think
about them daily and try my best to live my life by them.

CONTENTS

AUTHOR'S NOTE

Surnames in Iceland follow the patronymic tradition of our Viking relatives. A father's first name becomes a prefix for his children's. Gender determines the rest. All of us are *"sons"* and *"dottirs."* My dad is David, so I am Davidsdottir and my brother is Davidsson.

In 2009, CrossFit was still a curiosity to people outside its ranks. That summer this fanatically enthusiastic community gained a curiosity of its own—the country of Iceland—when Annie Thorisdottir burst onto the scene at the second annual CrossFit Games. Two years later she brought home the title Fittest Woman on Earth.

Over the next decade the dominance of Iceland's female athletes grew with the sport: Annie, Sara Sigmundottir, and I all fighting for the top spot at the Games. Thorisdottir, Sigmundsdottir, and Davidsdottir. One country. Three hundred thirty thousand inhabitants. Ten podiums. Four championships. Two silver medals. Four bronze. All Dottirs.

The Dottirs are no longer a curiosity at the CrossFit Games; we are a dominant force. The word itself has become symbolic of power, strength, and greatness.

The proud tradition of Icelandic Dottirs goes back long before CrossFit on our tiny island, but the ethos of the CrossFit community fits in perfectly with our culture.

We value capabilities over looks. We value hard work and respect. Feelings of oneness and community unite us. Additionally, Iceland has the most gender equality in the world, so it means a lot to me that men and women at the CrossFit Games have the exact same workouts, prize money, and television airtime.

I am so proud to be part of all this. I love how every female in Iceland can relate to this and wear the name "Dottir" with pride. It brings me so much pride that I thought it was only fitting for my book to carry the name as its title!

I hope that reading about my journey gives you confidence in your own capabilities. I hope you believe that with hard work and persistence, you, too, can accomplish anything you dream of. I hope you find the same inner strength and power for yourself that "Dottir" gives me.

Here is to you being the *best* you!

SLED DOG

SLEÐAHUNDUR

In her first year competing at the CrossFit Games, Katrin Davids-dottir finished in thirtieth place.

She fared slightly better the following year, finishing twenty-fourth at the 2013 Games.

In 2014, she didn't compete at the Games, having failed to qualify during the Meridian Regional.

At this point, lots of other people in similar situations might have seen the writing on the wall and quite reasonably concluded, "Maybe this isn't for me." After three years of training and competing to become the Fittest on Earth, Katrin seemed to be moving backward.

Certainly, many people lose interest after a lot less. Would-be golfers pack it in after a couple of lessons when their progress stalls. Scores of people give up piano when they don't become a concert pianist after a year of practicing. From where she stood in 2014, it would have made sense for Katrin to conclude that she just wasn't destined to be among the elite of the elite.

She might have shrugged and gone back to the gym, content with being a "Games Athlete"—an extraordinary group of humans—and just enjoyed the experience year after year. Or she might have quit, discouraged by the level of discipline, training, and sacrifice it takes to be mediocre at the CrossFit Games.

Katrin did something else.

Katrin dug her heels in. She decided that she did want to be among the elite of the elite, and she was willing to completely reinvent herself to do it. At the age of twenty-two, Kat went pro. She left the familiar comforts of her family, friends, and country behind and started a new life in Boston, training like a professional athlete with me at my gym, CrossFit New England (CFNE).

The way I build an athlete is from the inside out. I have no idea if this is the right approach, but it's the way I do it. It starts with character first, and there are four traits in particular I look for when deciding to take on a new athlete—coachability, confidence, positivity, and passion. From the beginning, Katrin has embodied these qualities better than any athlete I've worked with.

Before she moved to Boston, Katrin had been to CFNE a handful of times for various training camps. During these early visits, one of the things that stood out to me was how coachable she was. She *wanted* to be coached. She *loved* feedback. So many athletes receive coaching cautiously, or even painfully. As their performance is being critiqued, you can see it in their eyes—they're wondering what your criticism means in the bigger picture. *Does Ben not think I'm a good athlete? Does this mean Ben doesn't like me? What if he doesn't want to coach me anymore? Does he think I'm not trying hard enough?* From the beginning, Katrin was different. When Katrin absorbs feedback, she takes it at face value, with no thought other than how she can use the information to get better. If there is the smallest chance it might make her better, she wants to know about it.

Over the years, Kat's coachability has evolved into a super-power. She understands and truly believes in the notion that "you win or you learn." To her, it's never about "passing the test," because in her mind, there is no test—everything is simply an opportunity to learn or improve in some way. It's the reason that, even as a two-time champion, she's continued to grow and improve, and it's what makes coaching her so exciting.

The second thing I look for in my athletes is confidence, but it's not most people's understanding of confidence. To me, "confidence" is not walking onto the competition floor knowing you can win. Confidence is going out onto the floor knowing that no matter what happens, you'll be able to deliver your best; that no amount of adversity can prevent you from meeting your potential. Katrin not only does this, but has internalized it as part of her worldview—"be the best me" is a phrase she's popularized. Kat has figured out something that few competitors grasp: that the best result she can possibly hope for is the best she's capable of, and that other people's results have nothing to do with her best effort.

The most poignant example of this occurred at the 2015 Games, during a legless rope climb workout in which she finished in fifteenth place. Despite multiple top-five finishes that year, Kat regards that legless rope climb workout as her best performance of the weekend because of the way she was able to stay confident in *her* abilities, ignore what was happening around her, and deliver the best result *she* was capable of. It's one of my proudest memories as her coach.

The third quality I look for in an athlete is positivity, for the simple reason that what we focus on we see more of. If an athlete can look at a "bad" situation and see opportunities instead of obstacles, they'll perform better. Most people understand this in principle—of course being positive is more productive than being negative—but putting it into practice is much more difficult. Katrin has learned how to shift from a negative headspace back to a positive outlook better than anyone I've ever met. She never hangs on to the negative and, as a result, is always moving forward.

During the 2016 Games, for example, several athletes were asked by a documentarian how they were feeling before the beach event. The day before had been brutally long—even by CrossFit Games standards—with travel to and competition at a rugged off-site venue, followed by unexpected delays on the return trip that kept all the athletes up until 1 a.m. When asked, one of the women described how much harder this year was compared to years past. She complained about the early flight, the brutal workouts, and the limited amount of sleep she had gotten because of the delays. When asked the same question, Katrin answered with her patented positivity, noting how much she had been able to sleep during the delays and how fired up she was to be competing again already. As ever, her perception of her circumstances allowed her to see advantage and opportunity where many of her competitors saw adversity and difficulty.

The fourth thing I look for is passion. At least it was, until I started working with Katrin. Passion, I reasoned, was crucial to enduring the level of work, sacrifice, and discomfort that success in this sport demands. But Katrin isn't passionate. When it comes to training for the CrossFit Games, Kat is 5 or 6 degrees past passion, in a land most people would call obsession. Over the years, Katrin showed me that to be exceptional, passion is not nearly enough. She didn't go from being a mediocre Games athlete to winning back-to-back Games championships by being passionate—she got there by being obsessed.

As amazing as she is as an athlete, Kat is an even more extraordinary person.

She is whip-smart, perceptive, and thoughtful. She smiles easily and often, and has a laugh that sounds like confetti and makes everything funnier. Katrin doesn't say anything she doesn't mean, or talk just to make conversation—whether you're talking about chronic disease rates in the United States or Taylor Swift's latest music video, Kat will have a thoughtful, well-reasoned opinion and won't be afraid to tactfully disagree with yours.

More than anything, though, Katrin is an incredible friend. There are two kind of friendships, I think. There are the kind of friends you hang out with and talk about the workout, the weather, and how the Patriots are doing this season. And then there are the friends you share your hopes and dreams with. The kind you talk to about your fears and your insecurities. The kind who know your triumphs and your struggles. Anyone who has the privilege of calling Kat their friend will agree that she doesn't do superficial friendships. Katrin is thoughtful, selfless, and empathetic in a way that very few people are, and she has a way of making the people she loves feel important, appreciated, and understood. Hanging out with Kat makes you feel like you're in a really small gang, and that together, you can do anything.

Her friendship is especially meaningful to me because I don't have a lot of friends. I have a small handful of people that I'm close with, and Katrin is one of them.

I think one of the signs of a deep friendship is the ability to have long silences without them ever feeling awkward. On Cape Cod last summer, my daughter Maya observed that Katrin and I can, and often do, sit at the breakfast table in complete silence for upward of thirty minutes. She was right—almost every morning on the Cape started this way. Katrin would sip her coffee and eat her bowl of precisely measured macros while I tucked into whatever Paleo Power Meal I had pulled out of the fridge. Every once in a while one of us might make a comment, but mostly we just sat and ate together in contented silence, completely comfortable just being in each other's company.

The same level of trust that allows Katrin and I to sit together in comfortable silence also allows us to be vulnerable with each other. In the moments immediately following the conclusion of the 2017 CrossFit Games, I knew Katrin's disappointing results were largely my fault. I hadn't been able to see it until that moment, but I realized with a sinking feeling that I had been distracted all year, had said yes to too many things, and hadn't given her the attention she deserved. In short, I hadn't held up my end of the bargain. It broke my heart to realize that she had given me everything she had, and I had let her down.

The easy thing to do in that situation would have been to sweep those sentiments under the rug. I could have presented Katrin with some made-up reasons to explain why she hadn't been able to perform the way she always had, and she might have believed me. But I've always believed that deep friendships demand more of you. The fact that I was afraid to tell Katrin that I had let her down meant that was exactly what I needed to say. An emotional, tear-filled, twenty-five-minute apology was the hard thing to do, but it was the only thing worthy of our friendship.

One of the reasons I can say anything to Katrin is because we're on the same path. I think all deep relationships are characterized by a kind of oneness—a shared vision or set of priorities. With my wife, Heather, this is our love, our family, and our passion for health. With Katrin, it's a shared vision for what we're trying to create together, which is maximizing her performance as a Cross-Fit Games athlete.

My oneness with Kat started when we unknowingly decided to "go pro" at the same time. The timing could not have better—I was ready to invest everything I had into being a better coach at the exact same moment that she was ready to invest everything she had into being a better athlete. We began this journey together, at the same starting point. Our partnership has always been on equal footing; we figure things out together, test and tweak them together, and get better together.

A lot of this has taken place during car rides. Due to the nature of our jobs, Katrin and I travel a lot together—we drive to training camps, competitions, seminars, and sponsor events. Over the years, these trips have become analogous to a Vulcan mind-meld, and are part of our secret sauce.

One of the first times this happened was on the way to Power Monkey Camp in 2015. Katrin and I had been working together for a few months, and we spent the entire ninety-minute drive through the backwoods of Tennessee talking about mind-set principles and how they applied to our approach to the CrossFit Games. We talked about what it means to be a competitor, and the importance of your inner coach. It wasn't like I was telling Katrin these things—we were sharing our thoughts and formulating the principles that would become the foundation for how we would operate going forward. We bounced ideas back and forth, let them roll around in the car with us, and slowly stitched together a vision for what we were trying to create together. By the time we arrived at Power Monkey, we felt like we had discovered a fourth law of gravity. We had tapped into a new power source that has continuously sparked us both forward professionally, personally, and together.

Part of the reason I'm so close with Katrin is because I've spent so much time around her. When she first moved to Boston, she lived with me and my family for a year. Even when she got her own place, I would see her for three to four hours a day while I coached her. One or two days a week, I coach her for the entire day, then she comes over to my house and has dinner with my family. In the summers before the Games, she comes with us to

Cape Cod and lives in our summer home. Somewhere along the way, Katrin became part of my family. She is one of Heather's closest friends, and is like a sister to my daughter Maya and my son Jonah. My youngest son, Bode, has grown up watching Katrin and doesn't know any world other than one full of strong and capable women. My youngest daughter, Harley Love, wants to be an Icelandic princess just like Katrin when she grows up.

You know her as Katrin Tanja Davidsdottir, two-time CrossFit Games champion and one of the fiercest competitors on the planet. I hope that by reading her story, you get to know Kat—the Kat I have had the privilege of calling my athlete, best friend, and *Dóttir*.

Every training session I've ever had with Katrin has ended the same way. After we've debriefed the day, she always gives me a hug and thanks me. "Thank you for coaching me today," she'll say, with her trademark fifty-megawatt smile. Kat, the most grateful person I've ever met, is always thanking someone for something. But the truth is, we should be thanking her.

Thank you, Kat, for everything.

—*Ben Bergeron*

DOTTIR

1

YOU WIN OR YOU LEARN

Þú Vinnur Eða Þú Lærir

August 6, 2017

Momentarily, I forget where I am. The ceiling looks unfamiliar, the bed feels foreign. I start to wake up; the sheer soreness I feel hastens the process.

It's Sunday—the final day of competition at the 2017 Reebok CrossFit Games in Madison, Wisconsin.

I fight my eyes open. Gravity was absent in my dream; now it feels as though its strength has doubled in my consciousness. "Tired" falls devastatingly short of describing my physical condition. I stretch my arms and wince in pain. I feel every movement from each of the ten events of the previous four days. Everything hurts—quads, calves, hamstrings—all vibrate with a consistent, dull ache. The smallest of muscles whose existence I previously ignored make their presence known with sharp, stinging intervals. My forearms and biceps feel bruised. I swear there's a knife buried between my shoulder blades.

I'm twenty-four years old. Right now, I feel like I'm sixty-four.

I'm no stranger to pain. My chosen profession as a CrossFit

Games athlete forces me not only to make pain a habit but to find new and creative ways in which to experience it. I've been here before. And I don't mind it. It's my life's work to be here—at the "ultimate proving grounds for the fittest athletes on Earth."

The Games are first and foremost a celebration of the world's largest fitness community and of the athletes who represent the pinnacle of that community. In practice, the Games take inspiration from all disciplines of modern sports and combine them with manual labor and mental-fortitude tests borrowed from U.S. Navy SEAL training. What the World Cup is to soccer, the Super Bowl is to football, and the World Series is to baseball, the CrossFit Games is to fitness.

The Games crown the Fittest on Earth through tests that assess athletes' competencies by any and all conceivable measures of fitness, which CrossFit defines as increased work capacity across broad time and modal domains. To speak plainly: It combines the marathoner, the gymnast, and every type of weight lifter into one tidy package. It is observable, measurable, and repeatable. And, therefore, testable.

As I gingerly test each sore limb, it occurs to me this might be my last day as "Fittest Woman on Earth." I don't know exactly where I am on the leaderboard, but I know enough to know I'm going to have to fight today. I try to dismiss the thought as best I can.

Control what you can control, Kat, I tell myself.

The old me would have thrown herself a pity party. But I've grown substantially as a person and an athlete; my 2014 self wouldn't recognize similarities. When I began my professional career, I was immature and reactive. I didn't realize there was any other way. Much of the credit goes to my coach, Ben Bergeron. The mental toughness I developed under Ben's coaching is the reason I'm here, attempting to become the only woman in history to win the CrossFit Games three times.

I'm still braiding my hair when Ben knocks on my door. Ben has become accustomed to this. I'm always late. While he's transformed nearly every corner of my mind, he has yet to cure my chronic lateness. Unfazed, he picks up my bags and takes them downstairs. He comes back and sits on the edge of the bed, the only surface not overrun by piles of clothing.

As I stand in front of the mirror, I imagine an alternate reality where I'm not a professional athlete. Maybe my hands aren't covered in calluses. Maybe I'm an engineer, as I once set out to be. Or a lawyer, like my grandfather. Maybe I have a dog. Maybe I have a boyfriend.

A throbbing pain in my biceps reminds me I chose this life instead. I'm a professional athlete. I've chosen to live by a code that permits only a narrow bandwidth when it comes to lifestyle: diet, rest, training, recovery. I've studied how champions live and I've done my best to imitate their best practices. What I want requires laser focus and discipline. I must tightly control all my activities. Winning the Games has required monumental time and effort on improving myself. I don't consider myself selfish, but I want to be justified. As the best CEO, writer, or diplomat makes intentional choices on where to focus their effort, so, too, must the fittest athletes on Earth. This a choice, not a sacrifice.

Finally, my hair is battle ready. Ben and I leave the hotel to walk across the street for breakfast at a small café called Gooseberry. We order the same thing we've ordered every morning all week: eggs, greens, oatmeal, and coffee. Ben, a known crazy person, doesn't drink coffee.

We don't talk much during breakfast. The silence is comfortable. It's a sign of profound friendship, I think, when the quiet feels just as soothing as deep conversation. Ben became my coach in 2015, and after years of mutual struggle and countless hours of tinkering, he is so much more. Our relationship involves the familial bonds between mentor and student, athlete and coach, confidant and friend. To me, he's family.

The drive to the venue is the last piece of our pre-competition ritual. Within the confidential confines of the car, we detail strategies and make necessary reinforcements to my mental preparation. It's been this way since 2015. Ben makes a joke, and for a second I forget my nervous butterflies. I used to fear my butterflies, but I've become friends with them over the years. Being nervous is a good thing. It means you care. It means your body is physically preparing for the coming task. Welcoming the butterflies is my first order of business when heading to the venue. At the end of the day, what you feel doesn't matter—it's what you do that makes you brave.

This year, the drive is different. Everything is different— from the sights and smells to the venue itself. Most notably, the drive is far shorter than in years past. As a result, so, too, is our preparation time. Over the previous five years I had learned to navigate Games competition at the StubHub Center in Carson, California. The layout, staff, and protocols had become familiar. I had a routine there. This year, I was navigating new territory.

I was unsure about Wisconsin. I felt like my safety blanket had been snatched away. I wasn't scared, but I didn't feel safe. Until this year, the StubHub Center was all I knew when it came to the Games, and I had so many emotions tied to that venue. I transformed as a person and an athlete while competing there. So many of my greatest moments and memories took place there.

All year long I had come to crave the magical combination of sights and sounds that seemed intrinsic to the bowl of StubHub's Tennis Stadium. Just by closing my eyes and thinking about it, I could hear the roar of the crowd resonating in my bones, sending tingles up my spine. I often replayed times when I would seemingly lose control of my body and feel as if I was floating under the

Friday Night Lights. In training, I would often try to conjure that rush of adrenaline—the deafening roar of the fittest, most enthusiastic crowd on Earth carrying me over the finish line. Would that magic be transported to Wisconsin?

As a matter of team policy, we don't spend time or energy on the leaderboard. That is a well-established truth among those who know me. But I'd be lying if I said I was oblivious to my current standing at any given point in the competition. Short of going blind and deaf, that would be impossible. Massive, on-field screens display fancy graphics and scoreboards. Indefatigable on-field announcers amp up the crowd with real-time standings.

"Katrin Davidsdottir has some ground to make up, if she wants to get back to the podium!"

A constant stream of cameras and interviews seek information for fans at home.

"Kat, you're the two-time champion. You're currently 110 points back in fifth. What will you change for tomorrow?"

If that weren't enough, where you stand on the floor is where you sit in the overall points race. Competition lanes are reshuffled prior to each event. The leaders are featured dead center, with their chasers cascading out to the perimeters from first to worst.

The trick, then, is not to waste your energy dodging interviews, closing your eyes, and plugging your ears. Rather, the trick is to filter the information appropriately. The leaderboard tells a story of what happened. It's in the past. We constantly move forward with our game plan and focus only on the next right move. Everything else is background noise. The next moment, the next rep, the next event are what we can control. What's done is done, and dwelling on mistakes or "shoulda, woulda, coulda" scenarios is a waste of time and emotional energy that competitors can't afford. Easier said than done.

Sunday mornings at the Games have traditionally been my jam.

The events usually feature grunt work, requiring grit and the ability to grind after multiple days of physical challenges. They also tend to feature a lot of running. Sunday mornings are special to me, and I enter the final day determined to fight. It doesn't occur to me that I might be out of the running to win even with a miraculous day. This morning's event—the Madison Triplet—shares DNA with the Sunday events of the past. This is where I excel. I can feel it. This is where I dig in my heels. Now, I fight.

MADISON TRIPLET
5 rounds for time:
Run 450 meters
7 hay–bale clean burpees (70-pound sandbag for women,
100-pound sandbag for men)

I'm amped. I cruise through my warm-up in the massive exhibition hall that houses the athlete warm-up area. I'm anxious to get on the floor. Pacing on the self-propelled Assault Air Runner, I visualize the competition rush and feel adrenaline dripping into my bloodstream. I'm picturing myself sailing past the other women and being first over the finish line. Suddenly, Ben snaps me out of my visualization. That's when I realize I've gotten carried away. I'm pushing my pace in my *warm-up*—and I've been at it for twenty minutes. That's the same amount of time I'd have to complete the Madison Triplet. I've made a mistake.

Soon after I dismount, Games staff usher me and the rest of the athletes in my heat between multiple metal barricades to march us across the parking lot, into the venue, and to the starting line. For this particular event, Games director Dave Castro, a retired U.S. Navy SEAL instructor, is exhibiting his flair. Stacked hay bales are a nod to the Midwestern locale, while obnoxiously yellow 70-pound sandbags pay tribute to the host city's famous cheese curds.

My plan is to use the first two rounds to feel out the event and settle into an aggressive pace I can maintain. The 450-meter run is modest. It takes us out into the open space north of the stadium on the perimeter of the broadcast compound, where dozens of cameras and hundreds of people are sending images to television and social media platforms.

Sam Briggs—the 2013 champion known for her endurance prowess—leaves the stadium like she was shot out of a cannon. I'm immediately faced with a split-second decision: Latch on to the lead pack or take a gamble their pace will falter. I accelerate for ten steps. But my body is downshifting, and a wave of panic floods over me. I'm in a no-man's-land behind Briggs and the leaders and in front of the main group of women. Something isn't right.

When I arrive at the burpees, they feel more taxing than annoying. Unusual. The cadence is awkward: throw the sandbag, drop to the ground, hurdle over the hay bales. I have to concentrate to avoid throwing the sandbag and immediately hurdling over the hay. Mistakes are costly.

By the second round, the imaginary tether connecting me to the event leaders snaps. My body is throttling down my speed, and I seem to have no say in the matter. I fall back into the middle of the pack.

What is happening to me?

My running feels like trudging. The burning, tingling sensation of lactic acid spreads rapidly throughout the muscles in my legs. My quads and calves are screaming. My feet feel like concrete blocks. I'm familiar with all these sensations but they typically appear when I'm close to finishing, not in Round 2.

In Round 3, the crowd noise sinks to a whisper, and my field of vision slowly evaporates from my peripheral. All I can see is what's directly ahead of me. I'm laser focused on the competitor just beyond my grasp—more for directional guidance than competitiveness. I'm pretty sure I'm going to pass out.

The final two rounds are a blur. I'm going through the motions, doing my best to minimize the damage and, more important, to stay conscious. I fall farther and farther back on the runs. My push simply isn't there. It's like I'm running in quicksand or navigating a dream in which my body disobeys every order I send it. As I enter the stadium for the final round, Sam Briggs finishes the event.

I finally stumble across the finish line and collapse. I'm shell-shocked. This is the most disappointed I have ever felt in a Games event. I immediately search my brain for answers. Maybe I'm sick. I was like a stranger in my own body for the entire event. The fatigue slowly subsides on the walk back to the athlete warm-up area. That's when I remember: My twenty-minute warm-up. As a two-time champion, I had made a rookie mistake.

I sit by myself, processing the weekend so far. Good, bad, or indifferent, I always allow a brief moment to indulge my reaction and assessment. It's the only way to successfully compartmentalize emotions and effectively move on. Now I allow myself to be disappointed. How could I have been so stupid?

I choose to refocus my attention on two things: First, there is no more room for mistakes. To be the champion, I'll have to be flawless and aggressive. Second, it's not over. In the Sport of Fitness, anything can happen. Ben's notion of competitive excellence is so ingrained in my psyche, it might as well be tattooed on my brain: We give our best effort regardless of circumstance. Where you are on the leaderboard is irrelevant. We have one speed—all in.

The inverse also applies. My favorite training partner, Mat Fraser, is having an experience the opposite of mine. Basically, he is destroying the competition. Barring an injury or a lightning bolt shot from heaven, Mat is on track to win his second consecutive championship by a record points margin. Regardless, after every event, he focuses on opportunities for improvement. He could complete only the minimum work requirement for the remainder of the competition, but instead he continues to push. He's hungry for improvement, even after event wins. His scenario and mine are both opportunities to display competitive excellence. If I'm being honest, though, I'd prefer to be in his shoes right now.

Shortly after the Madison Triplet, Game staff gathers us competitors in the warm-up area for the briefing on our next event. Head judge Adrian "Boz" Bozman is curt and brief as he explains the standards for the next event: 2223 Interval. The event is the first of its kind. There will be periods of work followed by one-minute rest periods:

2 minutes on, 1 minute off:
2 rope climbs
7-calorie SkiErg
Max-rep overhead squats (105 pounds)

In the fourth round, the time period extends to three minutes. The rope climbs and SkiErg are formalities—busy work, really. The endgame is to accumulate 75 reps—a staggering volume for which Dave Castro jokingly apologizes in light of the beating our bodies have already sustained.

More than anything, this event is a test of strategy and pacing. Any surplus of overhead squats gained in an overzealous first or second round will be squandered if you fail to recover in the one-minute rest period. This is a test of how well we can flirt with the edge of our capacities.

Boz has finished explaining the event flow and is about to

review the movements when I raise my hand. He looks bemused. Boz has answered just about every mundane and ridiculous question in athlete briefings such as this one. More often than not, they come from rookies. But right now, curiosity is burning a hole in my mind.

"What if you finish your overhead squats on the third interval?" I ask.

Boz cocks his head to see if I'm joking. Seventy-five overhead squats in six minutes, on top of rope climbs and SkiErg work, sounds like science fiction. But I'm dead serious.

"No one will do that," he says, laughing.

Now I'm pissed.

I raise my hand again.

Boz looks mildly annoyed.

"Okay. But, what if?" I persist.

We still have to finish the final rope climbs and SkiErg, he explains.

Good to know, I think.

I have every intention of proving him wrong.

After the briefing, I huddle with Ben to review our game plan.

Ben, who typically composes himself like a Zen master, is atypically excited.

"Just go," he says.

"No matter what?" I push back.

Typically our game plan has more variables: If this, then that.

"Just go," he repeats.

His voice is loaded with something out of place in this context. Anger? Excitement? I'm not sure. But it's contagious, and I feel my stomach fill with good nervous energy. The kind that makes magic.

"What about the—" I start.

I want to analyze the structure and possible approaches to the event. He forcefully cuts me off.

"Katrin. Just. Go."

This is an order.

He's right.

My back is against the wall. I have nothing to lose and everything to gain. I'm a dangerous competitor when I cut the brakes. And that's exactly what I plan to do here. Before we part ways, Ben says one last thing.

"We compete with excellence."

That's all I need.

The Alliant Energy Center's Coliseum is Madison's answer to the StubHub Center's Tennis Stadium. The differences outweigh the similarities nearly enough for me to avoid comparisons of any sort. One very critical exception, however, pits them as opposites in my mind. The Coliseum hosts the exclusive access nighttime events, previously hosted in the tennis stadium. From as early as 2010, these events have become the stuff of legend at the Cross-Fit Games and have always been close to my heart. Given this, Madison's Coliseum was fighting an uphill battle to win my affection, even before I arrived. Then my debut in the building earlier this week produced my second-worst finish since 2013 and sealed the deal.

Still, I admit that the Coliseum brings the Games a new kind of swagger. The building has a roof, allowing for control of the atmosphere. A laser light show dances on screaming fans and the music is so loud I feel the bass vibrations above my rapidly beating heart as I walk onto the competition floor. We are called out one at a time. Few feelings are better than your name being called as the fans drown you in cheers and support. My adrenaline peaks, my fears dissipate, and, for the first time all week, I feel like myself.

Standing in my lane, I'm looking down the field of play. Towering above my lane, a mountain of steel is lurking. Its beams meet in an A-frame, and it spans the width of the stadium floor, enveloping all the lanes from edge to edge. Ropes dangle from the structure, and we are staged on red crash pads so massive I feel like I'm on a trampoline. A manila rope dangles in front of my face. I know it's 20 feet long, but it looks endless in this light, with the top of the rig disappearing into the darkness of the stadium's rafters.

To my right is Annie Thorisdottir, my countrywoman and the only other female to win back-to-back Games titles. More important, Annie is the woman who ignited my passion for CrossFit and set me down the path that has led here. Now, six years after her first championship, we are both fighting our way back to the podium shoulder to shoulder. "Comfortable" is not the right word, but being next to Annie feels like home.

The interval format creates a unique tension between effort and recovery. This event is also peppered with land mines. Playing conservatively can put you at a deficit too far to reclaim at the finish line. But an overly aggressive pace can spell disaster if you implode.

I do lots of intervals in training, and I love them. One of Ben's many talents is formulating combinations and rep schemes that fall just outside my abilities. I'm forced to exceed my limitations, suck it up, and go again. More than anything, this enhances my mental ability to succeed or die trying. There is an expectation in these workouts that I will fail. It's part of the learning process that ensures I will not fail when it matters, right now—at game time. Those failures are why I am supremely confident I will finish the squats in Round 3.

From the moment the buzzer sounds, I'm in attack mode. All the women are even after the first rope climb but I jump up for my second rep first, before everyone else. I'm the first athlete at the SkiErg. I decide I'm going to try to break it. I've put dozens of hours in with the SkiErg, and I know every nuance of this machine. I know I can ride it hard with little effect.

With the calories completed, I sprint to the bar and rip it from the ground without hesitation. There is no pacing. My eyes are fixed on the mat in front of me, where the number of reps to complete is marked. In Round 1, we advanced the barbell every 10 reps.

A lifetime of handstands and gymnastics training have rewarded me with strong and flexible shoulders. I remember Amma, my grandmother, razzing me as a child because I spent so much time walking on my hands.

"The only suntan you'll ever have is on your ankles!" she would say.

It's paying off now. I wish she could see me.

I keep my grip narrow and focus on keeping the weight balanced. The first 10 reps feel smooth and methodical.

I advance. It's clear I'm in the lead. My legs are feeling the soreness of the week, but my pace remains unchanged. I finish 20 reps. Beside me, Annie advances in hot pursuit and it spurs me on. With the interval winding down, I step forward once more to bank one more rep. I end the interval in the lead with 31.

"That is a big gamble," TV announcer Chase Ingraham says to viewers at home.

He's not wrong. I am gambling.

But I know this event is stacked in my favor. I live on intervals. I'm going to break this workout in half. I can maintain my suicide pace, and the other women are going to be forced to make a decision: match my pace and risk disaster, or watch me collect 100 points.

Image isn't everything, but it's important. I made a point to look strong during the rest period. No slouching, no hands on the hips, no obvious signs I was feeling pain. I grab my chalk and immediately return to face my rope.

Everything goes smoothly again through the rope climbs and the SkiErg in Round 2. I run to my bar slightly behind Annie and another Icelandic competitor, Sara Sigmundsdóttir.

"For the two-time defending champion, it's risk versus reward," says announcer Brandon Domaigne.

I've decided I want both.

I hoist the bar up at once, ignoring my instincts to extend my rest. I'm aware of fatigue in my arms, but I don't care. The transitions are more frequent now that we are north of 30 reps; we're moving forward every 3 reps. From the corner of my eye, I can see Annie. She's chasing me from a few reps back.

After the second interval, I jog back. I have 49 squats in the bank when I begin Round 3. The rope climbs are becoming challenging, but my mind has gone into autopilot and the movements are happening automatically now. The crowd erupts as I leave the SkiErg for my barbell.

There you are, I think, as the rush of endorphins pushes away my muscle fatigue and I feel a tingling sensation run up my spine. *There's my magic.*

"You've been asking for it all weekend. Where's the Katrin we saw in 2015 and 2016?" Domaigne says as I jump onto the finish platform and beam a platter-sized smile. "We see her again in event number 12!"

I'm grinning like a crazy woman for the duration of the event. I can't erase it. I never want it to go away. I find Ben immediately when I exit the stadium floor and shout to him excitedly through a smile.

"I know it's Sunday, Ben. And I know that it's late, but I found my magic!"

It's in this moment I realize what I had been getting wrong all along. All this time I had been waiting for some external force—the venue, the crowd, a wand-toting fairy godmother—to re-create the intangible feelings of invincibility that led me to victory in years past. I had been waiting for it to happen *to me* instead of making it happen *for me*. I had to create my own magic.

"My only question," Ingraham asks, "is why is this happening now, in Event 12? Why haven't we seen this for the eleven other events?!"

It was the question we had been pondering the entire weekend. Ben and I now agree: Ferocity was the missing ingredient. We had caged the lion. We had changed the winning formula by playing it safe. In training and in competition, we'd been conservative. But it was aggression and some recklessness that had earned me two championships. This event had reminded me of my abilities. I feel reborn heading into the final.

The walk from the Coliseum back to the main athlete area takes us through a short underground tunnel that emerges into the beer garden: an airplane-sized hangar sporting a 100-foot-high widescreen where viewers enjoy food, drinks, and the competition. As we enter, the crowd erupts. They have lined the barrier to greet us with an ocean of high-fives and selfie requests.

Once we reach the athlete area, recovery time is short. After a quick celebration of my event win, our team maximizes the time by focusing on carrying the mental edge into the final event.

"You gotta fight, Kat," Ben tells me emphatically.

"I know," I reply.

"I'm serious. You're not out of the running," he says.

His eyes are penetrating.

"I know," I repeat.

"Katrin, you really need to—" he starts.

"Ben, I know," I interrupt.

He's trying to convince me to fight when there wasn't a doubt in my mind I was going out there to fight and win for the final event, the Fibonacci Final:

3-5-8 reps of:
deficit handstand push-ups
5-8-13 reps of:
124-pound kettlebell deadlifts

Then, 35-pound kettlebell overhead lunge 89 feet to the finish line.

In past years, I had taken Amma onto the field with me for the final event, symbolically. I had felt her presence the entire weekend and now, more than ever, I pictured Amma standing alongside me, encouraging me to fight to the end.

More than ever, I had felt her presence throughout the weekend. The love-ball necklace she and my grandfather, Afi, had gifted me is my prized possession. It has accompanied me onto the field for the final event the past two years, and I hold it in my hand now as I look to the sky and meditate on words of encouragement from the notes she often wrote me.

"You are the strongest of anyone in the world, and together we are even stronger than that . . . can you even imagine?"

I lay the necklace next to the parallettes where I will perform my handstand push-ups. It isn't an event that lines up well for me on paper. Deadlifts have been a weakness in the past. These are heavy—124 pounds in each hand—and there are a lot of them. But I've overcome staggering odds before. It was in a final event similar to this one that I took the lead from Sara Sigmundsdóttir in 2015, deadlifting my way to a gold medal with these exact same kettlebells. Sara enters the final ahead of me again—this time in fourth. Annie and I sandwich her on the leaderboard.

The point separation is impossibly close among the top five women. This single event will decide who takes the gold.

All the women in the race are virtually shoulder to shoulder as we charge through the handstand push-ups and deadlifts. Entering the final round, it's clear the overhead walking lunge is where the event will be won. Any stumble could spell a loss.

I feel unstable the moment I send the bells overhead. I try to focus on the finish line and the screaming crowd urging me toward it. Annie is already ten lunges ahead of me. From the corner of my eye, I see Sara a few lanes away in lockstep with me as we begin our lunges. Annie's and Sara's presence jolts my brain to override my exhaustion and I charge down the lane, my trailing knee driving into the ground and my lead leg shaking with each lunge. Annie falters. When her bells go down, I dig for one final push. I know Sara is feeding off this surge, too. I grit my teeth. I pass Annie at the very moment she picks up her bells and returns to lunging. We charge, together now, toward the end of the competition.

Annie overtakes me two steps from the finish line. My knee fails to hit the ground. I am forced to retrace 5 feet before continuing. Sara and Annie lunge on to victory. I take third in the heat and fourth overall in the event. I collapse. I know I've given everything I could. I sit, dumbfounded on the finish mat as I watch Tia-Clair Toomey fail her final rep of lunges, then recover to tumble over the finish line alongside Kara Saunders (née Webb). They're separated by nineteen-hundredths of a second.

I'm proud of my performance. But an emptiness is filling me. I realize the Games are over and I haven't done enough. I experience a terrible new emotion—regret. I stand helplessly on the finish mat and wait for the results to be tabulated. It's agonizing. Dave calls Annie's name for third place. She's elated. She flashes a 100-megawatt smile around the arena. Then he brings

Kara and Tia out onto the floor and it sinks in that not only have I not defended my title, I'm not going to be on the podium at all. Dave calls out the name of the 2017 champion, and for the first time in two years, it's not my name. I watch, heartbroken, as Tia celebrates her victory from the middle of the floor, the same place I had stood last year and the year before.

This is the hardest moment for me. I've been in Tia's shoes. I've heard my name called. I know the overwhelming joy of that triumphant moment. My heart breaks.

The massive leaderboard flashes the official standings. I'm in elite company. It's an honor simply to be among this group of women. It gives me perspective. But it doesn't make me feel any better. I join Tia on the competition floor to congratulate her. I hug her through my tears. She's crying, too—from joy.

I'm surrounded by people, many of them my friends, but I suddenly feel overwhelmingly lonely. Wistfully, I scan the crowd for a friendly face. Someone who loves me. Will everyone still love me now that I'm not the Fittest Woman on Earth? I wish Amma were here. She'd be screaming her face off, cheering for me—unaware or unconcerned that I didn't win. Amma was always so proud of me.

When I walk off the floor into the tunnel, Ben is waiting for me. My eyes well up with tears again. He hugs me.

"I'm proud of you," he says.

I endure the awards ceremony, but I'm dying inside. The pizza tastes bitter. It tastes like fifth place. I go through the motions of my obligations: interviews, a press conference, drug testing. Then, I slowly pack my things in the warm-up area.

You win or you learn, we like to say. As Ben and I drive back to the hotel, I can tell he wants to wait before debriefing the week. But I'm ready now. I was ready the moment I finished the Fibonacci Final. We start talking, looping through downtown Madison as we consider the minutiae of each moment, eventually pulling over into a parking lot when it's clear I want to examine deeply.

"We were too conservative," Ben says. "I thought if I got you here healthy, we'd be okay."

He miscalculated, he continues, and takes complete responsibility.

An hour later, we have outlined a plan for the coming year. But the big questions in my mind are still unresolved:

How did we get here? What went wrong? And, most important: *How do we fix it?*

2

FAMILY

FJÖLSKYLDA

What makes a Great Sled Dog?
Breed, Ambition, Tough Feet
—JANE J. LEE

The below-freezing temperature preserves every exhalation, exaggerating my respiration rate as long, drawn-out clouds that hang at eye level. The result is a dramatic accentuation of the already icy edge to a rivalry that has been seven years in the making.

We both know what's at stake. The implications of victory or loss in this setting go beyond any trophy or ribbon. My stomach does more than backflips as I approach the start. Side flips, indos, corkscrews.

I've run this course a million times. It's a short sprint with no tricks. But it feels alien in this light. The bank of the second turn has amassed substantially, compliments of a consistent wind that has built over the course of the week, and the waning light of the Icelandic winter afternoon betrays the slightest shimmer of black ice just beyond the finish line. I do my best to choke back the doubt as we take our spots on the starting line.

The call to action comes from my left.

"Ready . . ."

Focus, I think.

"Set . . ."

The familiar count is taking an eternity today.

"Go!"

My mind goes blank. This is it. This is me.

My confidence returns once the race begins. This is always when I'm at my best: in the moment. Just let me work. My spring off the line goes flawlessly and within five strides, I'm at top speed. I can feel my competitor off my left shoulder, ready to pounce. We speed down the course in the formation, like we've been lit on fire—clear of thought, driven by emotion. It's not fear of losing that drives us but a distaste for it.

Every muscle in my body is on high alert as brain chemicals that served my ancestors in battle course through my body. My head is tingling, my thoughts are clear. For some, this would be punishment. It's the place I'm most happy.

With the finish line in reach, I falter. Clumsily, I've clipped my own heel, something I'll later blame on the ungainliness of the boots I'm wearing. I recover partially . . . one step, a half hop, my left foot finds purchase. Nope. It's hopeless, I'm coming in hot. I'm going down. My hands search for the ground as I sprawl, but this is destined to be awkward, potentially painful. Definitely dangerous.

For better or worse, my competitor is entangled in my mess. We are locked as a unit in the chaos, flailing onto the ground and across the finish line in a ball. Our winter clothes provide a small buffer from the concrete, but the impact is still real.

After it's determined that no one has been hurt, we collapse in laughter. After all, he's my little brother Jack, and the lamppost that marks the finish line is just one of many arbitrary markers to which we would race on our walk home from school. I gave him a minute or two to collect himself before we carry on racing to the next. That one was a tie, and I still want to beat him.

Jack is two years younger than me and the truth is, he would be just as happy not racing around like a crazy person, but he could never escape when I was in search of a competition. Poor guy. I don't think he minded that much, but he also would have been happy playing on his own.

I came out of the womb hypercompetitive, and even that is understating it. If there wasn't a physical challenge available, I created one. I loved competition then as much as I love it now.

When I was home by myself, sometimes I would put a clock on the floor and try to hold a handstand, then I'd try to beat my own time. At school, I would challenge my classmates to see who had the most pencils in their pencil case. Competitiveness is written deep into my genetic code. It came as part of the package.

Home videos of me as a baby are family legend. There is one where I am an infant, still crawling, trying desperately to get up a step. I fail over and over and over again. When my grandmother comes over to help, I defensively push her away. Another shows me on the playground, attempting to climb a slide from the bottom up. The older kids are zooming around me, irritated by my presence. I'm so slow. Still, I refuse any help. Two-year-old me is determined to make it by herself.

My mom encouraged this early determined streak. She was sixteen when I was born. Because she was so young, she was often told she wasn't ready to be a mother and that she wouldn't be a good mom. Instead of internalizing it, she went on a mission to make me a wonderbaby. She read countless books on parenting and bought nearly every learning toy on the market. If children were supposed to say ten words by the age of one, I was going to say thirty. If I was supposed to be 50 pounds at a certain age, I would weigh 60. If I was supposed to walk, I was going to run. It was her mission to see me surpass normal goals and reach for greatness. I internalized this drive for excellence into my athletic future.

I was born in London, where my grandfather Helgi Ágústsson was a diplomat. He was stationed there as the Icelandic Ambassador to the United Kingdom. My mother takes pleasure in reminding me I was two weeks late in being born. A sign of things to come, she teases, because of my reputation for running a few minutes behind.

We moved to Iceland when Jack was two. My grandparents stayed behind in the United Kingdom. I was sad to leave them, but I visited almost every other month.

Iceland is a great place to grow up. Hafnarfjörður, the Reykjavik suburb where we moved, could not have contrasted more sharply to the metropolis of London. Like nearly everywhere in Iceland, it was clean and safe and everyone knew each other. Children can stay outside all day and often do, even well into the night. We lived on a circle drive where there were tons of other kids, and we would play massive games of hide-and-seek and tag.

The year after we moved home, my little sister, Hannah, was born. I can tell you that the world was not ready for that force of nature. If Jack and I are cut from the same black-and-white cloth, Hannah is a purple-and-green, polka-dotted butterfly. From birth, she had the attitude of a hurricane. No one can tell Hannah what to do or when she can do it.

Hannah has no fear. She doesn't have a filter, either, which got her in trouble a time or two when she was younger. She is also very strong—way stronger than me—but her aversion to conformity wasn't a good fit for organized sports. Or coaches.

When we were kids, our personalities clashed. But as we've both grown up, our differences have actually made me love her more than ever. Hannah is so funny and gregarious. She pulls me out of my shell.

As kids, the outdoors were like one huge playground to us. Unless I was at school or it was time to eat, we were outside. When we got bored of each other, my siblings and I would go knocking on doors to recruit friends to join us for games and adventures. My mom would call us in for dinner but afterward we were right back outside. Even in the winter, our parents gave us the freedom to roam, but they were strict with curfews: 8 o'clock in the winter and 10 o'clock in the summer.

Like most Icelandic children, we were encouraged to experiment with lots of sports. I loved sports and trying new things, but to this day I cannot figure out how my mom managed our chaotic schedule. Jack, Hannah, and I were all participating in *at least* one activity at any given time. My mom would drop me off at gymnastics, head back to town and grab Jack at handball, then transfer him to soccer or piano before picking up Hannah, who played soccer and participated in gymnastics as well.

My mom was really plugged in to what we were up to. That's the kind of mom I want to be. She always wanted to be involved and helpful. She knew my friends and my siblings' friends. She would check in with them and be genuinely interested in what they had going on. She wanted to be involved, and we knew she cared deeply about us.

I think it's cute how much she loves talking about her kids and finding out about other people's kids. It always makes me laugh when we're at the CrossFit Games or Regionals and she would come home with stories of meeting other competitors' parents, trading stories with them and forging new friendships.

"Guess what," she said to me after a day of Regionals competition. "I hung out with the Vellners today. Did you know that Pat's brother is in the Cirque du Soleil?!"

I remember being proud she was younger than most of my friends' parents. I wanted to do everything just like her. To me, she was the coolest person in the world, and I looked up to her. She had red highlights, so I wanted red highlights (which she did not allow). She had a belly-button piercing, so I wanted one (which she didn't let me do, either). She also had the cartilage of her upper ear pierced, which I was dying to get. This, she actually did allow me to do!

Because all her songs were my favorite songs, she made me a mixtape—yes, an actual cassette tape—featuring Madonna's "Music," Oasis's "Wonderwall," and Deep Blue Something's "Breakfast at Tiffany's." I still love those songs. I can't remember if she was entertained or annoyed by the attention, but I was her shadow; she couldn't shake me.

When I was six, gymnastics entered my life. It was my first love. Within a few years, it was my sport. I spent four hours a day, six days a week training, on top of school and homework. My first gym, called Bjork, acted as my second home from age six until sixteen. I remember the pride I felt walking through town after practices, my shiny uniform glistening under the lights.

Gymnastics taught me discipline. Even at a young age, coaches set expectations. I also learned perseverance—because nothing came naturally to me. When I watch an athlete such as Simone Biles perform, it blows my mind. She looks like a cat. She always seems to know exactly where her body is in space. Biles can perform a double flip with a triple twist and know just where she is.

I was virtually the opposite. Any type of twisting caused me to lose all sense of awareness. I was basically flying through the air, guessing when I would hit the ground and unsure which body part would make contact first. When I was learning *any* new skills, not just twists, I always landed on my head *at least* three times. I had friends in gymnastics who would just try stuff and land on their feet with nothing more than a stumble-step to the side. Not me. I was always on my head. But I would get back up and try again.

What I lacked in natural talent, I made up for in grit. I was always a hard worker. As a gymnast, I thrived on conditioning and the endless practice our Russian coaches prescribed. I loved the sweat and the discipline, but sometimes my affinity for hard training made me an outcast among the other girls; no gymnast loves conditioning, especially when you're a kid.

Ironically, I wasn't driven to compete in gymnastics. It was the one thing where I never felt competitive drive. I wasn't trying to be the Icelandic National Champion. I was simply trying to get better, and I loved the challenge and the process that led to success. I learned resiliency through failure. Gymnastics taught me early on that failure is part of the process. I would land on my head, go try again, fail, and then try again—over and over. Finally, the third, fourth, or fifth time, a lightbulb would go off and I would think, *Ah, yeah, now I get it!* But it always took me those failed attempts to learn.

This arduous process was the same no matter what I was learning. It was a priceless lesson that success doesn't simply appear; it takes hard work, passion, and resilience. I learned that I could succeed in anything, if I was willing to commit myself to it.

My mom taught me how to laugh at myself, and gymnastics reinforced that. It would become one of my greatest assets in life, especially later, as a professional athlete. I have always taken my sport seriously—I respect my coaches, my competitors, and my teammates. But I refuse to take myself too seriously, and this I'm certain I inherited from my mom. The ability to giggle when I mess something up royally is a priceless gift. To advance in any skill, you need to be able to shrug off mistakes and smile at them. Having fun and laughing, even if it's at your own expense, makes the process enjoyable.

My parents got divorced when I was in second grade. My dad decided that he would be moving back to England. We kids stayed with our mom in Iceland. Around the same time, I learned that my grandparents would be moving away. Afi, my grandfather, became the Icelandic ambassador to Denmark, which required them to leave Iceland, and leave me. I was young and sensitive and the stress was too much. I often got migraine headaches as a child. Usually they accompanied stress or sickness, and hospital visits were required if they were especially intense. The combined stress of my parents' split and the departure of my anchors, Amma and Afi, landed me in the hospital with a migraine. The diagnosis was a headache, but I know it was my broken heart manifesting itself.

I wasn't away from my grandparents too long. Mom took me to stay with them for a few weeks not long after they left. Over time we would also settle into a rhythm of visits to my dad. From then on, I would divide my summers between visiting my grandparents in Copenhagen and visiting my dad in England with my siblings.

My dad has been a mathematics professor at a college since before I was born. This meant that he had the same holidays as us kids, and we would always go on fun trips. Dad would fly to Iceland and pick us up when there was a break in school. On trips to London, we would usually go to stay with his parents; I called them Nanny and Granddad.

Every single summer we would take a big trip. My dad loves seeing the world and showing us the world. We went to places like Italy, India, and Thailand. My dad is a collector of experiences. He's an amazing teacher, loves his work, and he is my gold standard for work ethic. All his professional life, the *only* day he took off was for his father's funeral. He's a very committed man.

I'm precariously close to being a perfectionist in most things. I credit my dad for fostering that quality in me. In school, especially, I always took my job as a student seriously. I finished my homework religiously and without any oversight. I loved taking exams and seeing how I stacked up against my peers. I was a good student. I was unusually focused for my age, liked to work, and found pleasure in achievements. The downside was a serious demeanor that didn't necessarily reflect my inner thoughts. Parent-teacher conferences often produced comments like, "Katrin needs to relax a little."

My dad has a rational, analytical mind paired with a teacher's ability to reframe situations, making you believe everything is easier than you are making it. He makes things sound so simple and achievable.

He looks at the world through a prism of "How can this be better?" This coaxed excellence from all of us kids, especially in academics. Instead of celebrating top marks (even 9.5 out of a possible 10 points), he searched for opportunities for us to improve. He acknowledged the result was good, but as a teacher he is hardwired to fill voids of understanding. He wanted to teach us what we got wrong, worried we might go through life not knowing that last half a point.

I never saw my mom's and dad's differing approaches to parenting as being in conflict. In fact, I believe they were perfectly complementary. I like to think that I adopted characteristics from both of them. In academics I mirrored my father. I internalized his drive toward constant improvement. Perhaps to a fault.

My mother tried to teach me how to soften the laser beam. When I burst through the front door and charged straight for my room after school one day, the opposing forces were on display.

"What's up?" my mom prodded.

"I got a nine on my exam," I said through clenched teeth.

"Kat, that's really good."

"No, it's not."

She countered with a perfectly logical argument that I simply did not want to hear.

"If you get nines, or even eights, in college, or especially in university, it's a fantastic result!"

"Maybe for you," I huffed, insinuating that she did not value perfection. Even at twelve years old I wanted it like I wanted to breathe air.

I see a lot of my father in Jack, as well. He is very calculated and analytical. I'm certain he would tell you that he's the most intelligent sibling, but I'll fight him for that. He is very smart. He was always very athletic and played soccer growing up. Even on the pitch, Jack was constantly analyzing. He would get angry when the other kids were playing bunch ball instead of running the plays he was trying to draw up for them. He just wanted them to follow his directions.

The skill set would serve him well in adulthood. He now coaches the women's soccer team at his university in England. His girlfriend told me recently that even when he's in the shower, he can't shut down his analytical brain. She catches him drawing plays in the steam-fogged shower glass.

I credit both of my parents for instilling a drive to succeed. My grandparents had a lot to do with that as well, of course. My school average was never lower than a 9.5 out of 10, and I graduated a year early. Any time I received a grade lower than 10, I would focus on the question I got wrong. It didn't matter to me where I placed in relation to the rest of the class or that my grade was the highest. I wanted to *know* and understand everything. I would hound my teacher for an explanation so my understanding would be complete.

More important than any of that is just how abundantly clear my dad makes it that he loves his kids to the moon and back. He passionately and actively shows us that he cares and goes out of his way to check on us. He wants to make sure that we are doing all right. He is so loving that it drives my sister crazy, but I can't get enough of it.

My baby brother, Bjorgvin, balances the force in our family. Where my highly driven, type-A personality needs to "Go, go, go," Bjorgvin is happiest at a slower pace. Bjorgvin was born when I was eleven, and we didn't live together for long. It's fun for me to see him as a young adult and how different he is from me, Jack, and Hannah.

He takes after my mom a bit more. Bjorgvin has the typically affable qualities displayed by the baby in most families. He is easygoing and sweet. He gets along with everyone and is nearly impossible to fluster.

I watched Hannah intentionally try to get him fired up by making fun of his hair. He was so unperturbed that she became upset and stormed out of the room. Nothing can burst Bjorgvin's bubble. He will literally giggle when someone tries to get a rise out of him.

I had a hard time understanding him for quite a while because he is not super competitive, which simply does not compute in my mind. But that's just Bjorgvin. He's like a cool breeze, calmly watching the world before he reacts. My constant competitiveness and drive for perfection are as alien to him as they are natural to me.

In most ways my parents were opposites. But their personalities as parents actually complemented each other perfectly and rounded out my siblings and me. It wasn't just my parents, either; I was lucky enough to have incredible grandparents, too.

Having so many supportive people in my family provided me with a strong foundation of security and confidence. My competitive nature was nurtured and encouraged by a coterie of loving people all around. My family knows me, loves me, and gives me faith in myself. Because of them, I was able to put myself out there and test what I'm really made of. There came times in my competitive life when I had to question everything, but thankfully I had my family as my rock.

3

GRANDMA AND GRANDPA

AMMA NAD AFI

One look, and I had found a world completely new
When love walked in with you
—GEORGE GERSHWIN, "LOVE WALKED IN"

April 14, 1962

It was the sixties: John F. Kennedy was the president of the United States, the Cold War raged with Europe stuck in the middle, the Beatles released their first hit, "Love Me Do," and Brazil won the World Cup for a second time that year. In Iceland, though, a band was playing in midtown Reykjavik on a clear and beautiful spring evening. Helgi Ágústsson tapped his foot to the live band at the Hotel Borg. It was a popular place to socialize and go dancing and Helgi had arrived early with his friend Halldor Sigurdsson to enjoy the jazz band before the crowds drifted into the venue and the night began in earnest.

The scene revolved around dancing. Real dancing—the kind that required social skills, athleticism, and chivalry. These old friends, Helgi and Halldor, had all three in spades and were frequent fliers at the Borg. Each would encourage the other's confidence to ask for dances with attractive young ladies when confidence faltered. They were perfect gentlemen and even better dancers.

When the band took their first pause, the boys decided to take a stroll around the small lake in downtown Reykjavik. Just before they returned to the Borg, they stopped at a small corner shop to buy a plate of chocolate.

With chocolate in hand, they nearly collided with two beautiful girls who were exiting a taxi. The girls said yes when they offered some chocolate, and a conversation ensued. They talked all the way into the dance, where they shared a table. Helgi and Halldor bought the women soft drinks and they danced all night.

Helgi felt an unshakable connection with one of the women. Her name was Hervör, but her friends called her by her nickname: Heba. She was an especially talented dancer and very beautiful.

Helgi knew the bass player, Omar. After a few dances, he requested the song "Love Walked In." Omar agreed and complimented Helgi's taste, perhaps for the Gershwin, perhaps for Heba. Most likely both. The song had great meaning to Helgi and he was hoping that she would understand the message he was trying to send.

"Do you know this song?" he asked.

"No," she replied. A bit crestfallen, he realized he would need to try something else.

He walked her home that night and a few days later they reunited to see a movie together. Within months they were shopping for pots and pans.

In my family, this day is known as Chocolate Day, the day my grandparents met. We celebrated it every year for fifty-four years. Helgi and Heba are my favorite love story of all time; they are my gold standard when it comes to relationships, love, and respect.

My grandparents are my world. I call them by their Icelandic titles: Grandfather is "Afi" and Grandmother is "Amma." As a child,

I constantly fought for more time with them. Because they took such an active role in my upbringing, we have always been tremendously close.

My mother was still finishing school when I was a baby. Amma watched me during the day back then and our bond grew stronger. Every morning was the same: Amma taking her coffee in her Finnish Moomin mug while I played, practicing handstands and cartwheels under her delighted gaze. We would walk to Mom's school to visit with her when she had a break, or just go off on our own adventures. Amma and I were always doing something— walking in Hyde Park or exploring local shops. There was never a dull moment; we were always on the move.

Being an ambassador is a highly distinguished support role to the prime minister, and I was proud of my Afi. In Iceland, our politicians are constantly on television. My grandfather's position was enough to make him recognizable and respected, without being famous. When I joined him for lunch at work, I recognized the most important faces of Iceland's government. In my formative years—and even when I was little—this made me want to pursue law and diplomacy.

As a young girl, though, I was often annoyed at my grandparents' popularity. If we walked down any of Reykjavik's main streets, it became a parade of handshakes and hugs. They seemed to know everyone.

"I can't walk anywhere with you," I would complain, wanting their full attention.

A large part of the ambassador's job is entertaining guests and attending events. I remember watching my grandmother as she prepared for these. My legs would hang over the edge of the bed. I was enchanted by her and I would covet her pretty dresses and jewelry.

"Amma, when you're old, can I have that dress?" I asked her when I was five years old.

It was a gorgeous emerald green gown and she looked stunning in it.

"Of course," she replied.

This became one of her oft-repeated stories because of what came next. I followed up with something less conventional.

"Amma, did you hang out with the monkeys?"

My father had recently taught me about evolution. He gave me the rough concept but had left out critical details—like the time-line. In my young mind, it was perfectly reasonable to suspect that Amma was there with them. She laughed so hard at my erroneous question, enjoying my innocence. Memories of her laughing in that gown, of her positivity, and of how she taught me about love remain at the forefront of my mind, encouraging me in the quiet moments.

My life story feels punctuated by my grandparents' work posts. I have lived in Iceland since I was four. I consider it to be my base and my home. But when I look back at my life, my sense of time is anchored by where I spent my summers. When Afi's station in London ended, my grandparents returned to Reykjavik. I had moved back from London a year prior and I hadn't realized how much I missed them.

Amma was an incredible storyteller. When I was young, she would sing to me and tell me stories. She had such a vivid imagination, I wish she'd written children's books. She recounted fantastical tales about the adventures of the terrible trolls and magical elves of the Icelandic countryside, filling my head with wild dreams as I dozed off.

When school was out, we traveled to our summer house, about an hour and a half east of Reykjavik in a place called Ida. My grandparents simply said, "We're headed east," and I would get giddy. It's deep in the countryside and it's been in my family for two generations.

Along the way, my grandmother would pick up her troll tales and fairy fantasies, pointing to the parts of the landscape that were inspiration for her magical stories. There was one huge boulder on a mountainside that she would point out on every trip. I could never see what she meant. Once when I was seven, she was frustrated when I told her I couldn't see the troll and immediately stopped the car, swerving to the side of the road.

"Have you no imagination, child?" she scolded.

The boulder immediately turned into a horrible grimacing troll in my mind's eye. She cured me—for a moment—from my overly analytical mind.

My great-grandfather built that house out east in the wide-open space near the bottom of a rolling hill. The mossy plot stood close to a river teeming with fish. The walls seemed too small for the vaulted ceiling when I was growing up, but the space is so peaceful. It's the kind of place that produces energy. You can go there weary and return fully energized.

Some of my fondest memories came from summertime visits to Ida. Amma baked waffles with jam and whipped cream. Even my grandpa would try his hand at cooking when we were there, something that never happened at home. He actually set the kitchen on fire the only time he cooked at home. During the day, Amma played badminton with me. At night, my grandfather, my little brother Jack, and I would play cards and watch murder mysteries. They called them "whodunits."

I wanted to be around them so badly that being away for even one night was too long.

"Please let me sleep with you," I pleaded in a note. "My room is so close to the trees and I'm allergic to trees!"

While my eight-year-old tactics were less than compelling, they still let me sleep in the middle of their bed from time to time. In reality, I loved the trees. Outside, my grandparents had planted an army of them decades before I was born. They had grown to be enormous by the time I started visiting Ida. We call them "The Guardians" because they surround the house, protecting it from the harsh elements of the Icelandic countryside. No matter how nasty the weather gets outside, it's always peaceful in our cottage in Ida.

Denmark, 2003

Shortly after my parents divorced, Amma and Afi moved to Denmark for Afi to start his new role as the Icelandic Ambassador to Denmark.

The ambassador's residence was magnificent; I felt like royalty when I was there. There were enormous spaces for hosting parties and galas. As a bonus, it was walking distance from Dyrehavsbakken (Bakken for short), which is the Danish equivalent of Disneyland. Opened in 1583, Bakken is actually the world's oldest amusement park. We used to go every once in a while, but I was just a little too short to get on the rides, which was devastating at the time. I was fearless but had no way to prove it.

The first floor of the ambassador's residence is not for living. It's for hosting hundreds of people. There are ballrooms and enormous kitchens. It's large and ornate, and decorated with Icelandic art and entertainment. Amma loved hosting and she could talk for hours about art and culture. Amma loved talking about the house, but I loved the garden—so large you could get lost in it.

Everyone in Denmark bikes everywhere. Bike lanes have their own bike lanes. Fast, commuter traffic stays in the left bike lane, while the right bike lane is for parents with their kids in tow on their way to school drop-off and for the slow-moving tourists. My last summer in Copenhagen, my grandparents took me to a bike shop and bought me my very first bicycle. It was shiny and red with gears. I can remember how special and grown-up I felt, riding a bike with gears! I rode that bike constantly, all summer long, the feeling of freedom and adventure coursing through me.

Benzipan and Suunkit worked at the residence in Copenhagen every day. They had served many ambassadors before Afi, but their stories focused on their homeland: Thailand. Suunkit was an old man but Benzipan had a daughter my age. She still lived in Thailand and I loved to ask about her as Benzipan showed me pictures and told me about life at home. Seeing pictures of this little girl, I imagined she'd be my friend if she lived here and the adventures we would have together. When my grandparents weren't there, Benzipan would take me out to the amusement parks, either to the Tivoli or even Bakken.

Benzipan and Suunkit cooked the best food, curries and soups, full of amazing spices that were all new to me. I would stuff myself full because it was so delicious. Any time there were big receptions, Benzipan and Suunkit would decorate the house and carve the fruit into ornate presentations for guests.

I admired them; tremendously hardworking, they made a stark impression on my young mind. Benzipan ended up creating such a strong bond with my grandparents that she and her daughter traveled to the United States with them when they finished their time in Denmark.

After Denmark, Afi's next station was in the U.S. capital, Washington, D.C. I was eleven at the time and thought it was so cool that my grandfather was going to be the ambassador to the United States!

I wasn't a little girl any longer and during the summers that I visited D.C., I would attend training camps at a local gymnastics gym called Arlington Aerials. It was very different from my home, the opposite of the pristine Icelandic gyms I was used to. Arlington Aerials was more like a gym, less refined, and it actually smelled like a gym. I loved the foreign feeling that the camps offered. They operated with a more rigorous system, with higher expectations put on each athlete. They trained a lot more frequently, with more intensity than I was used to back in Iceland.

The American girls were surprisingly open and friendly, but I didn't make many friends outside the gym. I had it good with my grandparents and I preferred spending time with my family. Most days my grandfather was busy with work, and Amma would take me shopping. If another ambassador's family had kids my age, we would all go together.

Summer 2006

During my grandparents third and final summer in D.C., my mom and I stopped in D.C. on the way to a gymnastics camp in Alabama with my Icelandic club team. I was trying hard to disguise it, but I was in tremendous pain.

Both of my wrists were killing me. I had never experienced anything like it and the timing was terrible. I never complained about injuries, biting my lip and carrying on instead. Getting sidelined was more terrifying to me than the injury itself. I let the situation deteriorate to the point where I couldn't move my wrists. I was even using a closed fist to do round offs and back handsprings. That caught my coaches' attention and they forced me to rest. This was a nightmare for me. I was at a huge training camp with Olympians as coaches and now the whole opportunity was in jeopardy.

Doctors determined that there were no visible breaks on the

X-rays. I got a cast, a prescription for anti-inflammatories and directions to take it easy until the cast came off. I missed the remainder of the camp. When the cast was finally removed, I remember feeling so nervous and unsure. I treated it gingerly until I was confident that the healing process had been successful. I cartwheeled around the house in celebration.

Although I was limited in my movement, I had an amazing summer training every day. My grandparents were busy, so I would put on my leotards and shorts and head to the gym. My grandfather's chauffeur, Francisco, drove me to practice. He made every day like carpool karaoke, singing at the top of his lungs as we rolled for forty-five minutes across town.

When he was a kid, Afi helped build a three-story housing complex, and then lived there growing up with his parents. When he and Amma were newlyweds, they lived on the second floor, over his parents. So when it came time for my grandparents to move back to Iceland it was an easy choice for them—they purchased an apartment in that same building.

My mom moved to another town, even farther from Reykjavik, which made it hard to coordinate transportation, especially when I had exams and needed rides from school. When my mom was unavailable, Afi picked me up on his lunch breaks and took me to his office. I would sit in his office and study until it was time to go home.

I've always wanted to be like my grandfather and these days would reinforce my admiration for him. Sometimes I would have lunch with him and the prime minister, which really impressed me. I thought I was so cool. In my mind, I wanted to be an ambassador or the prime minister. Maybe even the president.

I still lived with my mom, but on days when I was in Reykjavik,

I would stay with my grandparents. I was at their house often enough that Amma kept an inflatable mattress for me to sleep on in the living room, which made me feel welcome. They provided me with security and stability, though I was constantly moving around.

My mom's husband got a new job and the whole family moved to Norway. I was still serious with gymnastics and I had switched gyms. I had just gotten into the college where I wanted to study. College in Iceland is what Americans might think of as prep school. It's a nonmandatory preparation for sixteen- to nineteen-year-olds in advance of university. My life and my best friends were all in Reykjavik. So, I moved in with my grandparents.

In gymnastics during my college years, my love for conditioning was as strong as ever. Among the other girls in my class, however, the unpopularity of our Russian coach and his methods were at an all-time high. Girls were melting down and crying in training. They would complain incessantly behind the scenes.

The coaches would tell us, "Look, you're doing the conditioning for yourself. Don't short the reps. You're not doing them for me."

Some girls would cut corners, but it ran against my nature. I wanted the conditioning. I thrived on it. Eventually, the other girls made enough of a stink that my coach was transferred and instructed the younger girls instead of us. Ironically, many of those younger girls wound up as some of the best in Iceland. Our Russian coach was replaced with Romanian ones.

If you watch the Olympics, you'll see that Russian gymnasts are strong, well built, and powerful. The Romanians, on the other hand, are thin. They are very graceful but far less powerful. Instead of a double flip, they will opt for a twist. They will focus on the artistic side of the sport and incorporate ballet.

Romanian coaches put a premium on the routines. For conditioning, the coaches would instruct the athletes to do more reps of the routines. Instead of traditional conditioning, the coaches believe that bars will strengthen your core and floor routines will increase your flexibility.

Only gold medals can say which method is the best, but I can tell you with confidence that the Russian methods favored me. I am not small, light, or graceful. I'm a bigger athlete with Viking bones and I needed the strength work and conditioning. Every time I requested more, the Romanian coaches replied that I needed to lose weight. They emphasized weight loss. They even discouraged us from conditioning because they were afraid we would gain muscle mass.

I've never been a rebellious athlete, but I was very unhappy with what we were doing. Moving in with my grandparents meant I was moving away from Hafnarfjörður to the heart of Reykjavik, which gave me the perfect opportunity to try a different club.

I moved to a club called Armann. The moment I walked into the modern, airy space, I liked it, but I was also intimidated. The head coach, Vladimir, was Russian and had a reputation for being extremely strict.

I was terrified for my entire first training session. Vladimir called me Tanja, either because he couldn't remember my name or liked this name better. I didn't dare to correct him and so the name stuck with me for two years because of my refusal to speak up. By some stroke of luck that day happened to be a conditioning test. I performed extremely well and actually enjoyed the session. We did push-ups until our arms were going to fall off and hanging pike tests that were borderline torturous.

The move over to Armann was the right move at the time, but I missed my friends from Bjork. Many of them are still among my best friends to this day. Over time, the girls from my team at Armann also became my best friends. It wasn't until years later that they told me over lots of laughter that they had not been happy with me that first day. They had scoffed, asking, "Who is this new girl who shows up and just keeps going?!"

I trained with them the entire summer. Summers at Armann focused on conditioning. In the afternoon sessions, we did some skill and apparatus work, but mostly it was about getting strong and fit.

In August, we attended a training camp in Denmark for two weeks to prepare for the coming season. We literally lived in the gym. Everyone slept on huge mattresses on the floor and we spent most of our waking hours training. Every morning we would wake up and go out for a jog before breakfast. A massive session followed and led directly to lunch. We would practice on the apparatus until dinner was served and then sleep like rocks before we repeated the whole process the following day. I have never seen as much improvement in such a short time as I did in that two-week period. It worked perfectly for me.

Six months later, I injured my ankle. It was a big sprain with lots of swelling and constant pain. It seemed small at the time, but it had a lasting impact on the direction I would take. I started putting school in front of gymnastics. I would take the day off if finals were coming up to study. My ankle gave me an additional excuse to stop moving, and I lost momentum.

For months, Amma cleaned up my bed each day. I was still an extended-stay guest. A visitor would never know I was living there. Amma decided it was time for me to become a permanent resident. It took two years, but finally we made an official room for me. The TV room chairs were switched out for a sleeping bed. I had a closet of my own, a desk, and everything I could need to live comfortably.

Living with my grandparents was a blessing, but it also presented some unique challenges. My mom had been so strict with what I ate when I was growing up. I was never allowed to eat anything unhealthy unless it was a cozy night or candy day. It was something we did on special occasions and I was used to the regimen.

Grandparents, on the other hand, live to spoil their grandchildren. Grandparents don't say "no." Grandparents don't stop you from eating sweets, which is okay if you're not living with them. I had to ditch the excuse that it was okay because "I'm with Amma and Afi," and I set my own boundaries. Harder than it sounds. I did my best to be strict with my diet, but they always had cakes around. Afi is the son of a baker, and he loves his pastries. Our little thing at night was making hot chocolate. We would make fresh "Icelandic bagels" (*Kringla*) and dip them in.

The morning routine included everyone waking up in shifts, then eventually meeting in the kitchen. My grandparents had their second cup of coffee while I ate breakfast. Grandpa would take me to school on his way to work, then take me to training later.

At the time I knew nothing about diet. My strategy as a gymnast had been to eat as little as possible. If I could skip breakfast, I was pleased. I would have a really light lunch and maybe a banana before training. Losing sight of my diet was not the end of the world, but between the stress of my exams and the lack of exercise it did present a problem. A pattern developed as this cycle continued. I started to gain weight.

I remember when I finally recognized that the *Kringla* were a problem. It was an ah-ha moment that we were having these "treats" every day. I had to have the conversation with my grandparents that I couldn't do this anymore for fear of derailing myself further.

When I finally did return to training, I was surprised to find that I was not enjoying it as much. I felt like all I was doing was attempting to get back to where I had been. Progress wasn't even in the discussion, it was a foreign concept. I felt sluggish and heavy and lost the fun I had previously found in the sport. It was clear in my mind that gymnastics would not sustain my athletic future. I knew I would never be the best in the world. My lack of enthusiasm led me to explore other options. That was the end of my gymnastics career. I needed something new. At sixteen years old, after ten years of living and breathing gymnastics as training and sport, I looked for something to replace it.

The lack of direction in my post-gymnastics era made me feel miserable. I spent most days bored, contemplating what my next move would be. It was a difficult time for me. I'm a high achiever and I thrive on waking up with a goal in mind and attacking my day with a purpose.

Later in the summer, I decided to try my skills at track. I had always been a natural runner but had never experienced the intensity of track intervals on the oval. I found that events like the 400-meter and 800-meter races could beat me up in the same way as the hardest days of gymnastics conditioning.

Track in Iceland is divided into four seasons, a repeating cycle of build-up seasons and competition seasons. I joined the club during the build-up season, which involved conditioning all the time. Perfect. I was going six days a week and spending a majority of my free time on the track.

It wasn't until the competition season arrived that I realized I didn't have an actual event. This presented a problem. The competition season was organized around the event. Training sessions were lighter, with rest and recovery and maintenance days. The abundance of competing and lack of training was exactly the opposite of what I was looking for. I was just trying out events and never really knew what I was doing. I didn't have an event of my own and I didn't like all the stumbling and failures. I endured the competition season and did another build-up season, which I loved. The coaches taught me a little bit about how I should be eating and I was feeling good about how I looked and felt.

I wanted to do the heptathlon, but my mind-set was a little bit skewed. I had tried my hand early on with the long and high jumps with very bad results. In my head, I thought this would clearly eliminate me as a contender from the heptathlon, so I moved on. My close friend is nationally ranked in the heptathlon. When I told her that story, she laughed at me and pointed out that she had been training in these events since she was six years old. I walked in off the street and quit because I was unsuccessful on my first try. Without the diversity of the heptathlon I was certain that I would get bored with a single event, and my track career ended shortly after. You can't be unhappy with yourself if you hadn't put in the hard work, but I had yet to learn that.

That summer I came back to the States to visit my family in Atlanta, Georgia. I always worked particularly hard in the summer, but now I had nowhere to direct my efforts. Even when we had breaks from gymnastics growing up, I filled any gaps in training by exercising or creating my own routines every single day. I have always loved exercise.

I joined a local globo gym and hit it hard all summer long. I would take multiple classes a day like Spin or Body Pump, whatever fit my schedule, really. I would also run every morning, which forced me to get up before sunrise to avoid the oppressive Southern heat. By now I was very conscious of what I was putting in my body. I drank tons of water and leaned heavily on smoothies and salads. I was deathly afraid of carbohydrates.

I had natural athletic talent and boundless energy, but I couldn't decide what I wanted to do with my athletic future. For the better part of a year, I had gone through the motions athletically. I would go back to gymnastics sporadically, but I didn't want to compete. I just wanted to train and to be there at the gym. I gave track another halfhearted attempt.

As directionless as I felt, the universe was diligently conspiring behind my back to align the stars that would lead me to CrossFit. While it can take me longer than I might like to find the hidden meaning in life's events, I have no doubt that everything happens for a reason.

My best friend growing up was a girl named Heiddis Anna Ludiksdottir. We did gymnastics together, but when I switched clubs she left to pursue pole vaulting. She was always telling me about this girl named Annie Mist Thorisdottir who trained with her. Annie was really good at pole vault, even though it was hardly getting a fraction of her attention. She divided time between Bootcamp classes and some "CrossFit" thing.

In the lead-up to Annie's trip to the 2011 CrossFit Games, a documentary about her was released. I had seen parts of it and was intrigued. This gave me a vague idea of who Annie was. My friend Heiddis Anna kept talking about her. She told me how good Annie was without even trying and how much potential she had, if she would just stop running off to this Bootcamp thing. She was notorious for being late to training because of other training. Apparently Annie was unstoppable.

I was always the one in gymnastics who constantly asked for conditioning. I craved it and exercise has always made me feel good. Annie was the same way. Heidis Anna would often remind me how similar the two of us were. Heiddis Anna was the first one who mentioned Bootcamp and encouraged me to try it while I was stepping between both gymnastics and track.

"You're a little crazy like her," she said. "You should do Cross-Fit."

For some reason I couldn't be convinced. I needed a spark of motivation badly. I was in my final year of college. I was uninspired and bored. Later that summer my motivation hit an all-time low.

That's when "Iceland Annie" brought CrossFit, along with a gold medal, back to the island.

4

THOR'S DAUGHTER

ÞÓRISDÓTTIR

*In the hotbeds the right butterfly wing flap
was causing talent hurricanes.*
—DANIEL COYLE, *THE TALENT CODE*

Fall 2011

Icelanders refer to ourselves as a unit.

"*We* qualified for the World Cup. *We* have such strong women."

We are very proud of the successes of our "*sons*" and "*dóttirs.*" That's how it was in 2011 when "We won the CrossFit Games" with "Iceland Annie" Mist Thorisdottir.

"*þetta reddast*" is a common phrase we use. It's the Icelandic way of saying, "It will all be good." We use it to remind ourselves that things tend to work out for the best, even if it's not "all good" at the moment. Most households and businesses will have the news on and everyone talks about it the following day. The news is less depressing in Iceland and just about anything can make it on air. If a lamb gets stuck in a fence and it needs saving, for example, it's on the news. Everyone knows everyone. Instead of six degrees of separation, in Iceland, it's more like two.

Annie's winning the CrossFit Games was all over the television and the newspapers. A documentary team had been following her on her journey, which added to the excitement. When she won, she became a national hero and an instant celebrity. She had traveled to the United States, performed what seemed to be every movement under the sun, and been crowned Fittest on Earth. Not in Iceland. Not in Europe. Not in the United States—on Earth.

This really put us on the map. Annie winning the Games validated for the world what Icelanders had held as a truism: that Icelandic women are mightily strong. There were parades and celebrations. Everywhere you turned, people were talking about it—cafés, shops, bookstores. You couldn't buy groceries without hearing about Annie Thorisdottir and her amazing fitness exploits. Her success was a boon for Icelandic sports and we were very proud.

CrossFit blew up in popularity as well, and everyone wanted to try the new sport. Because of Iceland's humble size the effects were magnified. Annie became a household name as everyone in Iceland talked about fitness, CrossFit, and the CrossFit Games. I watched, too, and was captivated by the images I saw on TV. Videos and pictures were shared all over Facebook and Icelandic websites. They featured athletes from many different backgrounds with amazing bodies doing crazy things. It was all set in a world-class facility under the sunny skies of Southern California. Thousands of spectators who looked like competitors themselves were clearly enthralled with the spectacle.

Annie was on display, climbing ropes, pulling sleds, hoisting weights, and doing movements I had never seen or heard of before. She looked untouchable, like a Viking shield maiden. But Heiddis Anna had already told me about her. "Iceland Annie" was just a girl from the nearby coastal town. We were more alike than we were different.

"Katrin, you could be so good at this," my mother and Amma observed. "Why don't you try it?"

I knew that they were right so I called CrossFit BC, the operators of Bootcamp, immediately. It was the gym where Annie trained. I was there the next day, ready.

With Bootcamp, it was love at first try. The angst I had been feeling after gymnastics and track were instantly a thing of the past. I felt like I had found my home. The sessions were massive outdoor beatdowns. They were heavy on cardio and bodyweight movements and mimicked military training. The trainers would act more like drill instructors than coaches. We would grind for hours on end and work so hard.

When I was a kid I was interested in the army. But I'm afraid of guns, don't like violence, and never wanted to fight. I just liked the idea of training professionally. I wanted to try my hand at all the cool stuff you see in movies. Bootcamp gave me a taste of that crazy that I'd always wanted to try.

The coaches loved challenging athletes. If I were holding a sandbag, they would come and exchange it for a heavier one. If your push-ups were strong, they would put a heavy load on your back and make you hold the plank position. Often the idea was to challenge you mentally. Everyone—and I mean everyone—will reach a physical breaking point sooner or later. Most Bootcamp sessions taught you to realize what you can accomplish once you've passed that breaking point.

There was also a premium placed on competition. There was a lot of running. Coaches would pair me up with the fastest and I would kill myself to try to win. I was addicted: The mix of mental challenges and competition fanned the flame inside of me to a red-hot glow. I wanted to see how far I could push myself. It was a constant challenge and I was working out with so many people that it kept it fun in spite of the craziness. And there was always someone to compete against. I learned to seek hard work over everything because we didn't work on a clock. You would just grind and try to find new limits for yourself every day. Each session left me sweaty and filthy, exhausted but fulfilled.

Where Bootcamp lent itself to the formation of pure work capacity, I was told CrossFit would introduce me to more technical movements and challenges. The coaches suggested that I alternate Bootcamp days with CrossFit days.

I felt nervous about CrossFit. I didn't know a single person there, and the classes were confusing just to an observer. Watching people cycle through the gym made me dizzy. I couldn't figure out how everyone knew where they were supposed to be. Some were doing pull-ups, others were lifting weights. There were people with kettlebells buzzing around. It looked like fitness chaos. I could not figure out what they were doing to save my life.

My official introduction to CrossFit was far less sexy than my intro to Bootcamp. I was placed in the Elements class just like everyone else and I hated it. I caught on quick, so the pace of the class felt slow. It was too easy and I wanted to do more. But I kept my mouth shut and just waited.

The first time I saw Annie, I was participating in Elements. She was teaching a regular group class, and the workout featured handstands. I had lived on my hands for almost a decade. Handstands were my best party trick and I wished I could be in that room showing off my skills. Instead I was stuck in the side room, shoulder-pressing a piece of PVC plumbing pipe. I had not anticipated being so starstruck just by spotting her, but she was a pretty big celebrity, especially to me.

Oh damn, Annie's coaching, I thought.

I admired the way she carried herself and you could see that she commanded respect. She told me years later that she had been eyeing me up to gauge my potential as well, saying to herself, *Damn, who is this girl?*

I really looked up to Annie. I remember when she said my name for the first time. It doesn't sound like a lot, but what it represented to me was acknowledgment, and in my mind, it was huge. I do my best to use people's names now because of the impact that had on me. Interactions mean so much more and I can connect so much better when I remember people's names.

In Elements, we spent fifty minutes focused on technical work, followed by a short workout. I'll never forget the first workout I was given because I thought it was a joke at first. It was a five-minute AMRAP of box step-ups and push-ups, barely a warm-up for me. My inner sled dog was dying to run. But I knew the on-ramp classes wouldn't last forever, and I picked up a lot of information that helped me immensely.

After Elements, it was time to pay for a punch card and transition into the general membership of the gym. I didn't have a lot of money and I really had not enjoyed Elements. My plan was to gracefully exit CrossFit and only attend Bootcamp, but the coaches at CrossFit BC wouldn't take no for an answer. They included a three-month CrossFit card with my Bootcamp membership.

When I got into the classes, it was a completely different speed. I loved it more than anything I had tried before. I felt like I was born to do CrossFit. Everything about it made me happy. Each day presented a new challenge. It was a roller-coaster ride of huge improvements followed by even bigger ego checks. I had never squatted before I tried CrossFit. My only real weightlifting experience involved light body-pump circuits and core work. I had only touched a barbell a handful of times during track, when we did power cleans. I remember thinking that I would be good with the lifts because I had well-defined biceps. I had a lot to learn.

Just like everyone who walks into CrossFit, I quickly discovered my strengths and weaknesses. I was pleasantly surprised by my abilities on the barbell and distraught by some of the gymnastics skills that did not transfer over from my formal training. I was infatuated. This was the most unique challenge I had ever faced and it changed every day.

Success came extremely quickly with the barbell when I did finally get my hands on it. Within a month, I could snatch my body weight. Part of my success came from being fearless on the lifts. I would throw myself under the bar on a snatch without a second thought. I was also so new that I was trying to max out every single time I snatched. I would fail over and over again at maximum weight, then reset and try it over and over again until I was either successful or too exhausted to continue. I would never do that now, but experience is the greatest teacher.

My affinity for the snatch and clean and jerk gained the attention of the Olympic-weightlifting coaches in Iceland. I took them up on offers for a few sessions and learned a lot. There was no way that weightlifting alone could maintain my focus and drive, but I loved doing it inside the framework of my CrossFit training. My legs were surprisingly weak. I would make up for it by leveraging my back to whip the bar up. My power clean was solid and I could put anything that I got to my shoulder over my head.

Everyone who has tried it knows that CrossFit gives and CrossFit takes away. For all my success on the barbell, the gymnastic rings were my absolute nemesis. Muscle-ups were the first movement I ever encountered that I physically could not do. Other people were getting themselves on top of the rings and I couldn't for a million dollars. As an athlete, nothing made me crazier. I was following the formula and working so hard, and still failed to make progress. I would tell myself stories in my head, like that I was built strangely and that a limitation of my anatomy was probably to blame. I thought it was reasonable to believe I owned the only body in the gym physically incapable of the muscle-up.

Acquiring that skill became an obsession. I watched every single video on the internet of coaches teaching muscle-ups and athletes performing them. I watched so many videos of Canadian CrossFit athlete Camille Leblanc-Bazinet doing muscle-ups that I felt like we were close friends. Sometimes I watched them in slow motion, clicking through them frame by frame, trying to crack the code or witness the black magic that would make me move like her.

Carl Paoli, a former gymnast from Spain, was producing instructional videos out of San Francisco CrossFit. They were phenomenal and I worked on every single skill and progression I could find. I showed up early for training and work progressions. Of course, with a false grip, it's only so long until you're going to start bleeding all over the place. That was my process: I would drill every day before class until my hands bled. I would work on muscle-ups whenever I could. I was obsessed. On Fridays, I didn't start classes until 10 a.m., so I would drive to my old gymnastics gym and work on the rings continuously until it was time for class. It went on like this every day for two months. I couldn't figure out why girls who I surpassed in any other movement in the gym could swing around me like monkeys while I was cemented to the floor, watching.

In the fall, I was visiting Reebok CrossFit Thames, the gym owned by Annie's coach, Jami Tikkanen. Jami was out of town at the time, but one of his coaches was working with me after class. Maybe it was the right cue, maybe the pressure of being at another gym, or maybe it was just the product of all my hard work, but something sparked the magic and I found myself on top of the rings. I almost exploded I was so ecstatic. I kicked my feet spastically and screamed at the top of my lungs. I didn't come down for what felt like a minute. The feeling of working so hard and then succeeding was too sweet, and I wanted to live there forever. When I finally got down, I hugged everyone in sight.

I was smiling ear to ear and beaming on the way home, as happy as I had ever been. I felt victorious and elated until a thought occurred to me, *What if I can never do that again?* My joy dissolved into panic and I couldn't sleep. I showed up to the gym early the next day to see if my new skill had mysteriously disappeared overnight. It had not and I was happy again. This cycle repeated itself for a week. The joy of a successful muscle-up was followed by dread that it would be the last time I saw the view from on top of the rings. For months, I had to test the skill every single week to make sure I still had it.

Winter, 2012

When I was only a few weeks into CrossFit, three girls who had competed at the CrossFit Games on a team attended the class before mine. They wrote their times on the whiteboard and when I realized I had beaten all of them, my confidence surged. *Hey, I'm good at this.* When I spoke to my mom later on the phone, I remember declaring to her, "Mom, I'm gonna make Regionals." Of course she was on board. I was serious and determined from the moment I began CrossFit. Now I had goals.

Sometime around Christmas I remember setting my sights even higher, saying, "I'm going to make the CrossFit Games." At my cousin's house I had acquired one of the Livestrong bracelets that were popular at the time. I had no idea what it meant, but was attracted to the bright-yellow color that caught your attention and loved that it said "strong." My cousin parted with the rubber bracelet easily. I put it on and decided it would serve as my reminder that I was going to go to the CrossFit Games. This was the first time I used a bracelet as a reminder. Now it's a thing.

It was highlighter yellow and tacky. But I wore it on my left wrist no matter what, including to the school gala to which I wore a beautiful black sparkly dress, high heels, and a coiffed hairdo. It was always with me. When workouts hurt or school was hard and I wanted to quit, I would look at it to get motivated. After Bootcamp, I went to CrossFit where they had treadmills upstairs. I would do 10-by-400-meter repeats, picturing the CrossFit Games in my head and cranking the speed until I was nearly falling off. I often took myself past exhaustion and just at the right moment, my left wrist would pop up within view.

I would repeat to myself: *I wanna make it, I wanna make it, I wanna make it.*

Annie urged me toward competition. My first was a couples' tournament. I did it on a whim with one of my classmates because we thought it would be fun. In my mind, I wasn't taking it too seriously, but there were girls in the mix who had qualified to compete on teams at the CrossFit Games, so the bar was high. At the end of the competition, we were on top of the leaderboard. It was a welcome surprise, but I still had a lot to learn about the intricacies of this new sport.

I started actively seeking out competitions at the local level. I went to small weekend comps in the gym and the surrounding area. Competing stoked the fire inside me to train even harder, and I thrived, loving every minute of competition.

January 2012—Reykjavik; Eighteen years old

Progress came slowly but consistently. The skills I had honed through years of practice in gymnastics laid over the technical demands of CrossFit in a way that allowed me to excel. The slow nature of my gains made them easy to ignore, until I compared myself to my peers. The competitions I entered served as a strong reminder that what felt slow to me was a rocket ship of progress in the CrossFit world at large.

As I gained competence in competition, I was also gaining the respect of the athletes I looked up to. Annie had been paying attention and apparently thought that I was ready to level up. She invited me to train with her and her boyfriend, Frederik Aegidius, at Cross-Fit Reykjavik. I had been training around Annie for months, but never with her. I completely freaked out. Annie freakin' Thorisdottir had asked *me* to train with her. Frederik was also a heavy hitter and he was on the cusp of qualifying for his first CrossFit Games.

I had won a recent competition that paired a CrossFit workout with the total of your Olympic lifts, but I had tweaked my back in the process. I had enough experience to know that I wasn't injured, but my back was definitely lit up pretty badly. There was absolutely no way I was going to pass up this once-in-a-lifetime opportunity so I loaded up on ibuprofen, which I never do, slathered my back in Icy Hot, put a heating pad on it, and stretched for most of the night. I prepared for that session like I was going to Regionals, obsessing over what I should put in my gym bag before I went to bed and then tossing and turning nervously before falling asleep.

Annie and Frederik showed me a whole new approach to training, and I had a blast. On top of that I was forced to push myself further and harder than ever. I never had competition like this is in the gym ever. Despite the fact that I was an up-and-comer and a potential future opponent, Annie was the perfect mentor. I would eventually come to find that identifying potential and fostering it is a habit for her. This was the first of what would become many times that I witnessed her desire to help develop promising Icelandic athletes. Annie took me under her wing.

Training together became more regular. We both had very busy schedules, though, and seldom were able to actually coordinate. When we did, I got a much clearer picture of what an athlete at the top of the game looked and performed like. It was simultaneously humbling and inspirational. I was lucky to have this example so early in my career. It shaped the way I train and compete. Annie often shared her experiences and strategies from her already legendary career. We talked about movements and approaches to competition. I had stumbled into an apprenticeship with a master of her craft.

Not long into our training together, Annie and Frederik were scheduled to travel to Denmark for a competition called the Butcher's Classics.

"You should come," she said in passing one day.

I smiled dismissively. I thought she was absolutely crazy to think I could just pick up and leave. But she pressed the issue further, so I knew she was serious.

"It's a good competition and if you take first place, you win one thousand dollars, which is enough to cover your flight and accommodation."

I was absolutely floored by the idea.

"Oh my God," was all I could think to say.

"Think about it," she said.

I didn't stop thinking about it. The thoughts swam in my head and the pull of competition was magnetic, but this sounded insane to me. Traveling to Denmark on a whim? Looking back, it fell into place as if it was destiny. At the time, I was familiar with the CrossFit Games because of Annie. But I was not aware of the dedication it would take and how long the process would be until I saw how she trained. Then I realized that if she thought this was a good idea, I should seriously consider it.

I felt conflicted, but my grandparents were supportive. They tracked ticket prices with me to find something I could afford.

At this point, I didn't have two pennies to rub together, much less enough to make it to Denmark. My grandpa was still filling my gas tank and I lived at home. Any extra money went toward clothes or food.

That Friday there was another huge gala at my college. If I went to the competition, I would have to miss it, which was a big deal. At the time, it was one of the biggest decisions of my life. At school the next day, I shared the dilemma with my class. They were so overwhelmingly supportive and thrilled for me that I decided to go. Everything about it made me nervous and excited. This was the most spontaneous thing I had ever done.

At the last minute, Annie and Frederik had to change their plans. I was now headed to Denmark on my own. They arranged for me to sleep on an acquaintance's couch. On my flight, I realized I knew her name but nothing else. No address, no phone number, nothing. My plane touched down around 10 p.m. I was kicking myself while I waited for my bag to arrive.

There was an element of excitement from the craziness of the whole situation. After I tamped down my feelings of dread, I logged into the airport WiFi and found her on Facebook. Luckily she responded to my message, but the directions were too vague for my sleepy brain. It took two hours, a few buses, one train, and a short walk before I arrived. It was well past midnight when I finally got to sleep.

The competition was just one day and the workouts were not announced until you were onsite. I was alone in Denmark; tired, nervous, and freezing cold. Still, I performed well and entered the final event with the top women. The final workout was similar to the CrossFit benchmark workout Fran, a brutal combination of thrusters and pull-ups with a repetition scheme short enough to allow you to sprint and inflict lots of pain on yourself in the process.

I was nervous because I didn't have butterfly pull-ups at the time. It wasn't my best event of the day, but I managed to hang on. I won the competition and it was covered by local media and a few websites. I was thrilled and shocked by how much fun I had. It was super competitive and I had stepped up to the challenge. The whole experience was a huge confidence builder. I had stepped way outside my comfort zone and I was growing because of it.

Open 2012

In February, Annie transitioned to CrossFit Reykjavik and eventually she asked me to join her. I was flattered but also terrified. She proposed that we train together three or four times a week. The remaining days I would be left to my own devices. I can imagine the intent was to ensure I didn't become a stage-5 clinger, but the uncertainty scared me. I was still so new and I was scared I wouldn't know what to do on my non-Annie days.

I think the owners of Bootcamp caught wind of it because they really started to pull me in and keep me around. They offered me incentives for staying, including free coaching and sponsorship to Regionals. They did come through with some coaching from CrossFit BC's cofounder, Elvar þor Karlsson. Elvar was great, but mostly he looked over my programming rather than hands-on coaching. Bootcamp was my safety net, which is ultimately why I stayed. I was breaking out of my shell, but I was anything but adventurous. I was very square and risk-averse. I felt safe there, so I stayed.

Fear held me back from moving on with Annie. It damaged our friendship for a while. I could tell that she was disappointed in my decision and I felt I had missed out on the opportunity to train with the best female athlete in the sport. We had become good friends, but after that we didn't talk for a while. I don't like to dwell on things, but if I think about it, I do have some regrets. I had already learned so much from her and I could have gotten even better. I was sad that it put a strain on our relationship.

I won almost every competition I entered that year and the momentum carried on into the CrossFit Games Open, the first qualifying stage for the Games. I was killing it. At the end of Week 3, my worst score for any workout was fourth place in Europe. It was me and Annie at the top of the leaderboard, then everyone else trailing dozens of points behind.

A media team had traveled to Iceland for an interview with Annie. The production manager reached out to see if they could meet with me as well while they were in town. I was shocked but flattered by the attention and agreed to the interview. I met them at Armann, my old gymnastics gym. It was my first interview ever and I was incredibly nervous. I rambled a lot and spoke with a British accent, which came more naturally to me at the time. I didn't know what to say or how to act, I was just a timid teenager who loved this rapidly growing sport.

I continued to do well on the remaining Open workouts and finished each workout in seventh place or better out of all the women competing in Europe. I took second place in the overall standings, just 10 points behind Annie.

The video didn't publish until after the Open concluded. I was so excited about it until I saw the title they had chosen. The chosen title was "Another Annie." I was sick to my stomach when I saw it. My relationship with Annie was already rocky at the time, and this certainly wasn't going to help. I know it annoyed Annie, too. I had nothing to do with the title, but I felt the tension when it posted to social media.

Beyond damage to our friendship, I was personally annoyed as well. I just wanted to be Katrin. Why did I have to be the next Annie? I hated the manufactured rivalry and the constant comparisons, but it was something I would have to get used to as Icelandic female CrossFit athletes continued to command attention.

5

ICELAND

ÍSLAND

I think, if the world can be saved, it will be by women.
—VIGDÍS FINNBOGADÓTTIR, FORMER PRESIDENT
OF ICELAND, AND THE FIRST DEMOCRATICALLY
ELECTED FEMALE HEAD OF STATE IN THE WORLD

When you drive away from the airport in Reykjavik it's easy to feel like you've been tricked. Where the brochures and tourist websites promised fjords, volcanoes, and natural beauty, the harsh landscape surrounding Keflavík looks more like a barren wasteland. Scrub brushes and moss hug lava rock flats as far as the eye can see down to the north Atlantic Ocean a few miles away. This harsh environment combined with inconceivable natural beauty that awaits just miles in any direction have combined to forge a population more resilient than any other that I know of.

Along with resilience, Icelandic people have a strong tradition of storytelling. Most agree these stories were born as a cure from the boredom that accompanied long, dark winters bundled around a fire. My grandmother loved the mythology of the island and recounted it for me when I was young. The rocks you see by the roadside, according to Amma, are unfortunate trolls who had been caught in the sun and turned to stone forever.

We also have a strong sense of pride, despite our small size. Iceland is a tiny country with only 334,000 inhabitants on the whole island. But we play big and we think we can do anything. In our minds we are the biggest country in the world and we are hypercompetitive.

From the moment you arrive on the island, you can feel its power. I am always floored by how empty the vast land can look. When you take the time to get a closer look, Iceland has some of Earth's most amazing natural phenomenon. I love taking visitors to see the Northern Lights in the wintertime. Science-fiction movies are always being filmed here because of the otherworldly features like black sand beaches, lava flows, and waterfalls. There are geysers, volcanoes, and hot springs dotting the whole island. It really is the land of fire and ice.

The weather changes from hour to hour and you can typically expect to encounter rain at some point during the day. We always prepare for anything when we leave the house. The same landscape under different conditions can look like a completely different world. The mountains can be cast in purple or pink with dark patches on the lava flows and a million different shades of green and gray. It's all so naturally beautiful that it takes the breath away. It's something I've never taken for granted.

Even winter days with subzero temperatures are beautiful in their own way. The ground is coated in ice or snow and against it the sky becomes as blue as the Icelandic flag. As kids, we would play in the snow for hours, taking breaks only when our fingers and toes couldn't take it any longer.

Summers were the opposite, bringing beautiful temperatures and nearly twenty-four hours of sunlight. The energy you feel from so much sunlight is an incredibly invigorating phenomenon that you have to experience to understand. Iceland is a late country year round, but especially so in the summer months. Activities will often carry on until midnight and it's not uncommon, even for families, to be out later than that.

Icelandic people are hearty. In the CrossFit community, especially, people frequently ask me, "What's in the water up there?" Ironically, part of the answer is in the question itself. Our natural resources are so pristine you can freely drink from wild streams without fear. It's become a tourist attraction to buy a cup and drink from the flowing water. We also have an abundance of quality fish, seafood, and wild game.

More important than what's in the water is what's in our blood. Iceland was originally settled by the Vikings as they explored westward in search of new lands and bounties. People who thrived here did so against the odds, especially back then. It's a harsh environment for everything—from farming to building. You have to be tough just to survive, much less thrive. There's something about the combination of inhospitable climates and cold weather that equates to a long and healthy life. Of course it's less so now, but there was a time in Iceland where you had to be fit just to survive, and that blood still runs in our veins.

Iceland has, arguably, the highest level of gender equality in the world. This means I grew up with amazing female role models and never once thought being a woman was a limiting factor for what I could accomplish. Gender equality is more than a buzzword in Iceland—it's built into our social contract. And we have gone to greater lengths than any other country to ensure equality is baked into our culture. In 2017, Iceland passed laws making it illegal to pay women less than men for the same job. Where it was already a social expectation, equality is now written into our laws. The law, which may sound like common sense, is the first of its kind in the world.

We also have a history of leading from the front when it comes to female leaders. Iceland elected the world's first female president, Vigdís Finnbogadóttir. She took office in 1980 and she was the president for sixteen years. I was three years old when she stepped down, but the mark she left on my generation helped to form how I see the world. She was a great president and is one of Iceland's most notable celebrities.

My grandparents were close with Vigdís through Afi's job. There is a video of me at eighteen months old performing a song-and-dance routine for her that I had just learned. I was shouting the name of the song at her and roping her into my craziness. Needless to say, she's an important role model. I like to imagine that dancing with the first female president in the world before I turned two somehow empowered my sponge-like baby brain and encouraged me to seek greatness in my own life.

The expectations of women in Iceland have been raised over the years, not lowered. Growing up, I was never told that I wasn't capable of something because I was a girl or that I shouldn't be as strong as the men. I knew that I could do anything that anyone else could do. It didn't mean it would be easy. But it was attainable. I was raised with this worldview and I would probably take it for granted if I hadn't traveled the world.

I notice gender roles far more in the United States. Women here seem to be told how to see the world far more than I was as a child: "Girls should like pink and play with dolls." Or, "They shouldn't speak their mind." Or, "Women should be skinny and look good for cameras."

Don't get me wrong; I am a girlie girl. I love to get manicures. I love sparkles and headbands and getting my hair done. But that's my choice, and no one ever told me I had to be that way. Just like they never told me I couldn't lift heavy weights or do pull-ups until my hands bleed. If I had wanted to do just about anything, I feel confident that I would have been supported. Young girls in the States seem to be pressured into a narrower funnel, which can be limiting. I hope that I can help to change that.

I have never been afraid to be strong. As a little girl I would watch a Swedish show called *Pippi Långstrump*. The same character was less popular but present in the United States, where she was known as Pippi Longstocking. She was the strongest girl in the world, and she was my absolute hero. She could lift horses and she lived alone in her house. I thought all those things—her abilities, her strength, and her independence—were so cool. When I played in the yard, I would pretend to be Pippi getting into adventures and saving the world. *LazyTown* was another children's show I watched. The name is a bit ironic, as it basically promoted healthy eating and physical education. I was always imitating the show's dances and singing the songs.

Icelandic female role models in sports, politics, and pop culture reinforced that women could take a strong lead. Our cultural influences told us to be healthy and to be strong, and also to judge on character, not gender.

I have never taken for granted how lucky I am to grow up in this environment. It's something I'm passionate about sharing. I want women to have more confidence, and to believe in themselves. You're never going to do something by accident. You have to believe in yourself to want to become something.

Icelanders believe they are the best at everything. When it comes to the CrossFit Games, it's a matter of fact. In a world of strong women the Dottirs have consistently dominated the semifinal round of qualification on multiple continents. Since 2015 the top of the CrossFit Games leaderboard has read like an Icelandic phone book. For a country of modest size, we are monumentally accomplished in the sport of fitness.

It was Annie who first paved the way. When she was followed by an army of Icelandic women—Sara Sigmundsdóttir, Thuridur Helgadottir, Bjork Odinsdottir, and me—the CrossFit World took notice. People wanted to know why the women from Iceland were so good. Fans of the sport joked about the "Icelandic Invasion."

One thing is obvious: Icelandic women are worthy of the hype. Despite the fact that only 1 percent of the total women's field is from Iceland, one in four female podium finishers is Icelandic, and one in 2.5 female *champions* is Icelandic. That means we win the CrossFit Games about 160 times more often than you would expect us to win by chance. Those are staggering odds.

With CrossFit, the small size of Iceland is actually an advantage. Top athletes have grown together and challenged one another along the way inside and outside of CrossFit. The term "small world" takes a whole different meaning in Iceland. Everybody knows everybody, and if you don't know someone directly, you definitely know someone who knows them.

In gymnastics I competed frequently against the little sister of Bjork Odinsdottir. Bjork became a frequent challenger at the Regional level and went on to appearances at the CrossFit Games as an individual and a team member. My best friend trained pole vault with Annie when they were younger. One of the most veteran team competitors in Iceland, Anna Ólafsdóttir, did gymnastics with her when they were younger. Our moms and teachers and coaches were either friends themselves or had friends in common.

Although we didn't train together, we knew what everyone was doing. When Annie would perform the impossible, we would raise our game to that level. The intimidation level was reduced because I knew of these high-performing athletes as people, including the Fittest Woman on Earth. They were Icelandic women from right down the road. They did superhuman things, but in my world they were very human.

We would compete head to head at the Icelandic Championships and smaller competitions through Bootcamp and local CrossFit affiliates. We would push each other so hard that athletes were continuously breaking barriers. Little by little, the quality of competition was improving across the board. The rising tide raised all our ships.

Most people are never able to mingle or compete with the best in the world in their sport. I never met Simone Biles when I was in gymnastics and Allyson Felix never came to my track club. If you are lucky enough to have that opportunity, though, a spell can be broken. When you see champions in the flesh, you realize they are humans who bleed red just like you. When you understand this, lofty goals seem far more attainable. Annie's rise to stardom fed the ambitions of the rest of us because we knew who she was.

If she can do it, we thought, *why can't I?*

We believe we can succeed and that's a huge part of our success. Even up-and-coming Icelandic athletes speak with confidence about their chances of winning. We all push each other to be the best because we all want to win. When Annie returned to Iceland as the world champion, she sparked the ambitions of a new generation of athletes. The natural talents of her compatriots have ignited that spark into an inferno.

CrossFit spread like wildfire in the wake of Annie's success as well. When she had first traveled to the United States in 2009 to compete in Aromas, there was only one gym in all of Iceland. Now there are twelve in Reykjavik alone. Annie's gym, CrossFit Reykjavik, services thousands of clients every day.

Having access to Annie early in my career gave me a leg up on the competition and was critical to my success. I had what was essentially an internship with the best female CrossFit athlete on the planet.

When you see someone performing under the competition lights, you can underestimate what it takes to get there. They make it look easy, when in reality, that person has spent years preparing. What is impossible to see on game day is the countless, thankless hours that had to come first. The 6 a.m. swimming sessions alone at the pool or the late-night runs in the snow. The tears, the doubt, and the struggles. People like to make excuses and tell themselves they're not the best because they lost the genetic lottery. In reality, it's hard work that makes champions—not genetics.

Having Annie there in front of me in the flesh, in the same gym, was priceless. I was able to talk to her and pick her brain. I was able to see that even though she looks and performs like a superhero, she is a girl just like me. Training with Annie and seeing her process took away my excuses. I could see she had the same number of hours in her day. I could see her workouts and the intensity she brought.

The biggest blessing of all was that it *didn't* look easy. It looked hard as hell and extremely demanding of your time. But it still looked possible—she was doing it. I believed that if she could do it, then I could, too. Annie was a legend. She was the reigning champion of the CrossFit Games, and she showed me exactly what it would take for me to get there.

By the end of the 2012 school year, I was obsessed with training. College was winding down and I had a severe case of senioritis. Any spare moments I had were filled with training. I thought they were joking when Elvar and the coaches at Bootcamp would force me to take rest days periodically. They were very serious and they could see my obsession. Competing was always on the forefront of my mind, and I would daydream about the upcoming Regionals.

Our graduation date for school was the exact same weekend as the Regionals. I went home and told Amma about the conflict.

"Oh, so you can't compete?" she said, faking disappointment, but grinning ear to ear.

"Oh no, Amma. You know I'm competing," I replied. The smile on my face grew to match hers.

May 2012

My first Regional experience was like something out of a storybook. I had been to a handful of local competitions but nothing could have prepared me for the experience that awaited me in Copenhagen at the Ballerup Super Arena. What I felt there was totally different from anything I had ever experienced and I fell in love with competing all over again.

All weekend long it was the Thorisdottir-versus-Davidsdottir show. Annie took five first-place finishes and one second place— to me. I was the only one who beat her in an event that year. It was the first Regional in which I never finished worse than third place in any event. I took second place and secured a place at the CrossFit Games. It was a good result to say the least, and I was exploding with joy at the end of the weekend.

What I had enjoyed about local competitions was amplified a thousand times by what I experienced in Copenhagen. I had the time of my life on the big stage. I felt like I had been put on this Earth to compete. I felt superhuman when the crowd cheered. I found that I could feed off the energy and the applause. I was doing things I never dreamed I could do. It was absolutely crazy.

My family made the trip over from Iceland, which meant the world to me. I could always find them in the sea of fans by listening for Amma. She was a superfan and had been to dozens of my local competitions. She was so loud she would embarrass my mom, who would move away from her to avoid guilt by association. I loved having her there to see me perform.

At Regionals I was in seventh heaven and I could not imagine how the experience could be topped. If the Regionals felt this good, then the CrossFit Games were going to feel like ecstasy.

6

ROOKIE

NÝLIÐI

The only sin is mediocrity.
—MARTHA GRAHAM

June 2012

"Did you really just go for a run?"

My friends were razzing me from their beach chairs, as they shielded their eyes from the midmorning sun over my shoulder.

"Yeah. Wanna join me for burpees and windsprints?" I poked back.

A few brave souls had accepted my offer over the past few weeks. None had lasted very long. Most people tried to make me feel like I was some obsessed fitness freak. I found this funny because I wasn't doing nearly as much training as I should be.

I had returned from Regionals on Monday and made a same-day turnaround for a graduation trip to Majorca. Three hundred Icelandic college kids would make the Spanish island home base for two weeks of debauchery and celebration at an all-expenses-paid resort. It was a typical postgraduation "get drunk" trip for everyone and they were sprawled in all directions on the Mediterranean beaches. Everyone except for me. That's why my friends were giving me a hard time.

Most people followed the basic itinerary of day drinking followed by night blackouts. Wake-up calls were very late, except for the professional partiers who would set their alarms for 7 a.m. to reserve a sun bench where they could sleep it off before revving back up. This was obviously not the recommended preparation for the CrossFit Games.

I had tried alcohol before but I wasn't drawn to it, and I was certainly not a heavy drinker. Even before I took CrossFit seriously, drinking was reserved for special occasions, and this didn't qualify in my book. I didn't drink a sip or party at all for the week I was there. It was a difficult position to put myself in. I was there with all my friends and this was a time we could never get back. But as much as I wanted to relax and have fun, my excitement for my first CrossFit Games overshadowed everything else. Dreams of competing in Southern California invaded my thoughts constantly throughout the day.

With limited time and equipment, I did what I could to at least maintain my fitness. I would get up early and try to do something healthy. It was hardly adequate and I was itching to put in actual work. I would get back from runs to a pile of humans, barely conscious after very little sleep.

It was hard to relax even when I did try. My mind was preoccupied with how other girls were preparing for the Games. I was eager to get back home and get back to training. There was no way for me to know that absolutely nothing on this island could prepare me for the next beach I would face on the California coast in less than three months.

The Majorca trip also signaled my move to the next level, academically. Lots of people leave school after college in Iceland, but for me it was a foregone conclusion that I would attend university. I was eager to learn and I came from an academic family. But I was facing dilemmas. I had always been a phenomenal student and had gotten good grades. Things came to me easily but I still put in a lot of work. In university, you had to choose how to direct your studies.

Choosing a path in university felt daunting, because it locked you into a specialty. This was the first step toward your chosen field, and to be successful and graduate you would have to stick with it. All my mentors pushed me toward engineering for its practicality. I had always been good at math and rational thinking—there was a direct career path. It just made sense.

I was completely lost when I entered university. My whole life I had wanted to be just like my grandfather. I grew up thinking that I was going to be a lawyer, and then a diplomat. Now I didn't know what I wanted to do and I was suddenly questioning my desires. For two years, medicine had interested me greatly, so instead of dedicating my extracurriculars to easy classes like some of my friends did, I took physiology and biology classes to bolster my knowledge of the human body and how it operated.

I have an excessive need for pleasing people and because of it I am fairly easy to influence. I was feeling lost already and honestly I found it easier to do what other people wanted me to do. It's a characteristic I work hard to combat, but my desire to please others sometimes supplants my own thought process. I still have a tough time making decisions and expressing when I'm happy or not happy with something.

My trusted mentors offered a mixed bag when I sought their advice. While my grandparents would talk extensively about my choices, they would never actually tell me what they thought I should do. My father, on the other hand, would tell me exactly what he thought I should do. He was always like that, I suppose. My mom split the difference fifty-fifty and would offer an opinion, but not a strong one. She was being rational and suggested I play toward my strengths.

My dad likes to push me, and since he was pushing the hardest, I thought, *Okay, I'll try what he's pushing for,* which was engineering. I'm pretty sure most kids who attend university go through something similar. I applied for engineering without really even knowing what engineers are and what they do. I told myself that it made practical sense because it lined up with my talents.

Where there was uncertainty in my academic life, my year in athletics had gone amazingly well. I was winning every competition and getting a tremendous amount of attention for it. Everyone seemed interested in my story and what I would be able to do when I arrived in California.

I had never been very good at gymnastics, so all the attention and success was new to me. My classmates all knew how well I was doing and would ask me all about it; my friends and everyone I knew were cheering me on. I felt like a celebrity, and I was so excited for the Games.

I didn't think I was going to California to win the Games, but in my mind I was going to be in contention, and I had good reason to believe I could do it. I had enough experience training with Annie to know that she could beat me head to head, but I had also pulled out some wins and kept her close when she finished ahead. I was confident that I would at least be in the conversation, and I was okay with that for year one. I expected things to play out like they had at Regionals. There would be lots of attention on me, which was good. I loved the pressure of being on the competition floor and my best performances came when I could thrive on the energy of the crowd.

I continued to train hard all summer and I thought I was doing everything right with my diet. I was neurotic and I would go so far as to remove the chocolate nibs from my trail mix. My intake, however, was completely unrestricted. I would eat handfuls of nuts all the time. I had no concept of weighing and measuring or concern for portion sizes. I set rules and followed all of them, but I was confused. Not one gram of sugar or one slice of bread passed my lips, but I was smashing almond butter and tons of cream in my coffee.

In my mind I was doing everything right. In my mind I was working so hard. But in reality I had no idea what was going on or what to expect. I could cycle a barbell easily and moderate time domains, but efforts that went over ten minutes would punish me, and I had focused less on running. Elvar had been doing his best, and would give me as much direction as he could provide, but ultimately he wasn't my coach.

Getting to the Games is also expensive, and I was a college student with no job. I didn't have any money. Flights alone cost close to $1,200 each way and we had to be there so early that paying for accommodations in that part of Los Angeles was going to be virtually impossible to cover. I ran fund-raisers all summer with the help of Bootcamp. We sold shirts; we had an executive chef who would buy meat in bulk and help me sell it off. We made trail mix to sell for members. We ran a competition and barbecue with a donation for admission. Training and recovery were obviously important, but if I didn't hustle I wasn't even going to get to California.

Sveinbjörn Sveinbjörnsson was an individual competitor at the 2009 Games in Aromas—the same year Annie made her first appearance. He and his wife traveled to L.A. with me to offer whatever help and wisdom they could provide. They were amazingly kind, but their presence was more for emotional support and logistics. He was the most qualified of all the people in the gym, but he had never coached an athlete through the Games.

When I arrived, I was starstruck immediately. I saw Camille Leblanc-Bazinet. I had spent countless hours watching Cami on YouTube while I obsessed over muscle-ups. She was the best in the world at them. I completely froze and did not know what to say. It was a weird feeling that was completely foreign to me. We had celebrities in Iceland and it wasn't a big deal when you saw them. This was different, and it intimidated the hell out of me.

I felt like all the girls had deep friendships and had known each other for years. I got the sinking feeling immediately that I did not belong here. I started to shrink into myself and shy away from everyone even more. I'm sure there were other girls just like me, but I was swimming in my own head and the competition didn't start for a week. I didn't speak to one person that year.

On Monday, Games director Dave Castro announced a surprise event at Camp Pendleton on Wednesday. There had never been a Wednesday event, and I had no idea what kind of a "camp" we were heading to. On Tuesday we were given the opportunity to test the water and practice using our gear in the Pacific Ocean. Swimming is a rite of passage in Iceland. We are great swimmers. However, we are brought up in pools. I had never swum in the open ocean. I was already on my heels and feeling nervous.

In the bus, on the way to the beach, Cami was laughing and talking to everyone from her seat in the back of the bus in the center aisle. "I am so happy!" she laughed. Whether she meant to or not, she got in my head and I began to doubt myself. She continued, "I can't believe how much time I've spent in the ocean this year. Last year I was freaking out so bad. I feel amazing this year!"

I was doubting everything: the choices I had made, the training I had done, and, worst of all, the training I had missed. I even questioned my own ability to swim. My mind was overrun by insecurity and doubt. I hid myself in the reclining seat, then I looked out the window and cried.

I barely got into the ocean that day and when I did I was unable to get past the atypically large waves of the shore break. My goggles and flippers felt bulky and uncomfortable and my mind was setting off alarms. I just stared at the ocean, playing negative scenarios in my head on a loop until it was time to go. I kept thinking about all the what-ifs. This negativity carried on way into the evening, and I had a hard time sleeping. This was nothing like Regionals. This was the big leagues and I was panicking. *This sucks.*

Despite surviving the swim at Pendleton, my brain had effectively surrendered and I stayed in survival mode for the entire weekend. I floundered in the first or second heat all weekend, with the goal of simply not being last. The spirit I had when I was competing at Regionals was gone. There was no energy or adrenaline and I couldn't find any of the magic that had gotten me here the first time. I felt like I was a constant disappointment, and I would do worse than I thought I should do every single time.

I was eighteen years old and emotionally unequipped to pull myself out of the funk. The time difference with Iceland made it virtually impossible to call home, which was fine with me. I didn't even know what I would say if I got ahold of my mom or Amma. The couple caring for me took care of all the logistics I needed to address. They would slather me in sunscreen every morning and feed me every night. They even bought me a watch and came up with strategies when the Camp Pendleton events were announced. They would wake up early to make me breakfast, but none of it was any use. The problem was that I didn't know exactly what I needed other than an invisibility cloak. I was embarrassed about the whole experience and just wanted it to be over.

After so much early success, I felt like I was shouldering the expectations of my friends and family. I felt like I was letting down the members of Bootcamp. I knew that there were expectations that I was not living up to. When I left Bootcamp, they had told me to, "Go get that podium." They were serious because I had done so well at Regionals. They had called me "Another Annie." I worried about what they would call me after this.

My early success had turned out to work against me. I had a false sense of security that had kept me inside my comfort zone and had offered unrealistic expectations of my abilities. My second-place finish at Regionals was a distant memory now, where my *best* finish in any event was seventeenth! There were cuts made after each event. Only twenty-four athletes advanced to the final day, and I was not one of them. I sat through the entire final day as a spectator. As I sat in the stands that year, I wondered what made those girls so much better than me. I decided I never wanted to be cut again. I wanted to be out there.

A moment of kindness and a new mentor were the two most positive experiences I took from Southern California that year. The kindness came at the end of an event called the Track Triplet, where I had to sprint my lungs out on the last 400 meters just to beat the thirteen-minute time cap. I had been no-repped consistently for the way I regripped on my bar muscle-ups; every single rep was a battle. My whole body was heaving in agony from the effort, and I was feeling sorry for myself again. Out of nowhere, I was approached by Lindsey Valenzuela. Lindsey was a powerhouse and fan favorite for years. After a rookie appearance in 2011, she had made a huge statement at Regionals in 2012 by winning Events 3 and 5 earlier and taking first overall in Southern California. I had been an admirer for years, but we had never spoken.

"Hey, I just want you to know that what you did out there takes a lot of heart and character. Last year I was struggling and I finished four seconds under the time cap. I know how hard it is to keep pushing when it seems like everyone else is cruising through it. Great job, keep it up."

She was so genuine and sweet that she caught me off guard. I stammered and failed to even respond before she disappeared into the athlete warm-up area, but the transaction meant the world to me. I couldn't believe that she had taken time out to come and pick me up mentally.

The other positive from 2012 was meeting a new mentor. That came in a more roundabout fashion. When I was recovering from my own bout with the Track Triplet, I sat backstage in the warm-up area and watched the men compete on the big screen. As the second of four heats entered the final round of the workout, something caught my eye. The 2008 male champion, Jason Khalipa, was holding his own on the run portion of the event despite a gait that the announcer described as lumbering. Jason is a hulk of a human being, and had more than one famous fail in the Games on running events. Now he was using the run portion to open up his lead. Through two more heats, his time stayed in the top ten. What a difference a year had made for him—I had to know the secret.

After swearing me to secrecy, Jason shared with me that he had been working with a running coach named Chris Hinshaw. Hinshaw had fallen in his lap, quite frankly. The former All-American swimmer has ten Ironman finishes, including a second-place overall finish in Kona, a second-place overall finish at the Ironman World Championships in Canada, and a first-place overall finish at Ironman Brazil. He was living his postprofessional athletic life in the Silicon Valley and training at Jason's CrossFit gym—NorCal CrossFit. When he approached Jason with the offer to train him, Jason had quickly seen the genius in Chris's programming, and now I was seeing the results for myself. If he could get those kind of results for Jason, I wondered what he could do for me.

I emailed Chris before the Games were even over. He has since influenced my aerobic capacity for the better and helped fine-tune my metabolic engine. His influence on the sport and training in general has been massive not only in my life, but on the entire community that coalesces around the CrossFit Games. Hinshaw is the most analytical player in the Games and the way that he can deconstruct the events at first glance has been a game-changer for me. I can't thank Chris enough for taking a chance on me and helping me elevate my game from those early days when he didn't know anything about me.

Looking back at my early years I did just about everything wrong. Instead of doing my best, I only placed my value on my ranking. I was constantly monitoring the leaderboard and comparing myself to the other women. In so many events I watched the other girls beat me and stand on the finish line while I continued to work. Afterward, I would look at the leaderboard to see how badly I was free-falling.

I walked in with expectations that were too high and knowledge that was lacking. Sometimes I have to adjust my perspective to realize it's not that I'm unfit, but rather that the workout is hard. And I didn't respect it. You always have to respect the workout. When things are hard, it's not that I'm not good, it's that I didn't respect the challenge.

There are so many factors, including body maintenance and nutrition, that have to be in place to compete at that level. I didn't understand the challenge. When you walk in with expectations and no knowledge, you're setting yourself up for failure.

I had unwittingly set myself up for disappointment. There were so many things that I struggled with and was unprepared for: movements, preparation, and mind-set to name a few. Not just one or two, but too many to count. I went back to Iceland with a bruised ego and a lot to contemplate. Very little changed the following year. Shining success in the Open and Regionals was followed by a lackluster Games campaign.

Simply put, I didn't respect the challenge of the Games in 2012 and 2013. I didn't even really know what it was that I was walking into, what the Games were, or what the competitors were capable of. I was always a hard worker, but I didn't know what real hard work looked like, or the best way to train myself for it.

If you combined my first two years at the Games, I competed in twenty-three events. Only twelve of those finishes were better than twentieth. Four times I was worse than thirtieth in a field of forty-four athletes. Those are not very compelling statistics. I was content to make it to the Games, but when I got there, I was outclassed. I would go to the gym and do the work to be good enough to qualify for the Games. Then I could say for the rest of the year I was a CrossFit Games athlete. I was content with that. Former CrossFit Games commentator Sean Woodland observed that "You don't know how good you have to be to suck at the CrossFit Games." Just being there was an accomplishment, but I was getting too comfortable being mediocre.

In June 2013, I visited CrossFit New England (CFNE) for the first time. I had reached out to James Hobart and asked him to help me with my programming earlier in the year. James was a member of CrossFit Seminar Staff and a key player on CFNE's 2011 championship team in the CrossFit Games Affiliate Cup. He suggested I come to Natick, Massachusetts, to train with him and meet the CFNE crew. I had a fear of the unknown and traveling to the States to train with strangers was way out of my comfort zone. I was compelled, however. Something inside me said, *I've had enough of being mediocre. Let's go.*

CFNE is located in Natick, about 20 miles outside Boston. The modern-day CFNE is squeaky clean in both reputation and presentation. In the days of my first visit, however, it was small, raw, and dirty. The combo made it feel like a fraternity house, but the professionalism and competitive zeal with which it was operated made it feel like an Ivy League school. When my body made contact with the floor, I would come up with black smudges all over my clothes. Most of the barbells were rusted and didn't spin at the collars. The homemade pull-up bar system had a corner that had broken free from the wall. The detached portion would squeak to the cadence of your pull-ups as it separated and banged back into the wall. *Squeak, bang, squeak, bang, squeak, bang.*

The owner of CFNE, Ben Bergeron, who is now the most sought-after coach in the competitive fitness space, was refining and tinkering with his coaching methods as well. Ben is a tremendously astute individual. He is approachable and easy, but his brain is in constant motion, and his eyes are always studying the situation. By 2013, Ben had already led his team to multiple top finishes at the CrossFit Games, including a championship in 2011. He was on the leading edge of a new era in coaching and was focused on a "whole athlete" approach. I was signing up as a guinea pig and I had no idea what I was in for.

In 2013, Ben made the rawness of the gym into a competitive advantage. The less comfortable or secure he could make you, the better. In fact, Ben would dream up creative ways to pit athletes against adversity just to make them practice leaving their comfort zone. For example, we weren't allowed to use a women's bar for an entire month in April—only the men's. The diameter was awkward and unwieldy for me. I had never practiced adversity like this and the departure from my comfort zone paid dividends. Little details of workouts were changed at the last minute, and even though they were small, it made me cringe because I was so uncomfortable. I didn't know it at the time, but Ben's mind games were critical elements to my development.

The culture was what really set CFNE apart in my mind. I was used to Iceland and CrossFit Reykjavik, in particular, where everyone took part in classes with the exception of the people invited to train in private with Annie. Here, five or more heavy hitters were guaranteed to be throwing down. Every day you would train alongside athletes with veteran status in both individual and team competition. James Hobart and Mel Ockerby were both standouts from the 2011 championship team. Rachel Martinez and Ben's wife, Heather Bergeron, were heavy-hitting individual athletes. Max Isaak, Ali Leblanc, Sean Tully, Conor Nugent, Ally Bushy, Tracy O'Donnell—CFNE was chock-full of talented, hardworking competitors. They were a strong unit, but there was also a sense of competitiveness to gain a spot on the team for CFNE. Ben would train ten to twelve athletes throughout the year, but only the top six athletes would make the roster to compete for the team at the Games. There was an edge to the camaraderie that made us all push harder. I got a taste of something different on that first visit. I thrived in the environment and made up my mind before I even left that I would return as often as possible. This place felt like home.

Another, very different realization came from my time in Boston. For all the benefit that came from training with Annie, I had subjugated myself to her. She was my hero, Annie Thorisdottir, the reigning champion. It was easy for me to put myself behind her in training and be okay with it. In metabolic conditioning workouts I would think, *I can't beat Annie,* so if I was ahead of her I would slow down. When the weights rolled out I assumed she would outlift me. I always made the assumption that she should be doing better than me because she is the World Champion. It was impossible to gauge my own potential next to her, because I wasn't testing my true limitations.

CFNE felt like a university course in elite fitness. Back in Iceland, my actual university was giving me a hard dose of the real world. I was not thriving. Suddenly I found myself in a situation where I was in a class with three hundred people, the classes are online, and no one is taking care of you. In college, there was a small group of people and the teacher ensured that you knew what to hand in, at what time. When you're in a lecture with hundreds of people, the responsibility is all on you. You could skip class completely, if you chose to. I always showed up, but I didn't understand what the professor was talking about. Things were moving so fast.

I was lost and not having any fun. The math that I had loved was long gone, replaced by something complicated and beyond my grasp, and no one was there to hold my hand. My dad was an amazing resource, buying the course textbooks and tutoring me over Skype. He would even go through my assignments step by step and teach me everything. Even with this priceless tool I failed to understand the concepts. I leaned on memorization instead. It was the first time I put things down on paper that I thought were supposed to be there without knowing why. I managed good grades but didn't understand any of it.

Everyone kept telling me to stick with it, that I was "doing the right thing." But the grind was stealing my motivation, and I started to really dislike my work. I realized that if I hated it this much, there would never be a job in this field that could satisfy me. I took my exams that year already knowing I was done with engineering. Something needed to change. I would come back to school with a different focus.

7

FAILURE

MISTÖK

Failure is simply the opportunity to begin again,
this time more intelligently.
—HENRY FORD

March 2014

On an extended break from school, I returned to Boston to train at CFNE. I had been captivated on my previous trip and wanted to replicate that experience. It was almost like I was living two lives. My school life was rooted in safety and expectations. My training life was passion driven and fulfilling. I was constantly drawn to it.

After meeting me only briefly during my short visit the previous summer, the Bergeron family took me in and allowed me to stay in their home. We were fast friends, and I loved being with them and getting to know their beautiful kids. Maya and Jonah were already in high school and we talked, teased, and loved each other like siblings. The little ones, Harley and Bode, made me want to be a better person and role model as they grew up watching me.

Ben liked to joke that I was trapped. I had no friends outside of the gym community, no car, and nowhere to go. In reality, I was thrilled by the situation. I had become part of the Bergeron family. We would drive to the gym together, eat our meals to-gether, and talk about improving as people and athletes. I was a sponge and I just wanted to learn.

Living with the Bergerons also simplified my life and opened new possibilities for training. It was my first taste of what it was like to be a professional athlete. I wasn't working and there wasn't any school to worry about. Heather is amazing in the kitchen and they surround themselves with such good people. All I really had to focus on was training. All the other pieces fell into place through my association with Ben and his family.

I also realized how much my training had suffered because of my other time commitments. It resulted in a huge lack of confidence. I had qualified for the CrossFit Games twice, but I felt more like an imposter than a legitimate CrossFit Games athlete when I was there. In training, I would bounce around between programs. I didn't really know how I should be train-ing. I would pick what I wanted to do day to day, and leave the rest.

Heather was also a coach at CFNE and I would typically ride with her to work. I would train all day, stopping only for lunch. There was a big group there, some of the familiar names from my previous visit and some new faces: Rachel Martinez, Tracy O'Donnell, Ali Leblanc, Max Isaak, Geoff Leard, Conor Nugent, James Hobart, and Mat Fraser—just a bunch of amazing athletes.

I would finish my final training session around 3 p.m., but Ben wouldn't finish working until 5. Since he was my ride, I had to find a way to kill the time while I waited for him. I started to use it to my advantage by focusing on recovery, relaxing, and think-ing about training. After a few weeks, I was feeling the advantages of the lifestyle. All the little things that were out of reach when I was in a rush to fit in work, school, and training fell into place when I was in Natick.

On the drive to the gym one day I expressed how much I was loving being at CFNE and training with the crew we had there.

"I really don't want to leave," I complained.

"Stay," Ben replied. He seemed serious.

So I did.

I was amazed by how much improvement I was making athletically. I limited myself when I was in charge of my own training. I think many people fall victim to programming to their strengths and I was no different. I would avoid conditioning, focusing mostly on what I was good at. I would gravitate away from the sustained high intensity of an elegant three- or five-round CrossFit workout in favor of less challenging "every minute on the minute efforts" (EMOMs), which I found less demanding. It was an honest mistake, but with Ben in charge the training regimen was improved. I was morphing into a completely different athlete, physically. I hesitantly returned to Iceland but I missed my training and friends immediately and before I left Natick I already had firm plans to return. CFNE was becoming more like my home, and Reykjavik more of a place that I visited.

Whenever I spent time away from my coach and my training partners and CFNE the more I realized how badly I needed a team. My raw capacity was unquestionable. My Regional performances spoke for themselves. But I need my energy to be bridled and directed.

My early success had turned out to be a blessing and a curse. I was a big fish in the small pond of Europe, so I could make it to the Games, but when I got there I was awkward and uncomfortable. It felt like I didn't belong, like I wasn't fit enough, which took all the fun out of it. My athletic goal was simply to make it back to the Games; that was it. I was happy to rest on my laurels for another year as long as I got that T-shirt.

To make ends meet, and to make matters worse in terms of time management, I began coaching at a local gym five days a week. I wasn't drawn to coaching by passion. It was another thing I thought I was "supposed" to do. In my mind, all Games athletes were coaches. And if you wanted to be a Games athlete, my logic dictated, you should coach, too. It was true that many Games athletes were coaches, but they were driven by passion or necessity. I had neither. I was following the herd, not my heart.

It's not uncommon to have a job while you attend university and lots of athletes went to school or had jobs while they trained for the Games in those days. The combination of all three, however, was killing me. I would got to school from 8 a.m. to noon, train briefly, and then coach from 4 until 7 p.m.

I love helping people learn because I've gotten the privilege of working with so many amazing coaches and I've learned so much from my CrossFit career. I was excited to find creative fixes that resonated with different people. The same cue seldom works for two people, even if they share the same issue. Coaching was a puzzle in that way and I loved playing around with cues and remembering what worked for my clients. No matter how much I enjoyed them, three classes in a row would drain me. I would be engaging and fun for my first hour, on a roll in the second hour, and exhausted by the third. Anyone who has coached can likely attest that after three hours the quality of your product takes an abrupt nosedive.

Afterward, I still had training of my own to do, not to mention hours of schoolwork to complete. All this on an empty stomach made me feel like I was just "on the clock" and couldn't wait for my coaching duties to end.

It stabbed at me to bring this negative energy to coaching. It wasn't fair to the athletes coming to my classes. When I coach, I want to give everything to everyone. I want to ensure that everyone who talks to me feels important. I want to make sure they know I am interested. You never know what someone is going through and for that reason I always want to be kind.

I felt guilty, but I couldn't snap myself out of it. I wanted people to walk into the gym and have the best hour of their day—whether they're having a rough time at work or a horrible time at home, even if they are just having a bad day. An unmotivated Katrin, waiting for the minutes to tick by, was a disservice to them. I wanted them to have a coach who was ready to give everything.

Meanwhile my own training lacked inspiration after an afternoon of coaching. I would head into my studies completely exhausted. I was falling asleep regularly while reading or studying, and then I would show up for school late without having read anything. The other option I entertained was to stay up late and deprive myself of sleep only to be tired all day. It was a bad scene and a recipe for disaster.

Worst of all, I wasn't enjoying or excelling at anything. I was doing lots of things okay, and nothing wonderfully. My training was terrible, my coaching was lackluster, and the combination was dramatically affecting my ability to perform to a passable level in school. Everything was going in the wrong direction. When I was training, I would feel guilty about not studying. When I was studying, I would feel bad about all the work I was not doing at the gym. I was always conflicted and unhappy.

May 2014

I returned to CFNE in May for a Regionals training camp. The Europe Regional was just outside Copenhagen the second week of May and I had my work cut out for me. Sam Briggs was the defending Fittest Woman on Earth and of course Annie would be in the mix. With only three qualification spots to the Games up for grabs, there wasn't much wiggle room.

The event organizers had released all the events for the 2014 Regionals on April 30, a few days before I arrived in Boston. Most of them lined up perfectly for me—except for the fifth event, which jumped off the page and slapped me in the face.

Legless rope climbs had debuted at the Games in 2013 in an event called "Legless." Every athlete struggled with it. Only two women in the entire field finished the event in its entirety. I was *exceptionally* weak, only completing one successful climb in ten minutes, for which I fought tooth and nail.

Event 5 became the center of my universe in a very bad way. I was overflowing with anxiety and I had trouble getting it out of my head. Becoming unnerved had become a yearly ritual. In other words, panicking was a part of my process and not at all surprising. Regionals was the worst, because it was the gatekeeper. Since my measure of success was simply qualifying, Regionals decided if I could maintain my death grip on the label "CrossFit Games athlete" for one more year. Once I was qualified for the Games, the worst that could happen was last place. A few small mistakes or one devastating event at Regionals could wreck my season and, more important, my sense of identity.

It would have been easier for me not to know. Having the events in advance wreaked havoc on my mind. Everyone in the CFNE camp practiced them repeatedly, gauging the stimulus and tweaking strategies. When I didn't execute perfectly in my practice runs, I'd lose my composure. I'd become overly analytical and anxious, then I would work myself up to the point of tears. I would literally cry right there in front of everyone in the gym. I was shameless.

My body was more fit than it had ever been, but the space between my ears was still a mess. I was nineteen, but I was acting like a child. I was immature and I needed strong boundaries, which Ben established in a very specific dose of tough love. I'll never forget the day or the impact it had on me. This was the singular event that started me down the path to a complete overhaul of my attitude toward life. It's the first time I remember focusing on improvement through character building and not physical exercise. It's when our coach-to-athlete relationship turned a corner as well.

While we practiced the long chipper slated for Sunday at Regionals, I went to the dark side. I tend to put everything into my back when I'm pulling from the ground. When deadlifts are light enough, I hardly even bend my legs. This leaves me fried when high repetitions have to come off the floor, and Event 6 included 100 deadlifts along with a boatload of other work.

The event was already brutal and now my back was on fire from my poor mechanics. By the time I got to the box jump-overs, I wanted to stop and cry. I wasn't happy with how I was doing or how I was handling it. When I finished the workout, I immediately took my weight belt off and threw it against the wall. I stormed out the side door of the gym and sat on the patio, upset with myself. Yes, I threw a temper tantrum.

Ben followed me outside, walked over to where I had planted myself, and descended into a squat so we were making eye contact. He was calm. And stern, like a caring parent who wants to guide their children.

"That's not what we do here."

That's all that he said.

I wasn't angry or defensive. I agreed, in fact. I felt like an idiot and wished I could do it over. I decided right then and there that nothing like that would ever happen again. It's not how I wanted to carry myself.

We don't do that here, I repeated silently to myself as I nodded. "Okay."

This was a wake-up call. My parents and grandparents had taught me that "how you do something is how you do everything." But I had fallen into some bad habits when things weren't going my way. It was time to focus on more than just the results of the workout. From the moment Ben said those words to me I have tried to be an example of poise. I want to represent myself proudly. Now when other people act childish or immature, I'm the one who calls them out. I'm the one who lets them know "That's not what we do here."

I effectively eliminated temper tantrums, which was easy enough with some dedicated focus, but I couldn't stop myself from crying every time we practiced Event 5.

This is the one, the voice in my head would say. *This will keep me out of the Games.*

After one of our sessions, Ben approached me while I was cooling down on the treadmill.

"Things are not going to go as planned," he said.

I was immediately defensive. What a strange way to start a conversation. I couldn't understand why he was being so negative or why on Earth he would say that out loud. I was already unsettled about the potential disaster that awaited me.

"I want you to picture that. Visualize things going wrong. How will you address them?"

I had always thought visualization meant that by picturing actions and events to perfection you could ensure a better outcome. If the wheels start to come off when you play the game in the real world, then you're toast. Your best bet is to hang on for dear life.

What Ben was trying to do was prepare me for things to not go smoothly, which is what happens far more often in real life. When "Plan A" isn't going well, how do you adjust? What is your

"Plan B"? This was five days before competition, and in my mind I was married to "Plan A"—pull and pray.

May 17, 2014—Copenhagen

When I arrived in Denmark, everyone commented about how different I looked and how much my fitness had seemingly improved over last year. My time at CFNE had more of an impact than I realized. I felt like a different athlete. I felt like I was truly fit for the first time in my career. But in the back of my mind, there was a constant terror that the rope climbs would expose my weakness on Day 2 of competition.

The first day could not have gone any better. The first two events were back-to-back gifts: snatching followed by handstand walking. On the barbell, I tied for third and set a personal record on my hang squat snatch. I didn't just win the handstand walk in Europe, I set the high water mark for the entire world. I exceeded my expectations in Nasty Girls V2, tying Annie for sixth place. I finished Day 1 tied for first with Caroline Fryklund. I was killing it, but all I could think about during my exit interviews and even dinner that night were the rope climbs that awaited me the next day.

I breezed through Saturday morning's triplet, preoccupied the entire time by what might happen if I failed to perform a miracle on the ropes. I went back to the warm-up area to get some rest and change clothes. I had an hour to unwind and all I wanted to do was relax and listen to music, but crazy took over my brain. I obsessed over the leaderboard, trying to figure out what sorts of epic failures my lead could survive. I was in first place by 5 points—not a comfortable buffer. In great detail, I repeatedly envisioned catastrophe. Sam Briggs, the defending Games champion, recorded twenty-sixth place on the handstand walk the day before and was fighting herself out of a hole. I hoped people would focus on her and not me. I wondered how the other girls would pace the workout, and studied them during warm-ups. I thought about all the wrong things.

I was terrified and forced myself to keep moving just to keep my brain occupied. I'm pretty certain this was not what Ben meant when he suggested that I visualize the possibility of *something* going wrong. I was picturing *everything* going wrong. It was time to warm up; I would be taking the floor soon. When Athlete Control lined us up for our heat, I felt like I was being marched out in front of a firing squad.

As the overall leader, my lane was dead center on the competition floor, sandwiched between Annie and Caroline. We stood next to our "chess pieces," four-sided, chest-high foam pads that we advance each round to show our progress for the fans. Right then I wanted to hollow mine out and hide inside of it. Better still, I wished I was invisible. Meanwhile, spectators poured inside to watch the top women's heat.

A loud buzzer started the event. I was shocked at how fast every other women in the heat took off. They were sprinting to the ropes. Had it been any other event, I would have chased them down. But I knew from practicing at CFNE that the reward of keeping up with the leaders would be short lived. I was slow but consistent in my approach.

My key to staying alive was time management. Wait too long and I would run out of time. Move too fast and risk a costly failed rep. Sam, Annie, and Caroline, on the other hand, were all done with three climbs in the first sixty seconds of the event.

My first two climbs felt far better than I had anticipated. I picked up my pace slightly but it still wasn't enough to make me breathe hard. I surveyed the other lanes while I commuted between the ropes and my chess piece. Sam lapped me on my third climb. She was on the attack and fearless. I was in awe of her. Her composure was almost annoying as she strode across the floor, smacking gum the whole time and staring stoically into the distance. Annie and Caroline lapped me at the chess piece, half a round behind Sam. They were actually speeding up.

The chess pieces painted a dreary picture of what was transpiring, with mine glaringly lonely in the leaders lane, two or three rounds behind the women in the surrounding lanes. I fought through my fourth rep, while Sam was on her eighth. She crossed the finish line in 4:31. She didn't just win the heat—she set a world record in the event. A handful of girls finished shortly after and crumpled to the floor with exhaustion. So much for the diversion I had wanted. All the attention would soon turn to me.

The top of the rope is a terrifying place. Fourteen feet above the ground doesn't sound that high. When you're exhausted, however, and your forearms feel like bags of sand, making your grip unreliable, you might as well be hanging from a hot-air balloon.

All I had to do was reach up and touch the beam. On my seventh climb, I had to fight hard against my instincts to release my grip on the rope and make the touch. I got it, but the increase in effort it required bounced around in my head.

Only three to go, I told myself as I started to believe that just maybe I could pull this off.

More and more women were finishing. I was going to have a bad finish no matter what, but maybe I could avoid a complete disaster and minimize the damage.

Four and a half minutes remained in the event as I walked from the chess piece to the rope.

You've got time, I told myself. *Get your ass up that rope.*

Then all of my worst fears became reality.

During my eighth climb, I found myself at the top of the rope but uncertain if I could successfully touch the beam.

This has to happen, I told myself.

A missed rep would spell disaster. I simply couldn't afford it. I wasn't out of breath, but all the muscles in my upper body were burning and bursting. I took a gamble, throwing my right hand up toward the crossbeam, using the left to death grip the rope. I missed by inches and was sent back to the ground in free fall. Survival instincts sent both hands in search of anything to grab. They found the rope, saving me from injury but scorching my hands with a friction burn.

That's it. I just failed to make the Games, I told myself before I made contact with the ground. Then, *Bang!*

The floodgates in my mind exploded open and a tidal wave of negativity engulfed my last remaining life raft of positivity. I felt embarrassed and exposed in front of all those people. Time stopped for a moment as the thoughts raced through my head, then everything came crashing down. To my surprise, I didn't even get up. I rolled over, sat on my heels, covered my face, and unsuccessfully fought back tears.

With three minutes and thirty seconds on the clock, I quit.

Sam had now been done with her workout for almost four minutes. She and Bjork Odinsdottir had walked back to the ropes from their finish line on the opposite side of the competition floor. Sam took a knee and talked me off the cliff.

"You've got one minute, then you go. Give me one rope climb, got it?"

Sam's thick Mancunian accent had no sympathy.

"Now get up," she said.

It was an order.

According to Sam's plan, I would jump up for my next attempt with two minutes remaining in the workout. I had forty-five seconds to collect myself. I walked toward the finish mat, away from the ropes. Annie approached me and offered her counsel as well.

Sam and Annie flanked me on the walk back to the rope. Then Sam counted down for me.

"Four, three, two, one—go!"

I stepped up to the rope and jumped. Surprisingly, my body had regained some energy. My pull stayed strong until I approached the top. Three strong kips and I reached the top! My hands pressed against the massive braided eyelet that attached the rope to the steel rig. All I had to do was reach out. It was less than a foot. But my mind wouldn't allow it. I had gained the height I needed on my next kip, but my hands maintained a death grip on the rope. The effort was just wasted energy. I tried again with the same result.

I lost all momentum and hung awkwardly at the top of the rope in a half pull-up. I was stuck like a cat in a tree. My target was right there, just above eye level. I could almost hit it with my head, it was so close, but the muscles in my arms belligerently anchored me to safety with every ounce of strength in my body. I stayed frozen there for what felt like an eternity before I conceded defeat and gave up. Gravity took over and the manila rope turned into a coarse fireman's pole.

I hit my knees again with ninety seconds remaining, waiting to be saved by the bell. I would have stayed there, but Sam wouldn't let me quit. She gave me a half-hug and hauled me to my feet.

"Katrin Davidsdottir is showing lots of emotion. I think she wants to get off this ride," the host of the CrossFit Games, Rory McKernan, told the thousands of people tuning into the live broadcast from around the world.

He was right. I was in a waking nightmare and I desperately wanted it to be done.

Sam coached me on how to correct my pull while Annie encouraged me and assured me of my abilities. Every single woman from the final heat was gathered around me now and the crowd was deafening with their support. It was a beautiful show of support, but I just wanted them all to go away and stop looking at me. I made a halfhearted final attempt but didn't make it halfway. I covered my face and I cried.

The twenty-fourth-place finish in the event sunk me from first to sixth. It wouldn't be a death blow except for the mental damage I had sustained. The way I had handled my failure and my reaction were silly. The competition was still going on and there was a full day remaining. People fail and overcome all the time, Briggs was evidence of that, but I had disintegrated emotionally in front of the world. It was a mental breakdown and it shouldn't have happened. I imagined what Ben would say if he were there: "We definitely don't do *that* here."

This paled in comparison to the fit I had thrown at CFNE. Annie walked with me across the competition floor back to the warm-up area, trying her best to console me. I heard everything but couldn't tell you anything she said. All I could think about was curling up in a ball and hiding from the world. I continued to cry in the warm-up area. When I finally pulled myself together, I did an interview before heading back to the hotel to lick my wounds.

With puffy eyes and a half-smile on my face, I framed the event as best I could.

"Of course I'm disappointed. Being in the lead, of course there's pressure. I hoped that I would do better, I hoped that I would get through this clean. I knew that I wouldn't be near the top, but, um, I got a lot of points. We've seen this happen in the Regionals. Stacie Tovar taught us all last week that we're gonna come back, we're gonna finish this smiling."

Europe competed in the second of four regional weekends. The week before, I had watched Games legend Stacie Tovar fail to qualify for her sixth consecutive appearance after a result in the handstand walk that two first-place finishes couldn't redeem.

"Sam Briggs has taught us that we're gonna keep fighting, we're gonna come back tomorrow," I continued.

Briggs was mounting a legendary comeback. She took first on two of Saturday's events and was the runner-up in the other.

"So whatever happens, however it goes . . . we're gonna end this with a fight. We're gonna leave it all on the floor."

I wanted to believe what I had said, but I was mentally defeated. The Games introduce new rules from time to time and that year there was a rule in place that allowed for a fourth qualifying athlete in the event that the reigning champion secures a qualifying spot. The rule was a way of promoting better competition at the Games while still ensuring that no one got a free ride without earning it. This allowed me more forgiveness if Briggs was able to make it to the podium. It gave me hope.

I showed up on Sunday still embarrassed. I prayed no one would ask me to talk about it. In the competition, I needed to overperform, but really my fate was out of my hands. The girls in front of me would have to do poorly on one of the two events for me to make up ground. I took eighth in the chipper that had led to the belt-throwing incident at CFNE one month earlier. It was a good result when I needed a great one. Likewise, in the final event, I gave everything, collapsing over the finish line two seconds behind Kristin Holte and ahead of everyone else. But second place in the event wasn't enough.

Even Sam Briggs couldn't save me. She missed the podium by 6 points, and would not be able to defend her title from the previous year. Even if Sam had clinched, I was too far back to save. That's the brutal reality in our sport. If you have a weakness you don't eliminate in training, it will be exposed by competition. The test of fitness at the CrossFit Games is always changing and athletes have to evolve along with it or get left behind.

8

SPREAD THIN

Breitt út þunnt

You can have everything you want.
You just can't have it all at once.
—OPRAH WINFREY

Post-Regionals 2014

I was traumatized by not making it to the Games. I would wake up every morning in disbelief that this was my life. I kept hoping there was some way to go back in time and alter what happened. Then I would relive the event again in my head. It didn't feel real to me and I couldn't come to terms with the fact that it had actually happened. It was a harsh reality to wake up to every morning, and the cycle continued that way for two more weeks.

Everything I wanted to do—all my goals and a huge part of my identity—were wrapped up in being a CrossFit Games athlete. I had cleared my schedule and declined a family holiday on the expectation that I would be competing that summer, so not only was I depressed but I was lonely, too.

My dad called me the day after Regionals. I assumed he wanted to console me. Instead, he asked if I had changed my mind about the family trip to Morocco now that, "You know, your plans have changed." I was so offended I couldn't even speak to him. He hadn't even let the body get cold! I just wanted him to grieve with me for a second. I was even more upset because there was no way I was going to turn down an invitation to Morocco.

Almost as if he had planned it with my dad, Ben sent a text shortly afterward.

> I know you may not see this right now, but this could be the best thing that ever happened to you.

I was furious at the nerve it took just for him to write it! How could he not understand how devastated I really was? It was a week before I responded with something dismissive. I didn't believe any good could come out of this situation. Little did I know that Ben was right. This would be one of the biggest turning points in my life.

There were other places I would have rather been, but Morocco turned out to be therapeutic. I'm not a big reader, but I read a lot on that trip. I don't even know how I acquired them but I took Michael Johnson's *Gold Rush* and Jim Afremow's *The Champion's Mind*. They would both become linchpins of my mental game moving into the future.

The Champion's Mind is a compilation of traditional sports psychology practices that reads like an instruction manual. I read and reread it endlessly, attempting first to commit the ideas to memory. Through anecdotes and real stories, Afremow highlights the importance of mental fortitude in sports. I found parallels in most of the stories he used to my own experiences. I had so many realizations while I read it.

Gold Rush is a sports autobiography by Olympic sprinter Michael Johnson. It highlights his lifelong pursuit of self-understanding, preparation, control, and performance. Johnson is highly decorated and considered to be one of the best sprinters of all time. He is the only man to win gold in both the 200-meter and 400-meter dash in the same Olympics, which is unbelievable. However, the story that resonated most with me was not from that historic year in 1996, but rather from the '92 Games in Barcelona, when Johnson, the clear favorite for the 200 meter, failed to even make the finals after an unlucky bout with food poisoning. His relationship with failure helped me reframe mine.

I couldn't believe how perfect *Gold Rush* was for me at that time. It was striking to read about one of the most dominant athletes in history dealing with failure. It made me reevaluate my own situation. If his failures didn't define him, why should I allow mine to haunt me? I felt like he was in the room talking to me, challenging me to grow from the experience and to work even harder and achieve even more. It's so easy to doubt yourself and so effortless to believe in others. I took a strange reassurance from his humanity, I suppose. The fact that champions aren't immortal really resonated with me and helped my mental strength.

I was able to understand that one failure in an event didn't define him. Michael Johnson himself was obviously not a failure. In fact, he had catapulted himself on to greatness after failing in that particular event. Through that lens I could see that I was living the same story. Yes, I had failed at Regionals. That did not mean I wasn't good enough to compete with the women at the CrossFit Games. It was just one event. Johnson's story made it clear that that failure was only a pit stop in a much longer athletic journey.

The concepts I read were like medicine for my emotional healing. I allowed myself to relax and recover in Morocco. I was more motivated than ever to work harder than ever in the gym. But to continue working on my brain I would need help. I didn't know where to start.

Reading and absorbing concepts from the pages of books was a great start. I was enthralled with the concepts of sports psychology, but to pull them from the ethereal and cement them in my life I needed practice. I wanted to engrain these ideas in my heart so that they appeared when I needed them most, in moments of deep physical pain and tribulation.

There is no way to "dry train" mental toughness. To truly stick, these ideas needed to be forged in the fire of training and competition. A mechanic cannot learn to fix cars solely by reading manuals and a doctor cannot learn to perform surgery from watching a YouTube video. The same holds true for an athlete who wants to build an unbeatable mind. For better or worse, the field of mental toughness is young and constantly evolving.

I needed somewhere to put it all to the test. And I needed help. "Better than a thousand days of diligent study," Afremow wrote in *The Champion's Mind*, "is one day with a great teacher." I felt a gravitational pull to CFNE, and Ben Bergeron.

Summer 2014

It was still hard for me to go to the gym. Other athletes had the purpose of training for the Games. It killed me that I didn't. What was I doing? Training for general fitness? Just going to the gym for fun? I wanted to have that goal of getting ready for the CrossFit Games. That was what my summers had been about. I managed to turn that around by literally pretending that I would go to compete with them.

My first goal became helping Annie finalize her competition preparation. I took on her training schedule. In a lot of ways I was the perfect training partner because my fitness was through the roof, but she didn't have to worry about meeting me on the competition floor at the actual Games. I trained as if I was still going to the Games, so while I was able to keep Annie on her toes, I was benefiting from the push as well.

When late June arrived and Annie traveled to California, I was heartbroken that I wasn't going with her. I stayed behind in Iceland and was miserable all week long as social media buzzed with updates from athletes and fans. I had to actively avoid my phone and turn off notifications to keep from going crazy.

I tried to get my updates directly from Annie by text in the evenings, but she was in competition mode. She was also staging a legendary comeback. After her back-to-back championships, a terrible back injury had forced her to sit out in 2013. It was so bad initially that one doctor told her she might not walk again. I watched her work diligently and patiently for over a year to get back, with people vocally doubting her along the way.

In 2014 she had started slow, but seemed to be getting better and better as the week went on. I could only convince myself to tune into the broadcast for the final event. Annie was making a charge—taking first and second in the previous two events. Games director Dave Castro had kept the athletes in an isolation room prior to the final two events and they were briefed on the floor that they would complete Double Grace, thirty clean-and-jerks for time, to finish the weekend.

Damn, I thought, *that would have been my jam.* It was also Annie's. The difference was that she was there. My emotions were so mixed. I was over the moon watching Annie annihilate the workout and return to glory. At the same time I wished so badly that *I* were there competing. Annie took first in the workout and second place overall. I was so proud for her.

I watched Camille Leblanc-Bazinet clean-and-jerk her way to fifth place in the event, clinching the championship. I closed my computer and went to bed.

When I awoke the day after the 2014 Reebok CrossFit Games, I felt like a million pounds had been lifted off my chest.

Everyone had a clean slate, no one had qualified for the Games, and the score was back to 0–0. It was now the 2015 season, and I was ready to go.

I was fired up, physically rested, and focused. If there was any silver lining to not qualifying for the Games, it was that I got a head start going into the 2015 season. While the other athletes prepared, traveled, and were ultimately throttled by the torturous workouts that year, I stuck to my regular training. Aside from the legless rope climb, I was leading the Regional in Europe. I was as fit as I had ever been.

Fall 2014—Law School

I returned to school with a new and ambitious major and the challenges that accompanied it. Ever since I was a child I had pictured myself practicing law like my grandfather. Now that I was done with engineering I would give it a try. My dad literally laughed at the thought of me pursuing a degree and a profession that relied so heavily on details and reading.

"What's the last book you read," he mocked. "*The Blue Cup*?!"

He was referencing the children's book he used to read to me at bedtime.

My trip to Morocco had reinvigorated my reading skills, but he had a point. In a family of avid readers, I had chosen to spend most of my time on the move. It wasn't my fault; I had to move.

The truth is that I had never finished a single book in school. I always had the best of intentions, but I never made it through. In spite of that, I was determined that if I was going to pursue anything in school, it was going to be law. I felt like it was something that I had to at least try. Afi was my hero and I wanted to make him proud, and initially I really enjoyed the classes. It was a subject that really came to life, so different from the mathematics curriculum of engineering. Law was relevant; it felt like it was happening right now. We studied real court cases and I could see how they played out, what evidence made a difference, and how strong arguments were formed.

Living in two worlds would not be as easy as I had hoped. My soul's focus was shifting away from school to training. There was a magnetic pull toward the gym and I was spending the majority of my free time there. When I wasn't there I was watching videos about how to perform better when I did get there. I was like an addict; I could not get enough.

Law never stood a chance. School didn't stand a chance. I was so heavily invested in my training and I loved it. When push came to shove, studying got the least of my energy. I saw how much work my classmates were doing and it dwarfed my efforts. Girls I knew from college would come to class having memorized the jury from A to Z. They knew everything, not just the surface details. It was clear they had studied, and that I was coming up short.

It wasn't long before my grades began to reflect my effort. I did poorly on exams. Meanwhile, a key upcoming exam was looming in December. It was the law school year one equivalent of Regionals, with a fail rate that averaged around 85 percent. In practical application this test is the gatekeeper for who will continue on in law and who will be forced to choose another direction.

Always the optimist, to a stubborn fault, I believed I could pass, despite my lack of preparation. I was like a novice CrossFit athlete trying to qualify for Regionals on sheer determination and no practice. I continued to push off my studies in favor of CrossFit. I just wanted to train.

December 2014

My back was up against the wall in school. I had let everything slide and now I was out of time.

Our big exam was right around the corner, and most students in my class were making final preparations. My girlfriends had used additional time to read, prepare, and attend additional tutoring sessions. For the first time in my life, I was forced to cram. I was used to studying a lot, but this was different.

I negotiated with myself to set hard deadlines. I allowed the hours from 8 to 11 a.m. for training. I forced myself to enjoy it as much as possible because after training it was lunch and then nonstop studying. The library booths at the Commercial College of Iceland are bright orange. I hate the color orange, but the booths are highly effective for blocking out sounds and distractions. I would sit there and study until 10 or 11 at night. This schedule gave me just enough time to get a little bit of sleep before heading back to the gym.

Since I started university, I had created some bad habits and traditions. One of those was an annual ritual of getting sick in December. Burning the candle at both ends always ended the same way. This time was worse than ever before, because I was cramming for my law test. I still wouldn't throttle back in the gym. Long days at school meant I was consuming the mediocre food available on campus. I was in bad shape.

By the time I took my exam I had a hard time staying emotionally invested in it. It was killing me and I just wanted it to be over. I was unsure whether my self-destructive cramming was enough to help me pass, but it was a relief to be on the other side of it. Within days I packed my bags and prepared for another trip to Boston for a CFNE athlete camp.

January 2015

When I arrived, my face wore the defeat of a sleepless, poorly fed student—not an athlete in pursuit of the world's largest stage. Six weeks of obsessive cramming for my exams had softened me. I was haggard, and Ben didn't pull any punches when he saw me.

"Oh shit, what happened?"

Ben's words had clearly passed his brain-mouth filter more easily than he would have liked, and he stared blankly, apologetically, after he delivered them. The slip was additional (unnecessary) evidence that I was wearing the look of my previous month's lifestyle.

While I did not appreciate such a high dose of honesty, I could tell it came from a place of concern. I was a complete mess and in no shape at all. I looked and felt heavy and sluggish. I was so tired.

Boston was able to rejuvenate me. When I was there, I was a professional athlete. It was nothing but training and recovery, with no distractions or obligations. Progress came quickly in this environment and my fitness returned to an acceptable level by the end of the month.

My grades were submitted while I was at the camp. I went online to check them and stared at the screen, frozen in shock. I had failed. It was the first time in my life that I had failed anything in school.

When I returned to Iceland, I met with my instructor to see where I had gone wrong. It turned out that I had only failed by a fraction of a point. The content they were looking for was there, but not in the way they wanted it presented. I thought that I deserved more credit so I argued my case, but to no avail.

I hated the feeling of failure. After Regionals, this felt like adding insult to injury. I felt an emotional tornado whipping up inside of me. I was disappointed in myself and mad at my instructors. It tore me up inside and embarrassed me to my core. It would take me a long time to understand why this had happened.

I had to face some difficult realities. Success had come easily in school and in CrossFit when my ambitions were low. Now they had both leveled. If I wanted to be the best, it would take my full and undivided effort.

My mom was the first one to suggest taking a break from school. I was shocked she even mentioned it. My family has an academic tradition; it put tremendous value on higher education. I wanted to please my family by following my scripted path. There were things I was supposed to be, and things I was supposed to do. I was even more astonished when my grandmother agreed with my mother.

"Katrin, this is what we're doing right now. It's not permanent. You don't know what you want to do with your life and it's okay to take some time off to figure that out. In the meantime," she said with a smile, "you go and train!"

I struggled with these notions before realizing that these people who loved me and understood me better than anyone might just be onto something. I gave myself permission to take off one semester.

But only one, I told myself.

9

COACH

ÞJÁLFARI

If you want to take the island, burn the boats.
—JULIUS CAESAR

I took the semester off and stopped coaching completely. I threw myself into my training with a laser focus on becoming the best possible version of myself. Ben likes to say, "You can only do the best you can in the place that you are with what you have available." In Boston, I would have the best tools in the world—coaching and training partners—at my disposal. During my extended stay in New England the year before, I had accidentally stumbled into living like a professional athlete. Now I was going to do it on purpose.

Without the burdens of school and work, I felt like a million pounds had been lifted from my chest. I was training with an accomplished coach full-time and I was paying attention to my diet. I took control of all the factors that were under my control, both inside and outside the walls of the gym. Most significant, I had no distractions or obligations. All I had to do was train.

CFNE operates like a fitness academy. The quality of the coaching and collective interest in learning made me feel like I'd transferred schools instead of leaving. CFNE creates and attracts excellent athletes. On any given day you can find elite Masters athletes, world-class teams, multiyear individual veterans of the CrossFit Games, and a handful of Regional-caliber athletes with ambitions for the Games sharing the gym and pushing one another.

The biggest difference was that CFNE's competitors weren't splintered into groups pursuing individual training programs. They were one huge elite group of trainees. And they had the desire to be led. I was used to Iceland, where group classes were the norm and elite athletes would isolate themselves—with or without training partners—to attack their personalized programming. They offered each other pointers and input, but not real coaching.

When I first came to CFNE, I wasn't looking for a coach. I was coming to train with a motivated group of athletes. I wanted to be in that environment to push myself. But the first thing I noticed was not the athletes' performances but their deference to Ben. He was regularly running classes with ten, sometimes fifteen, of the best competitors in the sport.

The realization hit me: I had never been coached in CrossFit. Not like this, anyway. This was foreign to me and what I missed most about my gymnastics career. The last time I had an athlete-coach relationship was with Vladmir at Armann. Like my Russian coach, Ben had the intangible qualities of a great leader. These qualities come hardwired into a person's character. They distinguish the good from the great and they can't be taught. I couldn't articulate it then, but Ben had a quiet command of the room that I had never experienced before. We were a pack of very fit alpha personalities, but everyone listened when he talked. Maybe because Ben doesn't say much, the athletes *wanted* to hear what he had to say.

No one really had coaches back then, but Ben *coached* us. After workouts as we were sprawled out on the floor, Ben would often talk about mind-set: "Guys this is it. You need to tell yourself that you worked hard. I know your legs are burning and your lungs are bleeding. We *love* this feeling. This feeling is why you're here; it's what's making you better." Lying on the floor, unable to find a position that was comfortable, I would think: *Yes! This is what I want*.

This was the beginning of my mind-set shifting. I was nineteen, and these practices and people were the best influences I ever could have found. The books I was reading presented new ideas and philosophies, and Ben and our practices at CFNE helped me to actually put them into play. This solidified them, it made them real.

Ben says only what he means, and he hands out praise sparingly. A "good job," from Ben is a rare event, and usually meant you had done something truly exceptional. Most of his feedback was reserved for areas where we could improve.

I liked that his feedback never had any hidden meaning. Ben has a way of presenting constructive criticism that makes that clear. I never worried that he might be second-guessing whether I belonged there or whether I was good enough, or that he might think I wasn't trying hard enough. Ben just told the truth, in a way that reminded me of my dad. This kind of feedback is actually quite rare, but I leaned into it. I don't need someone to tell me I'm great all the time, and it annoys me if all I hear is "good, good, good." Give me something I can learn from, or feedback that will make me better. I know when I'm good. I want a coach to tell me where I can be great.

There was no cheerleading during training at CFNE, just statements of fact. I'd be killing myself on hill sprint intervals, and Ben would very matter-of-factly read off the time that was ticking off on his stopwatch. "Fifty-four seconds . . . Kat; one minute . . .

Rachel; one minute, seven . . . Ally." I'd go again and the cycle would repeat. As an athlete, that taught me a lot. Without any external praise for my effort, I was forced to turn inward for the positive feedback I was so badly craving.

I was forced to constantly question my level of effort: *Am I working hard enough? Could I go faster? Could I have pushed more?* I came to realize that I was the only one who would ever know if my performance reflected my best effort. I was learning so much about myself as an athlete. I was starting to understand what it meant to truly work hard.

In many ways, the coaching I was getting at CFNE reminded me of gymnastics back in Iceland. It started with respect. The first thing we did upon arriving at Armann for training every day was salute our coach, make eye contact, and greet him by name. "Good morning, Vladmir." The exchange was a sign of respect. It would set the tone that you were there to be coached and you recognized he was in charge. You would thank your coach in a similar fashion when you left. This is how it was at CFNE: a big group of people who showed up on time ready to work. Ben was there to coach and everyone listened.

All the things I loved about gymnastics were present in some degree at CFNE. In gymnastics, the higher my coaches' expectations, the more I loved it. I didn't want happy and bubbly. I wanted them to push me and show me I could do things I didn't think I could. That was Ben. I loved that he would hold me accountable when I wanted to quit. I *wanted* to be held to that high standard.

When you have a coach who is there for you every day when you show up and, in return, expects you are going to deliver your best effort, it creates a bond. With Ben, it started to feel like we were training together and working toward a common goal. As we tried new strategies, things started to click. We were reading the same books and discussing the concepts. We were learning and practicing techniques for building a stronger mind. There was growth happening well beyond the walls of the gym, and I could feel the momentum starting to build.

I'm not the same athlete I was when I met Ben. Ben is not the same coach he was when I moved to Boston. Although he had experienced success and produced Games-caliber athletes, he wasn't where he wanted to be. It all came together at the perfect time. I was ready to learn, and I was excited to take in new ideas not just for my training, but for my life.

My biggest takeaway was that doing my absolute best is the ideal outcome. I realized I didn't have to do anything special. I just had to work as hard as I could work. I realized I'm only in competition with myself. It was around this time that I began to internalize the slogan, "Be the best me." I use this phrase all the time when I need to refocus.

For all the good things that had entered my world, life was not all sunshine and rainbows. My failure at Regionals—on the rope climbs, in particular—had left a mental scar that I battled constantly. I still had full-on panic attacks in the face of legless rope climbs.

To face this demon, Ben prescribed me three legless rope climbs a day. It didn't matter when or how I completed them. They just had to be done—before training, after training, or spread throughout the day. It was on me.

There were many days when I would stand in front of the rope and stare at it. I could not convince myself to jump up. I just couldn't do it. I felt as helpless as I had at Regionals. In the back of my mind I thought that if I jumped up, I was putting myself out there again—vulnerable, in danger of another failure. It's a loop I was stuck in. It didn't matter if the gym was packed or empty. The fear was there.

People carry stress in different places. For me, it migrates to my chest, just under my throat. It's a massive lump in my throat, like a ball I can't get rid of, and I just want to cry. I often got myself so nervous that I would lose physical strength. When I convinced myself to jump up I would lose all the strength in my arms. This went on for months. I would complete my three rope climbs, but not without issue. I felt weak and wanted to cry. After months of this, I was still waiting for the day when they would feel better.

It was a great lesson in patience. I kept waiting for the skill to miraculously appear, but it didn't come. I pressed forward regardless.

10

OBSESSION

ÞRÁHYGGJA

Perfect never gets the opportunity to become better.

February 2015

A year of full-time training with no distractions was bearing fruit. The 2014 Regionals had lit a fire deep inside me that was impossible to mimic or create. It was my raw, emotional response to the failure I had experienced. I had a passionate determination to never put myself in that position again.

I was obsessed with qualifying for the Games, and I trained like failing to accomplish that was worse than dying. I was working harder than ever before in my life. When I needed motivation, I imagined how hard my competitors were training. I was in the best physical shape I had ever been in and accomplishing things I never thought possible. I noticed that Ben's investment in my mental fortitude was paying off as well. The between-the-ears focus felt like windshield wipers for my brain—my mind was starting to feel so much clearer!

The whole year, I fed on this drive every single session of every single day. In training, I pictured my fiercest competitors next to me. It helped me to find the next gear. In my mind's eye, I would place them one step or one rep ahead of me and make myself catch up. *She wouldn't put the bar down, she wouldn't slow down on the final 100-meter stretch,* I would remind myself. I would challenge myself to chase them down, and in the process, I was crushing myself.

If I was on the track, I would picture Kristin Holte, the running and endurance phenom from Norway who had taken the third spot in the Games instead of me the previous year. I saw her next to me as I ran my final 400-meter repeat of a brutal session; just out of reach as I entered the gut check of the home stretch, her avatar would go for broke, forcing me to question how bad I really wanted to win. I approached every workout this way: as if it were a Regional event and I was fighting my competitors for a qualifying spot to Games.

Kristin was just one of my many imaginary competitors. I would conjure up whoever I perceived to be best-in-class for the challenges I faced that day. If the workout heavily featured a barbell, Annie Thorisdottir was there alongside me. If she could hold on for another rep, then so could I. I would squeeze the bar as tight as possible until it slipped from my hands and fell to the floor. When there were muscle-ups in a workout, I competed with an imaginary Sam Briggs.

In early 2015, I was traveling between Boston and home more often. While in Iceland, I had switched over to training at Cross-Fit Reykjavik. Annie and I were inseparable during that time. We had experienced less good times in the past and I was over the moon that those times were now water under the bridge.

She grew to be one of my dearest friends. In Boston, I had learned about surrounding myself with excellent people, individuals who forced me to grow and improve. Annie fits this mold perfectly. Quite frankly, she exemplifies excellence. She is a very whole person whom I can admire outside the walls of the gym as much as I do inside. The relationships she has with her family, Frederik, and those she calls friends are healthy and balanced. She works diligently in everything she chooses to pursue. Annie didn't need to earn my respect, but she constantly set the bar higher. Although Iceland was now the powerhouse for female contenders at the CrossFit Games, Annie was the first. She had blazed the path that we had followed.

In our sport it's hard to be close with your competition because you don't want to reveal any secrets. If you're sore or banged up, you don't want to offer a mental edge to anyone by confiding in them. Annie and I are notable rivals. We know how much we each want to win the Games. That builds our mutual respect. I want to win, but I want her to be second. The same rings true for her.

"If it's not me, I want it to be you," we always say.

We are very similar; we respect each other's work and we are able to build each other up. It's priceless to have someone who has gone through the same things. We have so many similarities with the pressures we deal with and the things happening around us. Ours is one of the most valuable relationships I have. In more ways than one, Annie is the only one who can empathize with my experiences. I love being around her. It helped that our relationship had evolved and, in my mind, we'd become equals.

Any time I was in Boston I was working as hard as I could without anything else in my way. I trained alone a lot. In that context, there weren't limitations. I had continued to improve because there was nothing there to tell me that I should or should not be able to do something. I just searched for my potential. What I found was astounding. I realized I was capable of far more than I had previously thought. I took that confidence into the 2015 Reebok CrossFit Games Meridian Regional.

May 29-31, 2015—Copenhagen, Denmark

Copenhagen was at a distinct disadvantage when it came to winning my affection. It was ground zero of my worst nightmare. If the work I had put into improving my mental strength over the last year needed a pressure test, I couldn't think of a better place to test it. Simply facing rope climbs in training continued to cause tremendous anxiety over the safety net of CFNE. Now I would compete on the same floor where I had felt naked and exposed less than a year before.

The Games are a young sport now, and were even younger then. In 2015, the Regional format shifted to account for trends in the competition landscape. Games organizers abandoned the Olympic model from previous years. The seventeen regions around the world would no longer be guaranteed representation at the Games.

Organizers combined regions into "Super Regionals." In 2015, qualifying athletes would face the best from at least one other regional as well as their own. As many as five athletes would qualify for the Games. The depth of competition doubled, but the number of qualifiers only slightly increased.

"You're only going to see the best athletes at the CrossFit Games. The ones who deserve to be there," Dave Castro explained.

For Iceland, this meant the incorporation of Africa and the Middle East. Locals from these regions had yet to produce Games-caliber females. However, a growing number of global expats—attracted by the generous salaries and training-conducive lifestyle offered by the CrossFit Kool-Aid drinkers from Dubai's upper class—were submitting competitive scores in the Open. Most had opted to go team, though. The majority of the ladies who threatened to keep me out of the Games were from my island.

Our combined Regional was scheduled for the third and final week of Regionals and, as usual, the organizers released the workouts. On paper the seven events were exciting and well balanced. Running was reintroduced after a four-year hiatus. The use of self-propelled treadmills would make the 1-mile run in Event 3 both twice as hard and standard across all regions in one fell swoop. There was a handstand-walk-and-snatch combination to close the second day. That boosted my confidence. Most important, legless rope climbs were nowhere to be found. While it didn't mean I would glide through the weekend, I'd be lying if I said it didn't come as a relief.

Still, ropes would be present on Day 1 as part of a larger theme: Hero Friday. CrossFit's Hero workouts are legendary. They stand apart from other workouts in both their difficulty and significance. Many, if not most, early adopters of CrossFit training methodology came from first responder, military, and law enforcement backgrounds. CrossFit was a natural fit for these professions, where unknown challenges with high physical and mental demands are likely to greet them during a shift and failure to prepare could mean the difference between life and death. The only downside of intimacy with these communities is the harsh reality that their work often calls for them to make the ultimate sacrifice.

CrossFit created Hero workouts for CrossFit devotees who were killed in action as a way to honor them and carry their names forward. This year we would face two of them in what Castro had dubbed "Hero Friday."

EVENT 1: RANDY
For time:
75 snatches (55 pounds)
Time cap: 6 minutes

The workout is a tribute to a Los Angeles Police Department SWAT team member, and it had everyone on edge. In stark contrast to many Hero workouts that are a long grind, the light-weight snatches were lightning fast. The event record was 2:26:7. The speed made the event volatile. Small mistakes were costly, and ten or fifteen seconds had cost top athletes ten to fifteen spots on the leaderboard in previous weeks. Anything outside the top ten was a less-than-ideal way to start the Regional weekend, especially in a group of heavy hitters such as the one at the Meridian.

Annie and Sara set an insane pace, and I did my best to chase them. Athletes were required to advance the bar forward after each set of 25 reps. At 22, nearly every woman to my right advanced, led by Sara and Annie. My grip was nowhere near failure, but I could feel my forearms expanding and fatiguing. I kept the bar overhead as I advanced it and went directly into my next 25. As Sara advanced to her last set of 25, I had fallen 6 reps behind. I fought the urge to panic and focused instead on my game plan. My pace had not changed for the first 50 reps, but now it was time to leave everything on the floor. I advanced to my final set and held on for dear life.

Our barbells were arranged to one side of the competition floor. After the final rep, athletes had to step over their barbells and sprint to the finish mat. Annie and Sara dropped their bars first and sprinted to a photo finish. Kristin Holte followed close behind. When I saw a fourth athlete, Bjork Odinsdottir, take off, I worried I could be in trouble. I had 3 more reps to go. My grip was slipping every time I pulled the bar overhead and my reps had slowed significantly. It was like an uphill sprint to the finish. But no one crossed the finish line between Bjork and I. I was fifth in the overall standings with Randy out of the way.

The next workout paid tribute to Navy SEAL Thomas Valentine. It featured thrusters and rope climbs. Lots of them. Although I could use my legs, I was still nervous.

TOMMY V
For time:
21 thrusters (75 pounds)
12 rope climbs (15 feet)
15 thrusters
9 rope climbs
9 thrusters
6 rope climbs
Time cap: 16 minutes

After the 2014 Regionals, I began to identify which workout stood apart as the biggest test for me in the context of the competition, which would require my greatest focus and effort to do well. I would call this my "rope climb event," whether the reference was metaphorical or literal. My "rope climb events" did their best to expose my weaknesses. Tommy V was difficult, but I managed my rest well and stuck to my pace regardless of what the women around me were doing. I was steady on the rope and strong on the barbell, taking sixth in the event. With the nerves of Day 1 gone, I settled into the rest of the weekend and started having fun.

"We are accustomed to a foot race, but here at the Meridian Regional, as the crowd rises to their feet, we are seeing a *hand* race," announcer Chase Ingraham said at the opening of Day 2. We were facing a 250-foot handstand walk for time.

He was only partially joking: Bjork, Kristin, Annie, and I ran virtually upside down on the first leg of the 250-foot course. I'm typically better at longer handstand walks, while short-and-fast efforts favor Annie. I went for the advantage and chose not to take a break at the turnaround. I had told the announcers I would finish the event in one minute thirty seconds. I crossed the finish line in 1:19 and took my fourth career Regional event win. Regionals was my first love when it came to competition, and now I remembered why. It was so exhilarating to hear the cheers of the crowd and to perform at the level I knew I was capable of.

After a one-minute-forty-second reset, we hit the 1-rep-max snatch event to close Saturday. I had successfully lifted 175 pounds in my warm-up. Now, on the competition floor, I threw 155 on the bar to see how the fatigue of the handstand walk had affected me. I was brimming with confidence and swagger; my shoulders felt really strong. I didn't want to make a silly mistake, but I was feeling fantastic. I opened with 173—6 pounds higher than Annie or Sara. I was deep in my catch, but I buried it. In the short reset period, I fought the temptation to look at the weight increases that Sara and Annie had taken. I stuck to my plan and loaded my barbell to 183.

When it was my turn to lift, I took extra time to sit back into my setup. Then I pulled with everything I had. I pictured myself throwing the bar through the ceiling. I jumped toward the rafters of the Ballerup Super Arena, then dove under the bar like I was dodging a punch. I threw my hands to the sky and for a moment time seemed to slow down. This is the magic moment in the snatch, when the bar is weightless for one split second. Gravity is your best friend as you force your body down and your worst enemy as you pray the bar will stay suspended above you. The moment of truth comes in the catch. My butt was nearly touching the ground when I felt the bar settle in my hands and the load began pressing down on me. Balancing a bar loaded with more than your body weight over your head is harder than it sounds. The balance point is similar to what I feel in a handstand, but with a barbell you are on the razor's edge. A small deviation forward or backward can be impossible to recover from. I was patient. I waited in this bottomed-out position until the weight settled. After the catch, standing up was no issue. I showed a look of determination, but a smile spread across my face in conjunction with the opening of my hips. I waited at the top for my judge to call it a "good rep," then squealed and jumped up with delight. Annie ran over and gave me a huge hug!

Her coach, Jami Tikkanen, would later joke that mine was a "miracle snatch." That description doesn't take into account the hundreds of hours we practice all the minutiae that goes into this highly technical lift. Jami, one of the best coaches in the business, was referring to the ferocity a lifter needs to succeed. The only way to make progress in the snatch is to take chances. In competition, I fearlessly throw myself under the barbell. This time it paid off, and it would inform the way I snatched in competition going forward.

"You never think she's gonna make it, but somehow she does," Jami laughed as we all celebrated.

Sadly for me, Oxana Slivenko, a Russian silver-medalist weightlifter from the Beijing Olympics, was competing in our region for a second time. She was in the heat before mine and had easily beaten me by 40 pounds on her first attempt. Regardless, I was thrilled, as I was having the opposite Day 2 from what I had experienced in 2014. And it was still pretty cool that such a highly competitive lifter was on the floor with us.

Annie and I were tied for first at the close of the day, and I was so happy I couldn't wipe the smile off my face as we were interviewed.

"We train together, we basically live together . . . it makes sense that we're at the top together." I giggled.

"I'm so proud of this girl," Annie told the camera. "She deserves all of this. She deserves to be at the Games."

On Sunday, the muscle-ups in the final event led to my worst finish of the weekend. But it was far from catastrophic. Thirteenth place didn't even drop me in the overall standings, but that wasn't what mattered to me. I had given my best effort and exceeded my practice times. More important, I knew I had accomplished my goal in the most competitive female region in the world. The domination by Icelandic women had reached its zenith at Regionals that year. Five women qualified from the Meridian. Four of us were from Iceland.

Before 2014, I had taken qualifying for the Games for granted. Sure, I had gotten scared, I even cried during training sessions, but I always believed I would qualify. I don't think I was cocky, I was just naive. I knew that failure was technically an option, I just didn't think it was a possibility. In my heart of hearts, I expected to be at the Games.

This year I could draw on both experiences: the joy of qualifying and the devastation of coming up short. When my name was called as a qualifier for the Games, the happiness I felt was overwhelming. This time I cried happy tears. I was so happy just to qualify, and that was my only ambition. It was different this time. I had expected it before. Now I relished the opportunity. I was overwhelmed with gratitude and pride.

I ended the 2015 Meridian Regional the same as I had ended the Europe Regional in 2014, crying on the floor of the Ballerup Super Arena wrapped in the support of Europe's fittest athletes and its wonderful CrossFit fans. This time, though, they were tears of joy. This time I was going back to the CrossFit Games.

With the stress of Regionals behind us, it was time to have fun. It was time for Games training. Training takes different shapes throughout the competition season. The final run up to the Games is far and away my favorite. The training volume goes up, the intensity reaches an all-time high, and our focus narrows to a laser beam. We would train all day long and Ben was teaching all the time. Before or after training, he would discuss concepts focused on the mental side of the sport. On my lunch break, I would sit outside and read *The Champion's Mind*. I wasn't just reading the words anymore, I was really internalizing the concepts. Everything felt like it was clicking.

Ten days before the Games—after training was done and I had been working on my travel list—I walked into Ben's office and made an announcement.

"I am so happy with the training that we've done," I told him, "I don't even care what my placement is and I don't care what happens. I am so happy."

I meant it. I had always invested myself so heavily in where I was on the leaderboard at the Games. I had wanted to be a "Top 10 Girl." If I really let myself dream, my absolute goal was to finish in the top five. Now I was just so happy with the work that we had done that I would be pleased with any result. I felt ready and confident. I found it impossible to imagine that anyone had prepared more than we had. I was excited to step back onto the floor and test myself against the fittest women on Earth.

FITTEST ON EARTH

FITTEST Á JÖRÐINNI

At the end of the day, only you know how hard you worked.
Make sure you gave it your best.

July 2015—StubHub Center, Carson, California

Training for the Games is a process of growing and competing and repeating that process continually as you try to perfect it. Could my nutrition be better? Could my sleep be better? You always want to maximize everything. Champions don't have balance, and the reason they are exceptional is because they focus all their time and energy on what they do.

I worked so hard in 2015 that I would go home so trashed every single day. Nothing makes me more happy than the feeling of complete exhaustion at the end of the day. There is a satisfaction in that for me that nothing else can replace. I want to eat well, I want to sleep well, I want to recover, and then I want to do it all over again. That's what our entire year looked like. When you get to the Games and you've worked that hard it's easy to be confident. It's not a confidence that you are guaranteed to go and beat everyone, but rather a confidence that you know what you're gonna go do. You're going to do what you've done every day in training.

You're gonna go hard and leave no doubt. It's the confidence that you could possibly be in this given moment.

My experience at the 2015 Games was different from the start. I had never enjoyed being at the Games, but my new perspective lightened my mood and made it all seem fun. The lobby of the Marriott, where in 2012 and 2013 I had hidden myself away, now felt energetic and alive. I smiled my way through the check-in process. I laughed and socialized with people I recognized from other regions and even asked for pictures with some of them. I was having fun.

The only Reebok representative I knew at the time was Jared Davis. He's an affable former Games athlete with a thick Southern drawl and a big heart who took care of athlete relations. Now I met Tal Short. As the senior product designer for footwear, he was the man in charge of creating the Reebok shoe line designed specifically for CrossFit. When our conversation turned to items on our bucket lists, I told him I had two: I wanted to run in a marathon and I wanted to have my own shoe one day.

"If you win the Games, I'll give you your own shoe," he said, joking, of course.

"Deal," I joked back.

Both of us laughed at the absurdity of it. I was there to compete and have fun but winning the Games was not on my mind. My aspirations were centered on maximizing this experience. I knew nothing could be taken for granted.

By 2015, CrossFit had effectively taken over the Manhattan Beach Marriott. It looked like CrossFit owned the hotel. I can only imagine the confusion of tourists who had booked that weekend simply by chance. Huge banners celebrating the festival of fitness were hung everywhere. Nearly every person in the lobby sported an athletic physique and bright clothing.

The lobby had huge vaulted ceilings and lots of open space. Reebok had adorned the entire lobby with beanbag chairs and recliners throughout that sported the CrossFit Games logo. Straight ahead as you walked in were a set of stairs that descended to the back patio and pool area.

For the first time, the lobby level also featured a huge CrossFit gym. Rogue Fitness had converted three adjoining ballrooms into a CrossFitter's dream. Every imaginable tool and toy you could possibly want or need were there. We were getting spoiled. I met Ben, along with Mat Fraser and Michele Letendre just outside the gym. The conversation focused on mind-set. Ben expanded on a concept he had introduced to me in 2014, before I was prepared to understand.

"When people visualize their performance, they picture everything going perfectly," he started. "Don't envision perfection. I want you to have a plan, obviously. But you also need a Plan B. If you're smart, you will also have Plans C, D, and E," he counseled us.

I flashed back to the conversation we'd had on the treadmill in 2014, right before the Europe Regional. I had been incredulous when he had introduced this concept then, but now I got it. In gymnastics, I would lie in bed the night before a meet and picture entire routines; in my mind, I played them out to perfection. If I fell on my head, I would rewind and start from the beginning until I had successfully completed everything to my liking. This, of course, is not how reality works. I had never made the connection in gymnastics, but 2014 taught me what it was like to be on the competition floor in the heat of battle with no exit strategy. I was paralyzed when the moment hit and I didn't know what to do.

Ben recounted a story from the 2011 Games. He had led CFNE's team into the weekend, and before the event, he met with the entire team just as he was doing with us now. He had them lie on the floor and visualize themselves on the competition floor. He invoked the sights and smells to put them in the moment as best he could. They pictured a flawless execution of the event. Everything was in sync; they felt strong and were communicating clearly and efficiently.

When they took the floor, however, reality struck. Everything felt different than CFNE's team had imagined it. Unprepared for things to go awry, the team members were unable to recalibrate their strategy. Frustrated and angry, they floundered in the event and finished close to the bottom of the pack. Ben shared the story because it had caused him to adopt a new method of visualization in which you pictured potential contingencies. You prepared yourself for the worst and pictured yourself solving the problem instead of crumbling to it. It was what Ben had encouraged me to do before the 2014 Regional, with no success. Now I understood why it made so much sense.

I feel like the Games really begin with the athlete dinner on Monday night. Dave Castro invites the athletes to a nice dinner during which he makes workout announcements or fills in details from workouts that had been partially leaked on social media. In my first two years at the Games, this dinner was nerve-racking. This year, it was fun to see the people I had been watching compete over the Regional weekends.

I had a new sense of confidence that didn't go unnoticed, for better or worse. When I brought my own food to the Monday night athlete dinner, people gave me a really hard time. It didn't bother me at all, and I knew it wasn't personal. I knew I was stirring insecurities that they weren't taking the competition as seriously as I was. I was set on controlling everything within my circle of influence this year and letting the rest of it roll off my back.

Dave outlined the new additions to the Games. Wednesday would be like playtime with some very creative workouts that could not have been more different. There had been speculation about the use of stand-up paddleboards at the Games. Dave told us we would be taking paddleboards into the Pacific Ocean at Santa Monica, but they were prone paddleboards. They were mixed in with two medium-distance swims. It was so different from anything I had done in my life and I had a blast, finishing near the middle of the pack in eighteenth. This was only one spot below my best finish in my previous two years at the Games.

After the paddleboard event, we returned to the StubHub Center for a throwback to the 2010 CrossFit Games, the first year the event was held in Los Angeles. We moved 720 pounds of sandbags from one side of the stadium to the other, jumping walls and climbing stairs to make it happen. To cross the stadium floor, Rogue had constructed an overbuilt wheelbarrow that felt heavier than all the bags combined. I had never used a wheelbarrow in my life before that. I loved that we were just doing lots of hard work. It was like Bootcamp had been moved to Southern California. There wasn't a lot of strategy, but before the event Ben taught me the best way to distribute the weight and I got the hang of it quickly.

Friday

Friday morning started with the Hero workout Murph. In a class of workouts known for their difficulty, Murph stands out. In honor of U.S. Navy SEAL Lieutenant Michael Murphy, who was immortalized along with his teammates in the movie *Lone Survivor*, which details their heroic fight for life in the failed Operation Red Wings, the workout calls for hundreds of repetitions of pull-ups, push-ups, and squats sandwiched by 1-mile runs. The whole time, athletes wear body armor.

MURPH

For time:

1-mile run

100 pull-ups

200 push-ups

300 squats

1-mile run

Murph shows up a lot in CrossFit gyms on Memorial Day in the United States. Even people who live outside the United States will hit the workout on holidays like the Fourth of July and Veterans Day. But as common as it is, there were variables in Murph at the 2015 Games that most of us did not consider.

The first was the format. Dave required all the work to be done on a single movement before moving to the next. In our home gyms, we would normally break the movements into 20 rounds of 5 pull-ups, 10 push-ups, and 15 squats, for example. In Dave's world, we were starting Friday with a mile run and 100 pull-ups in body armor. The second variable was the heat. The event took place on the soccer-stadium floor in blazing sunlight. Reports of the temperature on the grass grew into tall tales: from 110 degrees to in excess of 120 degrees.

On the field, Dave gathered us in a huddle and fired us up by talking about who Murph had been as a person and why this event was so important. We were so excited when the event started that everyone took off in a sprint. The run took us underneath the StubHub Center before looping around a side street and back the way we came.

Underneath the stadium, I closed in on Kara Saunders from Australia. Kara was a top competitor and as I pulled up to pass her, she cut sharply in front me, forcing me to cut back. When I tried to pass on the other side, she cut me off again. I couldn't believe it. But

I had enough energy to elevate my pace and pass her on the gradual ramp that led past the television trucks and up to the stadium level. She finished fifteen seconds behind me. When I crossed the finish line, I turned to see her swerving like she was drunk before collapsing on the grass. It was only then that I realized she hadn't been trying to block me. She was hanging on to consciousness by a very thin thread. Scarily, Kara blacked out and was carted away on a stretcher. I finished twelfth in the event, but more important, I was feeling fine. Some of the other girls were absolutely wrecked.

While we waited for the fifty-five-minute time cap, we sought out whatever shade we could find. People hid underneath carts and behind equipment. If there was a sliver of shade, someone was in it. People were devastated, had and underneath the stadium, it had turned into chaos. Girls were crying, some were angry.

On my final run, I was surprised to see medical staff helping Annie. I wasn't allowed to go check on her until after the time cap, when I found her in the medical room. She had suffered heat damage. She looked confused and couldn't finish the event. She said her vision was blurred and she could hardly stand on her own two feet. I had never seen her remotely close to this condition, and it freaked me out. Annie friggin' Thorisdottir doesn't get beat up by a workout. It was hard to see her so upset.

Medical staff gave Annie 2.5 liters of saline solution intravenously over the ninety minutes that followed. She took the floor for the next event. Kara also recovered for the next event, but neither woman would bounce back completely. Immediately after Murph, Dave gathered competitors on the tennis-stadium floor for another briefing. All I wanted to do was jump in the ice bath.

I sat between two of the more veteran Games athletes: the affable and funny Australian Chad Mackay and All-American Scott Panchik, who had finished fifth or better in three Games appearances before this one. We would face the Snatch Speed Ladder next. We knew the structure of the event. It was nearly identical to an event from the 2014 Games, the Speed Clean Ladder, only now the weight was going overhead. The stakes were literally being raised. Dave had announced this event in advance of the Games with few details. Now he filled in the gaps by briefing the weights we would be lifting. The final snatch weight for women was 180 pounds. I had snatched 183 at Regionals, but that was a 1-rep max. If I got a shot at the final barbell, it would mean I had already successfully completed fourteen bars, five of them over 135 pounds. I got up to leave, assuming Dave had already delivered his punch line.

"Wait for it," Scott said, pointing out that Dave was still glaring at us intently. "Betcha it's another Hero."

Scott was a student of the game and very familiar with Dave's style of showmanship. No sooner had he said it than Dave started to speak again.

"At Regionals we had Hero Friday. You'll do that again here now."

I slapped Scott Panchik on the thigh. He had guessed right.

"Tonight, we will do the Hero WOD DT."

He explained the format of another challenging workout, but this one featured the barbell. I was excited.

DT
5 rounds for time:
12 deadlifts
9 hang power cleans
5 push jerks
*All at 105 pounds

"That concludes the Friday-evening event announcements," Dave said. "You guys can go ahead and start warming up for your squat snatches."

I jumped up and walked away as quickly as I could. I wanted to get to the ice baths first. I was first in line, speed walking ahead and already thinking how I would approach the quarterfinal snatch weights. I was almost close enough to touch the 20-foot-tall entryway banner that hung across the cavernous mouth leading to the tunnel beneath the StubHub Center when Dave's voice stopped me in my tracks. I should have known it wouldn't be that easy.

"You know what? Turn around," he said.

He looked to the sparsely populated arena and told them they would be involved in the decision-making process for the event. We weren't going to do DT. We would be tasked with either Double DT—10 rounds instead of 5—or Heavy DT—the standard workout with 145 pounds.

"What you guys do tonight will be decided by the CrossFit community. Now you can go."

I loved the idea of a fan vote. The crowd that attends the Cross-Fit Games is unique. It gets lovingly referred to as "The fittest crowd on Earth." The fact that they are participants of the methodology that feeds the sport before they are fans creates a feeling of symbiosis and shared struggle unique to anything I know. When I am grinding through the end of a brutal event, the encouragement that fills the stadium comes from a place of understanding. The fans here have had to dig deep. They have felt the pain of a hard workout and the reward that comes after. When I'm in my deepest holes, it's the Games fans who can lift me up, because in a way, we have suffered through it together.

Now they would decide what challenge we faced. When I got to the warm-up area, I pulled out my phone and voted for Heavy DT. The 600 reps in Murph made me think that shorter was better, no matter how heavy it was. I focused on recovery and got what little rest I could before we hit the Snatch Speed Ladder.

By my new standards, I was already feeling like a champion.

On the leaderboard, however, my finishes were unremarkable: eighteenth, fourteenth, and twelfth. Things turned around in the Snatch Speed Ladder.

I felt good in the warm-up area. I was standing by Annie and I could see she was emotional. Her body was not following her commands, and I could tell it was really troubling her. I gave her a hug and told her it was going to be all right. She was fighting back tears and to be honest, I was impressed she was even standing there, ready to take the floor.

In the quarterfinal round my movement felt like butter and the weights moved easily. I breezed to a first-place finish. As the weight got heavier in the next round, I slowed my charge but made no mistakes. I fell behind Nicole Holcomb and took second in my heat. Between heats, we sat in the equipment tunnel and waited as the names of qualifying athletes were called. I was pleasantly surprised that we both were fast enough to advance to the final, where we would join the top performers from other heats. Annie was clearly disappointed not to advance, but she gave me a hug and celebrated for me.

As I walked out onto the competition floor for the Snatch Speed Ladder final, play-by-play commentator Sean Woodland made an uncharacteristic error to the viewers at home: "Two rookies and three vets in this winner-take-all final. The two rookies: Brooke Ence and . . . I'm sorry, one rookie and four vets."

To his credit, the statement was symbolic. No one at the Games expected me to perform well. My previous performances at the Games had been lackluster, and last year I was absent. In my mind, this was a rookie season as a brand-new athlete. Just by gaining entry to the final, I was guaranteed a top-five finish—the first of my Games career. I was thrilled. It was just another confirmation that my approach was working.

One of the vets he was referring to was Elisabeth Akinwale. She was incredibly fit and had a gymnastics background. At the Games, she had earned a reputation for her heavy-barbell prowess. It took everything I had not to be intimidated as I lined up next to her.

The snatch is technical. As weights increase, the smallest of deviations can lead to failure. The lift is similar to a golf swing in that even tiny distractions can submarine an otherwise good rep. I put blinders on and kept my gaze locked on the wall at the far side of my lane. I focused on burying every single rep. I would set up, take a deep breath, drop my hips, then pull. The "miracle snatch" from Regionals was back. I successfully threw myself under 160. Then 165 and 170.

I let myself get caught up in the excitement on the second-to-last barbell. Elisabeth and I arrived simultaneously and I watched one of the leaders, Nicole Holcomb, fail her first attempt as I addressed my bar. I pulled before I was set and although I got under the weight, I dumped it immediately on the ground in front of me. I recomposed myself and caught my next attempt. It was behind me, and my arms had to stretch like rubber bands, but I recovered. Good rep. Nicole and Elisabeth came with me to the final bar. Brooke Ence had failed her first attempt and we all were now back in a virtual tie. I took my time, chalking my hand and refocusing. Everything fell in place at 180 and I sprinted across the line, just two seconds behind Brooke.

Second place in an event at the Games. I gave Brooke the biggest hug and smiled from ear to ear. I was feeling the magic of Regionals again, only now it was magnified.

We laughed and danced a little bit in celebration. That feeling is what dreams are made of. But win, lose, or draw, it was time to turn the page. I went back to the warm-up area and celebrated with my team before we turned our focus to DT. The fans had opted for heavy barbells. It was a choice welcomed by the athletes, as we had already put in so much volume.

My momentum carried into the evening. The evening events inside the tennis stadium stand out from all the others; the bright lights bring intensity to an intimately small stadium and comp floor. There was always an electricity in the air from the anticipation of what's to come on the competition floor. As an athlete, I could feel it and it would propel me to my best performances. Before DT, Ben told me to start slower than I wanted to. I stuck to the plan even though I had a temptation to push. I finished 11 reps behind Sara. I felt fantastic.

Saturday

Everything was falling into place this year. For two years, I had floundered at the bottom of the CrossFit Games leaderboard. Last year I wasn't even here. Now I was gliding through the weekend. I was with a team that I loved, and I was having the time of my life at a competition where I had previously only felt disappointed and embarrassed.

I didn't check the leaderboard once, on principle. I didn't need it to know how dramatically I was exceeding my expectations. I would give my best effort, finish happy, and move on. Then repeat. I was in the zone.

But after two days and five events, my sunshine-and-rainbow walls threatened to crumble and bury me by Saturday afternoon. Although I was avoiding the leaderboard, I couldn't avoid the bright white jersey overall leaders must wear. It was pressure I didn't need. I was being tested.

We had just completed the Sprint Course 1 and 2 that included obstacles. I had underperformed, but I wasn't unhappy with my effort. I turned the page to move on. But it was harder this time. I was letting my brain take over; it was stealing my confidence.

The day's second event, the Soccer Chipper, includes flipping a so-called Pig that weighed 395 pounds a total of 100 feet, as well as 4 legless rope climbs and a 100-foot handstand walk. Legless rope climbs—the same movement I had repeatedly failed at last year's Europe Regional before crumbling into barely controllable sobbing as the whole world watched. To add insult to the injury, the ropes at this year's Games were thicker in diameter. It wasn't enough to ensure failure, but it wasn't helping.

In my head I started thinking about how fast the other girls were going to move. I worried about my placement and where I would finish in relation to them. Anxieties I thought I had put behind me were bouncing around in my brain when CrossFit HQ's Angel Forbes, part of the Athlete Control team, approached me. "Here's your leader gear. Congratulations! Please make sure that you're wearing it when you take the field for the next event."

I hoped it was a mistake. I had no idea I was in first place. It wasn't where I wanted to be. I had finished poorly on Sprint Course 1 and 2—a pair of twenty-first-place finishes. I was overcome with terror when I realized everyone was about to see me fail at legless rope climbs. It was all I could think about. *I'm going to be wearing the leader jersey and they are all going to watch while I fail again.*

To Angel's dismay, my eyes welled up with tears and I began to cry before she had even turned to leave. It must have looked more like she had handed me a note detailing how I was going to die than a token of my success. She tried to console me. Then I lost it.

I looked around frantically and saw Frederik Aegidius standing nearby. He saw the distress in my face and tried to help me.

"Just find Ben, please! I need Ben here!" I watched Frederik run off into the crowded warm-up area that was already in full preparation mode for the event that was about to end me.

When Ben approached, I was holding the leader jersey like it was a dirty diaper. Before he was close enough to hear me, I rattled off my mounting insecurities like verbal diarrhea. "I have to wear this thing and everyone is going to see me fail and I'm so nervous for this event . . . this is terrible."

He absorbed my babbling without reacting. He was calm—that made me feel better. But I needed him to say something. He waited for me to make eye contact.

"I don't care about the leader jersey. Neither do you. That thing doesn't matter. It's Saturday afternoon at the CrossFit Games. The leaderboard is irrelevant. You're just going to go out there and show everyone how hard you've been working."

Hard work was an understatement. We had been maniacal about training rope climbs.

I had been traumatized at last year's Europe Regional. Legless rope climbs had exposed an enormous weakness. I had been humiliated in front of the world. I had questioned my identity as a CrossFit Games athlete.

I got panic attacks when rope climbs appeared in a workout. The anxiety led to decreased physical strength and tears. When I stood in front of a rope, my arms went numb. Even in training, I would get so nervous I couldn't breathe.

I would jump up for an attempt and my arms wouldn't work. This strengthened my belief that I was terrible at legless rope climbs, so I would panic and then fail again. The vicious cycle repeated endlessly. Sometimes I had to leave the room just to breathe.

As a cure, Ben prescribed three legless rope climbs every single day. Progress had come slowly, but it had come. On the last legless-rope-climb session before the Games, he had me complete them for time. The first two went okay, but I got really tired. I looked at the clock and made a mental note. My final climb took me twenty seconds exactly, despite the fatigue I was feeling. I had made huge strides in the past year. That's what Ben was reminding me of now as I faced the Soccer Chipper.

"It's just like every other day in the gym. Just picture the two of us in the gym. Climb the rope."

I knew he was right. We had worked hard at this.

"Come down from your first climb and rest until I would tell you that you're ready again."

Ben and I have worked together so closely that we have one mind in practice. He can tell by my facial expression and body language how I'm handling the discomfort, how hard I'm working, and when I'm ready to go.

"All I want you to do is make two rope climbs."

It was a modest goal. Our strategy was to complete half the prescribed work.

Okay, I thought. *I can do that.*

Everything seemed to turn around in an instant. My worries about failing in front of everyone evaporated. Instead I was excited to show everyone how hard we had worked and how much I had improved.

I was smiling as I entered the stadium. There was nothing on my mind but two rope climbs. Then I realized that in my obsession with the rope, I had overlooked what preceded the climbs: a new implement called the Pig.

I won't have to worry about the rope climbs if I don't make it past this thing, I thought.

After flipping the Pig 100 feet, I had four minutes left for the rope climbs and a 100-foot handstand walk. The ropes dangled from a mountain of steel called Zeus that spanned the width of the soccer field.

I stood on my massive red crash mat and told myself, *Okay, this is it. I'm going to do this.* My first climb was successful. My confidence soared. I walked away to shake out the fatigue and chalk my hands. I had purpose, but I wasn't in a hurry. I couldn't afford to miss. I made my way back to the rope. In my head, I was in CFNE, my home away from home. It was just me and Ben. "Go now," I heard him say matter-of-factly.

After another successful attempt, I moved to the final rope dangling closer to the finish line. I felt a surge of pride, realizing I had already met my goal. I was already exceeding my expectations with ninety seconds left on the clock. I thought back to my training. I knew exactly how long a legless rope climb should take me under fatigue. Ready or not, I was jumping up with thirty seconds left. I was either going to make it or I wasn't, but not trying wasn't an option. I collected myself and watched the seconds tick down. I shook my arms and took a few deep breaths.

Then I jumped up and pulled like hell. I was laser focused at the top of Zeus. The crowd was deafening. At the far end of the field, a handful of women were racing on their hands toward the finish line. Halfway through the climb, I could no longer keep my arms flexed. I was hanging on for dear life, swinging my body for momentum and praying that my grip didn't fail and send me into free fall. I was barely gaining ground and my forearms felt like they were full of cement.

The top of a rope is a scary place. The final pull on a legless climb forces you to take a chance. You have to release one hand in order to slap the rig and receive credit. It's scary, and your brain will fight against you the entire time. If your grip with the hand left behind is not strong enough, gravity will take over. Of course there is a crash mat below you, but with an awkward fall from that height the best-case scenario is a rope burn and a bruised ego. You also have to fight your mind, which is trying its best to save your life. The natural tendency when your hand leaves the rope is to clench your thighs around it as a replacement. This would invalidate everything you've done to this point, which is as costly as it is heartbreaking.

I made the touch successfully with three seconds left. I was time capped halfway through the prescribed work. My judge, Denise Thomas, presented me with my scorecard for signing. I know her well from training in Boston. With an ear-to-ear grin I said, "Denise, I won!" There was an awkward silence as Denise looked into my eyes, shifted her gaze to the south end zone where a handful of women were celebrating, then back to me. She looked back at me quizzically, trying to assess if I was messing around or had sustained a head injury.

"Honey," she started before pointing to the end zone. "Those girls over there, they won."

I could hear compassion mixed heavily with her thick British accent.

"You all right?"

I ignored her and repeated myself, "Denise, I won!" I was louder this time, yelling through a smile that had a mind of its own.

"Okay," she conceded and gave me a hug after I signed my scorecard. She must have thought I was crazy.

I had actually never been more sane. For the first time in my life, I understood why this finish was a huge win. I had performed to the best of my abilities. Results and leaderboards be damned. And I had exceeded my expectations.

I looked up from the perfectly manicured grass field to the bowl of the massive stadium. It was a beautiful day. It took a second, but I found Ben and my agent, Matt O'Keefe. They were standing above the entrance to the massive tunnel that led from the craziness of the stadium to the underbelly of the arena. I was beaming when we made eye contact. These were the people who had lifted me up. I couldn't have accomplished any of it without them, and I wouldn't want to.

By the time I met them in the warm-up area, my face hurt from smiling. We hugged and we celebrated. They were the only people in the world who could understand what I was feeling. They had lived it with me. In that moment, the converted parking lot felt like a little slice of heaven.

This event will forever hold a special place in my heart. It's hard enough to take the floor for an event when you know it's not a good event for you. In the Soccer Chipper event, both the jersey and my placement in the center lane were indications to those watching that the viewers' attention should be focused on me. All this in an event that featured four legless rope climbs, my nemesis. In the past, it would have been a recipe for disaster. But armed with my new mental training and a reframing of priorities by Ben, I flourished. The Soccer Chipper event showed me I wasn't just a better athlete. I felt like I had become a better person.

There had never been a focus on the destination in our training that season. Ben and I didn't discuss winning the Games. Success like that isn't something you can control. Instead, we put all our energy into the journey. Ben has asked how I thought a champion would train. How would they eat, sleep, and recover? Then I would do it.

This is what Ben calls "the process," and I fell in love with it. I believe you have to. Without a love of the process, success at the highest level is impossible. Not because it's complicated or difficult to understand; it's the opposite of that. Ben and I identified what it takes to accomplish the small things required to succeed at the Games. We deconstructed the elements of a Games champion, then we dedicated ourselves to them. The process dictated my success. The daily discipline and practice are what had led to the moment I entered the stadium in the white leader jersey. And the concept solidified when I understood my fifteenth-place finish in the Soccer Chipper was a win for me.

In the athlete area backstage, Ben told me how proud he was.

"Well done," he beamed. "You know what the difference was? When you turned your thoughts around like that. That's the mental win. You were upset and you regained control."

My biggest victory and my proudest moment is still this fifteenth-place finish in the Soccer Chipper event. I'm proud because of what it represents—a better way to measure progress—*and* of how it was accomplished—by the endless pursuit of improving myself. Being the best me has taught me to navigate challenges with my own personal compass. To do the best I can with the tools I have available. My compass is calibrated to my skills, abilities, and gifts—not to other people or things.

I was forced to face all my fears when I took the white leader jersey. It became the biggest win of my life, not just of the competition.

I took two more top-ten finishes that day, ending in third overall. My body was wrecked, but I was on an all-time high. I returned to the hotel in a joyful stupor. After hours of body work focused on my arms, I got some tortured sleep.

Sunday

"Help! I need help!" The words felt like they were coming from someone else, but they were mine. My voice was weak and quiet, as the words rode on my panting exhalations. My chest was heaving, and my legs were wrecked.

I had pushed my body past its limits and collapsed at the finish line. I wasn't being dramatic. I wasn't looking for attention. Something wasn't right. I could feel my body shutting down. "In order to protect the host," as my endurance coach,

Chris Hinshaw, describes it, the brain will shut down less vital systems in the body and redirect blood flow and oxygen to where they are most critically needed. At that moment, my brain decided all the muscles in my body were less relevant than my heart and lungs, which were both heaving as if they were trying to exit my body.

The medical team reached me almost as soon as I dropped myself to the ground.

Oh no, I thought.

I was now seriously questioning my decision to hit the accelerator when common sense told me instead to reach for the brake as I played the event back in my head.

EVENT II: MIDLINE MADNESS
6 rounds:

400-meter run

50-foot yoke carry (380/300 pounds)

Time cap: 25 minutes

Sunday morning was the first time it occurred to me that I could win the CrossFit Games. I hadn't even considered it a possibility prior to this. My mind was blown that I was doing so well! The other two workouts that would come in the afternoon remained a mystery.

This could be my only chance, I told myself.

I made a quick mental contract to leave absolutely nothing in the tank. I set my sights on a level of effort beyond what I had ever produced in training or competition. The dark place. The pain cave. Hurtsville. CrossFitters affectionately refer to the post-workout misery that is only attainable by the sustained, high-intensity effort of a well-programmed competition event as a "destination." Once you have been there, it takes mental focus and determination to revisit. Like walking on fire. I had been there many times.

Midline Madness featured a running loop that took us up all four flights of tightly grouped, steep stairs on the north end of the soccer stadium, up and over the sloping hill that overlooks the field, and back down into the bowl on another set of stairs.

We were all assigned lanes based on our placement. Likewise, some people started closer to the stairs. I was in Lane 7. Just like a waterfall start in track, the distance is an illusion because it evens out when you return to the field. I knew this, but I was determined to make a move early. As soon as the buzzer sounded, I sprinted and immediately passed two women.

A bottleneck started early on the stairs, but I could see that all the women were lined bumper to bumper on the right-hand side of the staircase. A metal handrail was all that separated the left from the right and there were open segments in the railing where spectators could easily switch from side to side. I stepped into the left stairwell and put it in high gear, passing both Chyna Cho and Lindsey Valenzuela. On the final set of stairs, I passed Nicole Holcomb and joined the stronger runners on our first ascent of the berm. I take pride in my ability to take chances on the downhill and this was no exception. I passed Emily Bridgers and moved into third.

The yoke felt light and there was no issue. I knew right away this would be all about the run. On my second run, I arrived at the stairs at the same time as Margaux Alvarez and Stacie Tovar. The left side of the staircase was open again and I exploited it. At the top of the second berm run, I was officially in the lead, but Sam Briggs and Anna Tunnicliffe were quickly closing in on me.

As I started my third run, viewers at home were hearing the voice of the 2008 Games champion, Tanya Wagner, another Games commentator.

"I'm so impressed that Katrin Davidsdottir can hang in this event with Anna Tunnicliffe and Sam Briggs. This is not about who can move the yoke, it's about who can maintain that speed on the run," said Wagner.

It was a moment too soon.

The adrenaline was long gone now and as I arrived at the stairs, my lungs were fighting for air after being compressed by the heavy yoke. This time, I grasped at the handrail for help on my ascent. Sam successfully made a move here, jolting me out of my tunnel vision. I tied an imaginary lasso around her and willed myself to catch up. Anna and I were now shoulder to shoulder.

For the next two rounds, I kept them in my sights. Margaux Alvarez and an Australian rookie named Tia-Clair Toomey had closed in on me from behind. At the time, I didn't realize who they were, exactly, but their constant presence in my peripheral vision would remind me to push every time I wanted to let up. I wasn't thinking anymore. I was just competing. The top of the berm was refreshing not only because the role of gravity shifted from antagonist to assistant, but also because the slight breeze felt like I was jumping into a cold pool compared with the scorching heat on the soccer field below.

In the sixth and final round, I knew I had passed the point of no return. Even if I had stopped right then and there, I knew the waves of pain would continue to wash over me. So I decided to push even harder. It was the last conscious thought I had. My lungs felt like they had been dipped in gasoline and set on fire. My legs had either gone numb or my brain had stopped sounding the alarm bells after falling on deaf ears for so long. I kept running, trying to catch Margaux, who had moved just ahead of me. The entire summer I had competed in this very scenario with imaginary foes. Now it was real, and I had trained for this very moment.

How bad do you want to win?

I answered the question for myself with one final charge. Tia, Margaux, and I arrived at our yokes at the same time, sprinting them to the red line in the end zone. The crowd in the soccer stadium was deafening. Our time differences came down to hundredths of a second with me sandwiched between the two of them in fifth. That's when I called for help. The leaderboard placement meant little to me. I had found another gear that previously hadn't existed. In my mind, this was another event win.

CrossFitters affectionately refer to the anabolic hole that envelops your body after a dose of high-intensity training as "the dark place." I had visited this place in nearly every training session. What I felt now was a deeper level of self-induced pain. I was hurt. It made me nervous. Two heavily muscled volunteers from the medical team were now wrestling me to my feet. It was a terrifying feeling, but not one I was unfamiliar with.

"Today I will do what others won't, so tomorrow I can accomplish what others can't." That's a quote by the legendary receiver Jerry Rice that Ben often recites and we try to live by. "Today I will do what others won't" looks like pouring your soul into brutal sprint intervals up a lonely ski hill outside Boston in the heat with no one around to see. It means running so hard on every single interval that you can't stand under your own power for fifteen minutes. It means giving so much effort in training that newbies don't know whether to high five you or call an ambulance. Doing what others can't looks like finding another gear when your gearbox is shattered. It looks like giving more than you think you have. More important, it looks like getting carried off the field but still having the confidence that you'll recover before the next event and then do it again.

Ben met us at the tunnel. "She's fine," he told the medical

staff, dismissively, as he pulled me to my feet. I draped one arm around his shoulder and the other on O'Keefe's. "This is what she does."

I was reaping the benefits of those self-torture sessions. I reminded myself there was nothing to hold back. It was now or never. I started to come out of the fog, and I even managed to smile and wave to the camera before the medical staff escorted me under the stadium, one under each arm. My moment of self-doubt was over. Now I had to trust in my ability to recover. I had prepared for this. I had come so far.

By the time we reached the shade of the building, I was able to walk under my own power. After some coaxing, I convinced the medical staff I was fine to join the other competitors on the north side of the tennis stadium, where Dave was about to brief the final event. I found a sliver of shade next to Kara Saunders and hid from the sun.

"The last test will have something none of you have seen at the CrossFit Games."

Every year there is something that we haven't touched before. Odd objects and specialty devices, like push or drag sleds. I feel like it's one of my favorite parts of the test. You get to see what people can figure out on the fly. No one gets to touch it in advance. You have to use your brain, as well as your physical talents. It's an opportunity to show off your athleticism and how good you are at adapting to situations.

The introduction of unknown challenges is an element that's wholly unique from any other part of the season. In the Open, people are in their own gym with their own equipment. Before Regionals, there is time to practice the events and strategize. At the Games, we are all on equal footing and it's up to you to see how you will react and perform on the fly. Every year there is at least one moment where I have to stop and ask myself, *How am*

I gonna do this? And the only way to do it is by yourself. That's awesome.

"Let's reveal the rig," he said ceremoniously.

The Rogue equipment team pulled back the tarp to reveal tall plexiglass walls in each lane. They were peppered with a diamond-shaped pattern that repeated itself from bottom to top.

"What is it?" he quizzed us. "That's right. It's a pegboard."

I was pissed at myself immediately. There was a pegboard at CFNE that did nothing but collect dust when I was there. I had never once even considered touching it. Now all of a sudden I found myself wishing I had spent more time in that dark corner of the gym that no one goes to. I had knots in my stomach. The other part of me was excited to see what I could handle.

"Let's see it, Dave!" someone shouted from the crowd. The comment received laughs and cheers.

"What, me? You guys want to see me try it?" he taunted, and the crowd cheered back.

He agreed after making the crowd give him some love.

"I'm gonna guess that in fifteen seconds, this ends up on Instagram with me on my ass."

He didn't make it look easy, but he made it look doable. I would find out long after that that Dave was once a rock-climbing enthusiast and loves pull-ups and legless rope climbs over most other movements.

Dave finished his briefing of the final, which was composed of two, separately scored events. Each heat would stay on the floor and the events would be done back to back, with a brief reset. The event names, Pedal to the Metal 1 and Pedal to the Metal 2, told us how Dave expected them to play out. They would be fast and aggressive. The buy-in and buy-out for each was different, but both events featured calories on both the Assault Bike and the row machine in the middle.

PTMI

For time:

3 pegboard ascents

24-calorie row

16-calorie bike

8 dumbbell squat snatches (100/70 pounds)

Time cap: 6 minutes

PTM2

For time:

12 parallette handstand push-ups

24-calorie cow

16-calorie bike

8 kettlebell deadlifts (203/124 pounds)

Time cap: 7 minutes

As we walked to the warm-up area, all the women were massaging their biceps, a clear indication that they had similar concerns to mine. I was wondering how my arms could be expected to get me up a pegboard, when I could hardly even scratch my nose. All the women were having issues with their biceps. Mine were so bad that my bodyworker, Chad, was actually moving them for me to jump-start my warm-up. Every time he moved them, I wanted to throw up. We had eleven events under our belts and they had been performed in harsh conditions. The cumulative effect of a weekend that started with 100 weighted pull-ups in Murph was finally catching up. Now we knew the final hurdle that stood between us and the end of the competition.

We were the lucky ones, as it turned out. After her difficulty with Murph, Annie had soldiered on for as long as possible, but had now officially withdrawn herself from the competition. My heart hurt so badly for her. I hugged her in the warm-up area, but I couldn't find the right words to say. The emotions were overwhelming and I still had to take the floor for the final events.

Justin Judkins, a correspondent for the media team, caught me on the road to the warm-up area for a pre-event interview.

"Ka-treen"—no one knew how to say my name yet—"what do you think about the final?"

"I love it, love it! I love chippers and it has hard movements. It's so heavy at the end [I was referring to the kettlebell dead, of course]. I don't know . . . I hope I can do it." I stopped and shook my head at the momentary lapse in positive thinking. "I mean, I can do it! With the adrenaline on the field, I can do it. It's gonna be tough, but I'm very excited."

Athletes and coaches gathered around the big-screen televisions strewn throughout the warm-up area to watch the earlier heats. Many of the women in my heat watched as well. Being in the final heat is an advantage because they always save the best for last. Going last means you can glean successful strategies or make last-minute adjustments to event strategies based on what did or did not work for earlier heats.

The other advantage was you were competing head to head with the fittest women at the Games. There was no guesswork about where you stacked up. We would only take the floor this one final time. One of us was going to win this thing.

I skipped the TVs, but I did watch the women in the warm-up area. There was only one pegboard, so we were forced to take turns. All the women were struggling with the exception of Amanda Goodman, who would compete in the third heat, and Margaux Alvarez, who would take the floor with me. *At least it's possible,* I told myself. I've surprised myself before when the rush of adrenaline in my bloodstream took over on the competition floor.

There was so much excitement in the venue that it would pulse in waves to where we were standing backstage. Deafening roars erupted from the crowd each time an athlete advanced to their next station in the chipper. I imagine this was what street level must have sounded like outside the Coliseum in ancient Rome.

When the first heat of women advanced to Pedal to the Medal 2, I overheard a group of girls recapping what they had seen: No woman had completed a single repetition on the pegboard. Information taken from the competition floor can often be misleading, if not downright destructive, but I found this nugget to be very useful. Had I not known that the pegboard had decimated the early heats, I might have adopted a much different strategy. I went to Ben to talk about it.

"You need to get out there and you have to make *one* pegboard," Ben told me as we hashed out our game plan.

It would have sounded like a very modest goal, except for the fact that I had been completely unsuccessful with the movement so far, and the way the first heat had fared against it.

"You perform the best when you're on the field. Go out there and figure it out. If you can't figure it out in the first two minutes, you stop and rest, that's it."

I was surprised by this suggestion, but it really was the way the weekend had played out. I was exceeding my expectations in almost every way once I took the competition floor. Ben gave me one final piece of advice on strategy.

"On the handstand push-ups in part 1, be smart. If you can get off of those handstand push-ups first, it's your workout."

There was an intensity in his gaze that I hadn't seen before. We both knew I was in a position to win the whole thing, but neither of us acknowledged it. We had a job to do. I gave him a hug and said goodbye, the last part of our pregame ritual before my check-in with Athlete Control. I love hugs, but here they actually serve a purpose. Prior to the competition I feel like I can offload my excess mental baggage onto him. The physical gesture is symbolic of this exchange. The last thing Ben said to me is something I'll never forget, which tied it all together.

"Show me smart. Show me strong."

The starting mats were arranged on the north side of the stadium, facing down the field of play on the back side of the pegboards. We would have to navigate to the front of the massive plexiglass structure at the event start. Standing on the mat, I took a deep breath and closed my eyes. The competition jitters had left my stomach, and my nervousness had evaporated the moment I entered the stadium. I now felt the same overwhelming gratitude I had experienced at my first Regional competition.

At the beep, I ran to my pegboard, anxious to get to work. My first approach was humbling. My feet lost their purchase and shot out immediately. It happened so fast I wondered if something was wrong, and checked my shoes to make sure they could grip the plexiglass surface. The second attempt returned a similar result and my confusion turned to anger. I was determined to make it to the top or die trying.

On my third attempt, I was finally making ground. The holes on the pegboard are tightly arranged in a diamond pattern that repeats on the way up. The distance from one hole to the next is no more than 4 inches, but with no efficient way to anchor your feet, the task can feel nearly impossible. I had made four advances up the board when my biceps could no longer follow my brain's directions. I watched helplessly as my arms slowly went from a

90-degree flexed position to full extension, leaving me dangling from the wooden dowels with straight arms. It was a tutorial in how not to ascend a pegboard. Apparently I had not made as much progress as I thought. My feet were nearly touching the ground, but I maintained my grip.

I squeezed the dowel as hard as I could and pulled my scapula back and down. It was a movement that I did daily in warm-ups but had never incorporated into actual movement. To my surprise, it worked! I gained a peg, then repeated the motion on the other side. I continued in this fashion up three more holes. The progress was painfully slow because I was only able to gain the altitude of the middle holes, which were more tightly grouped, but it was progress nonetheless. I made it to the top of the board and I was over the moon.

A black line at the bottom of the wall marked a successful rep. To count, you had to go up and down. I was so focused on getting to the top that I hadn't felt how fatigued the grip in my hands had become. Every portion of the descent was a fight, but I felt like I could make it. My grip failed with what felt like inches remaining. I threw my dowels on the mat; it was heartbreaking to get that close. The muscles in my hand were cramping and I could barely make a fist. It was clear that another attempt would return the same result, so I stopped. There were less than two minutes left in the time cap and my grip was beyond repair.

When I made that decision, I immediately pushed the pegboard from my mind; it was now behind me. By the time my feet had left my crash mat, I was focused on the next challenge, which I had every intention of winning. A few women joined me at the start mats, but most continued to struggle with the pegboard.

After the time cap, we lined up for the final time at the Games. I have never been more focused in my life. My body was loose, but my mind was laser focused. I thought about Ben's advice, and his words echoed in my head as we started the event.

Be smart, I reminded myself as I dug in on the parallette handstand push-ups.

I broke them into sets of three or fewer, never allowing myself to come anywhere near failure. I minimized my rest between sets to keep my tempo up. On the twelfth rep I turned to advance. When no one came with me, I realized that I was in the lead.

"Yes!" I shouted, throwing my hands wildly to the sky as I moved on to the rower, unable to contain my excitement.

I'm going to win the CrossFit Games, I told myself, for the first time all weekend long. I then proceeded to pull the handle of the Concept2 rower like I wanted to break it off. Sam Briggs passed me on the Assault Bike and got to the kettlebells first. Out of the corner of my eye, I could also see that Tia-Clair Toomey had arrived at the bike just as I was finishing. I wasn't as worried about Sam because she was trailing in the overall standings. Tia, on the other hand, was breathing down my neck!

Go time, I thought.

Deadlifts are not my jam, and the final challenge of the event was daunting even for the best lifters. Two massive kettlebells that looked like huge cannonballs were the only things that stood between me and the finish line. I gripped them and hauled with every ounce of strength I could muster. To my surprise they came away from the ground more easily than I was anticipating. My first two lifts went surprisingly well, and I advanced immediately to the next station where I caught up with Sam. With every successful rep, the crowd came to life around me. I've never felt more energized in my entire life; it was like they gave me superhuman strength to finish the remaining deadlifts.

When I crossed the finish line, all my emotions hit me at

once. I saluted the crowd, covered my mouth, and let the feelings flood over me. I wasn't crying, but I was overwhelmed. I could see my Icelandic friends in the crowd holding up my country's flag. I was as confused as I was ecstatic. I knew I had won the event but had no idea what it would mean for the overall standings. Sara Sigmundsdóttir had worn the leader's jersey onto the floor for PTM1 and PTM2. She had failed to finish the Assault Bike calories when the time cap hit. This was shocking and muddied the water even further. The finish order of the other heats would factor in to the overall scores.

We stood on the floor for what seemed like an eternity while the final scores were tabulated.

Dave Castro hovered at the scoring desk. What felt like a lifetime of immense anticipation in the arena came to a close when he took the microphone and approached us at the finish line. I wanted to throw up.

"Ladies and gentlemen, the champion of the CrossFit Games is from Iceland."

It was either me or Sara. He paused.

"And her name," Dave started before pausing again for several seconds, "is Katrin Davidsdottir!"

I heard the first part of my name and lost it. I dropped down and started bawling. I can't associate a single feeling with this experience. This was the culmination of my entire life, intensely focused in that single moment. The second that Dave said my name, I felt the reward for the entire journey. The sacrifices my family had made. The late nights, early mornings, and long days at the gym with my team. All the tears, self-doubt, sacrifice, and struggle. All the little things that no one sees. It all came together on the competition floor.

I collected myself and searched the crowd. I was looking for my family and friends, but the abundance of Icelandic flags also made my heart swell with pride. People from other countries were draped in the sky blue square with the snowy white cross and the fiery red center. Growing up, it was a flag that was obscure on the international sports scene. Now I'm confident that most Cross-Fitters know exactly what it looks like. It's thrilling to see our flag attain iconic status.

My dominant emotion was surprise. Shock, even. Twelve months earlier, I had been relegated to the sidelines. Now I was the Fittest Woman on Earth. It validated the changes I had made over the past eighteen months, and it fired me up to go back for more. I found Ben in the stands and squeezed him as hard as I could.

"I was gonna give myself another year," I said.

He was silent.

"You're all of it. I couldn't have done this without you."

I thanked him for helping me turn everything around in my life and my training.

"I'm proud of you. You were smart, and that's why you won," he said.

[12]

HEARTBREAK

HJARTSLÁTTUR

Grief is the price we pay for love.
—QUEEN ELIZABETH II

Twenty miles south of Boston, a mass of hills, rich in history, tower above the surrounding landscape. The tallest among them—Great Blue Hill—is the highest point on the Atlantic coast between Boston and the Florida Keys. In the winter, lifts service snow skiers, taking a break from the bustle of the city. When the snow clears, we utilize the steep, unstable terrain to forge our mental toughness.

We refer to "Blue Hills" casually, but every visit there is all business. Blue Hills, and the work we do there, is a hallmark of Ben's CompTrain competitor camps, where aspiring athletes travel long distances to be coached by Ben and train alongside his athletes. The workout seldom changes. Neither does the horrific impact it delivers to your whole body. Ben stands, mid-mountain, hand raised in the air. Every three to five minutes he drops his arm and we sprint toward him like we are being chased, only to stagger down and line up for the next. The message from Ben is always the same.

"No one knows how hard you're working but you. Don't cheat yourself."

April 14, 2016

It was a beautiful spring day. There was a chill in the air, but the sun was shining bright. A recent rainstorm had left the north side of the rocky hiking trail visibly damp. In the areas close to the trees, where the shade never surrendered to the midafternoon sun, the ground was wet and soft. At the bottom of the hill, 20 yards of ground sloped gradually but appeared to be flat in contrast to the rapidly rising slope we would be running up. From that point there was no mistaking the extreme grade. It's straight up.

That day was unlike any other of the dozens of times I'had been to Blue Hills. I had been up all night. Crying for most of that time. I showed up at CFNE in a fog of grief. My body was moving, but my brain was ravished by pain. I have never wanted so badly to be somewhere else. All I wanted was to be in Iceland.

I went to the same patio where Ben had scolded me for my mid-workout temper tantrum. I had grown so much since then, but at that moment, I felt like a child. I was overcome with emotion. I wept until there were no tears left. I was broken.

Ben and Whitney Gelin, another athlete at the camp, tried comforting me, but I was inconsolable. I continued to cry for the entire forty-five-minute drive to Blue Hills, where Ben was holding an athlete camp. There was nothing anyone could say or do to make it better.

A gradually sloping two-minute walk over flat ground leads from the parking lot to a building, which serves as the major activity hub in the wintertime. In the summer, the building's only use that I know of is as a starting point for our sprints. My eyes were puffy from crying and my mind was racing.

I was oblivious to everything that afternoon.

On my walk to the starting line, I stepped into a mud pit that swallowed my foot and caked my right foot in heavy, wet mud—like a cast.

Any other day, I would have laughed it off and looked for a solution. At that moment, I wanted the universe to take human form so I could challenge it to a fistfight. I clenched my fists as my temper soared, then I took a deep breath and kept walking.

Whatever, I thought.

All of us athletes were lined up for the first sprint when Whitney shouted at the top of her lungs, scaring me half to death.

"Wait! Ben, wait!"

She was waving her hands in the air. I was embarrassed for her. I thought she wanted time to rest or prepare. Instead she took off running down the hill we had come from. She was headed toward the parking lot but stopped well within view of all of us—about 30 yards from where we stood. She found the mudhole that had swallowed my shoe and jumped in with both feet, sending mud splashing all over her shoes, socks, and legs. I laughed—and cried. Then she ran back to the starting line.

"Now we're ready," Whitney said with a toothy grin.

Even though it seemed so silly at the time, it was one of the nicest gestures anyone could have done. I worked myself into the ground in that session. I tried to take on as much physical pain as my body could tolerate in hopes of pushing out the mental pain. Despite needing Ben's assistance just to walk, my mental anguish remained. It would become a permanent fixture.

My mom had called to tell me that Amma likely wouldn't make it through the night. At noon I got word that she had passed. It was the worst day of my life. It didn't matter that I had known it might be coming. Amma had been battling health issues for months, but nothing could have prepared me for this.

Earlier That Year

In January 2016, I had decided to move to Boston full-time. I rented an apartment, which established a more permanent living situation that both eased the burdens that come with being a permanent guest in someone's home and helped to convince me that I was fully committed. It was hard admitting—to myself and to others—I was actually moving. When people asked about it, I would tell them I wasn't going or that I was just "visiting for a while." I didn't want to talk about it that way for fear that acknowledging the move would force me to face the harshest reality: I was leaving behind the people I loved the most.

I was upset about leaving my family. I had a habit of crashing my grandparents' bedtime routine every night. As they read their books, I would jump on top of their comforter and wedge my way between them—Afi on my right and Amma on my left—to talk about whatever was on my mind. Amma would always put her book down, but Afi kept his nose in his. On the nights he couldn't ignore us, he would join the conversation. After we knew I would be leaving Iceland, the conversations were lined with sadness. Amma would do her best to put it in perspective.

"Katrin, this is what we are doing right now."

She always spoke as if we were one person.

"We will miss each other, but we want to be the best in the world, and this is what it takes."

Amma had boundless imagination and creativity. She loved fairy-tale creatures and telling me stories about them. She had a collection of Finnish coffee mugs called Moomin mugs. They feature cute little elves and creatures hugging, playing, or having fun. The light and colorful images perfectly matched Amma's personality: young at heart. She had ten or fifteen that she would rotate through when we had our morning coffee. The day I moved

(left) Helgi Ágústsson (Afi) and me as a baby, circa 1994. This was taken in London, where Afi served as the ambassador of Iceland from 1989 to 1995. He served the same role in Denmark (1999–2002) and the United States (2002–2006). *(Courtesy of the author.)*

(below) Three generations of Dottirs. Me, my mom, and Amma in London, circa 1994. Afi was the ambassador to the United Kingdom. Mom was in school, so I spent my days with Amma. We would visit Mom at her school during breaks. *(Courtesy of the author.)*

(below) The Icelandic landscape is like nothing else on earth. Black sand beaches, geysers, volcanoes, and waterfalls make it feel like another planet. This is me by Goðafoss, one of Iceland's most visited sites, when I was six. *(Courtesy of the author.)*

(above) West Palm Beach, 2018, with my agent, Matt O'Keefe. His athletes call him "Dad," because he looks after us so well. He is a pillar of my support system, and I wouldn't be where I am without him. *(Courtesy of the author.)*

(below) Breakfast at the Games has become a tradition and whoever can make it will join. The only rule is that we don't talk about the Games. (L–R: Afi, my mom, me, Ben, and Heather Bergeron). Manhattan Beach, Marriott, 2016. *(Courtesy of the author.)*

(left) My youngest sibling, BKjörgvin poses with me and Annie Thorisdottir at the 2013 Regionals, in Copenhagen. Annie was not competing due to injury. *(Jens Koch)*

(right) We have a tradition of getting our nails done the Monday before the games. This time it almost made me late for the Monday Athlete Dinner with Dave Castro. Madison, Wisconsin, July 31, 2017. *(Courtesy of the author.)*

(below) With my father, David. Morocco, summer 2014. This trip followed my failure at the 2014 Regionals. Dad loves to see the world and show it to us. We traveled often with him. *(Courtesy of the author.)*

(above) Chris Hinshaw took a chance on me after the 2012 Games. His impact on my success has been enormous. Natick High School track, 2018. *(Courtesy of the author.)*

(right) Annie and Frederik encouraged me to fly and compete in the Butcher's Classic. It was my first big competition and I took first. I was thrilled by the whole experience. February 5, 2012, Copenhagen, Denmark. *(Jens Koch)*

(above) Amma cheers for my last rep at the Icelandic CrossFit Championship. She was always my best and most enthusiastic fan. She was often so loud that my mom wouldn't sit by her. November 3, 2014. *(Stefán Pálsson)*

(below) Post workout debriefing with Ben at CrossFit New England, 2018. His analysis and insights are invaluable to my development. He is more than a coach, he is family. *(Jordan Samuel Photography / @JordanSamuelPhoto)*

(above) May 17, 2014—
Europe Regional;
Copenhangen, Denmark.
Sam Briggs encourages me
to keep fighting in the legless
rope climb event. Neither one
of us would qualify for the
Games. *(CrossFit, Inc.)*

(right) In order to pay for
my airfare and hotel, we ran
fund-raisers all summer. This
was taken at one such event.
My mother (pictured) and my
whole family came to support.
Pre 2012 Games, CrossFit B.C.
(Mynd: Kjartan Einarsson)

(above) With my siblings London, circa 2001 (L–R, Jack Davidsson (6), Hannah Davidsdottir (3), and Katrin (8); BKjörgvin was not born yet. *(Courtesy of the author.)*

(below) Whitney Gelin's act of kindness was a light on my darkest day. I learned of Amma's death hours prior to this training session. It was fifty-four years to the day after meeting Afi. Blue Hills Ski Area, Boston, April 14, 2016. *(Jordan Samuel Photography / @JordanSamuelPhoto)*

(above) Arnhildur Anna is my closest friend. I describe her as, "The social to my butterfly." On breaks from training we like to meet at coffee shops to catch up and people-watch. Reykjavik, 2018. (Courtesy of the author.)

(above, right) Afi and Amma were amazing dancers and it brought them so much joy. At parties, the host would often ask them to showcase their skills. This was at an ambassadors ball in Washington, D.C., circa 2005. (Courtesy of the author.)

(right) I have always looked up to my grandfather. He has been one of my biggest supporters. This was our final moment before I took the floor for the final of the 2016 Reebok CrossFit Games. (Courtesy of the author.)

to Boston in January, she slipped one into my bag on the way to the airport. Inside was a handwritten note:

To you, my Katrin. Look . . . back at what you have already accomplished, up and believe the sky will become clear, down to be sure that you are always going the right way, and ahead to conquer every challenge you face. Just a little note from Grandma.

She drew a perfect smiley face next to her name. This scrap of paper became a prized possession. I keep it with me and still read it often, sometimes reciting it out loud. I live by the wisdom in those four guiding principles. It's more than a note to me, it's a manifesto.

I was embarking on the biggest adventure I had ever faced and I was overcome with fear. Amma's note forced me to recognize how much I had accomplished as an athlete over the past three years. Her words also gave me perspective on Event 5 from Regionals. I considered why I was drawn to Boston and if it was the right path for me. Sometimes I would read her words about conquering every challenge when I needed motivation in place of a pregame speech. I got excited to take on the challenges that surely awaited me in this new chapter in my life.

I had bought a one-way ticket to Boston and taken a leap of faith. There was no one there to hold my hand, or wave a wand and say, "Okay, you're ready to be the best in the world." I had to make my own way. Nothing was lined up for me. I ate at the gym, bummed rides to training, and relied on the good graces of other people. I felt a huge sense of purpose.

After I won the CrossFit Games, it felt like time was vanishing. Being the champion is time intensive, it turns out. In addition to frequent visits to Reebok's headquarters in Canton, Massachusetts,

I had dozens of travel obligations: an Open announcement in Colorado, a training camp in Tennessee, and a bottomless vortex of photo shoots, interviews, and TV appearances.

Before I knew it, it was March. I was homesick for Iceland. I couldn't believe it had been three whole months since I had been back. With Regionals rapidly approaching in May, it was clear that if I didn't go now, I wouldn't have another opportunity until after the Games.

It would be my first year competing in the United States for Regionals—in the East Regional—and my entire family was coming to watch. My mom was bringing my grandparents, which excited me beyond words. I was also nervous because Amma was having health issues and the cause was unclear. She had complained of headaches for months. In January, her blood work indicated elevated levels of red blood cells. Back then, she had explained that her doctor was prescribing a new medication.

"Don't be alarmed, Katrin," she said. "It's cancer medicine. He says that one dose could help me."

I felt my heart thudding in my skull. I was buried by a wave of anxiety. She assured me she didn't have cancer.

I had spoken with her nearly every day since. Now, four months later, she told me she was feeling so much better and appeared to be making great progress. When I upgraded my iPhone, I left her my old one so we could FaceTime. I laughed every time she wrestled with the technology, making me motion sick as she swerved the phone around before finally framing herself.

"*Guð geymi þig*" is how she would end every conversation we had—"God keep you."

April was about to hit when I had another realization. It was go home now, or don't go until after Regionals. I am a planner, and I hate spur-of-the-moment activities, but I had to get home. I would normally run travel plans past Ben so they didn't interfere with training. This time I didn't consult anyone. Instead, I let him know at the gym that day.

I was so excited to tell my family I was coming home. I called Amma to tell her I was coming, but she didn't pick up. Next I called my mom and told her.

"When will you come?" she asked.

"I'm looking at flights right now."

I booked a red-eye to arrive in Iceland the next day.

I started writing a text to Amma to let her know I was coming, but was interrupted by a text from my mom.

"Don't tell her," she wrote. "It should be a surprise."

I loved the idea, but now I was the one dodging Amma's calls for the rest of the day. I'm a terrible liar. I would've spoiled the whole thing.

It's four hours later in Iceland than in Boston, making it far enough away to throw you off your clock but not far enough to require a total readjustment. I touched down at 4:30 a.m.—long before sunrise at that time of year. My mom picked me up and took me home to rest until the sun came up.

She invited my grandparents over for breakfast and the big surprise. I was giddy with excitement. I was standing in the living room when my grandfather walked in the house. He had poor eyesight that would later require surgery and although he stared directly at me, he couldn't identify the blond-haired girl in front of him. In his mind, I was in Boston and there was no way it could be me. After Amma walked through the house passing out hugs to my siblings, I caught her eyes. She started crying immediately. It was the perfect surprise.

We spent an amazing week together, but my usually unstoppable Amma was uncharacteristically tired. By that point, she had left her job and had stepped down from the various boards on which she served. She was keeping busy as a nanny to a friend's four-year-old daughter. The girl had a medical condition that prevented her from attending playschool. It could be exhausting work. Still, Amma wanted to do it and she loved the little girl. She would recount stories of playing pirates with Lilja. At the time, I attributed her fatigue to running around chasing this little one all day.

On April 4, while I was visiting, she left a note for me on the nightstand while I slept.

Dear Katrin,

Stars are born, but Champions are made. This is a long and hard way that not a lot of people want to go. But practice makes perfect.

Love,

Amma

When I asked about it, she told me that Lilja had wanted Amma to play with her.

"Amma, let's go jump on the trampoline," she pleaded.

"I can't," Amma replied. "I've never jumped on a trampoline."

In seven decades on the planet, she had somehow missed the simple pleasure of bouncing.

"Well, you'll never be able to if you don't practice," Lilja countered.

That day, my seventy-four-year-old grandmother jumped on a trampoline for the first time. She lit up when she told me about it.

I lit up, too, because she had not been herself lately. Something was off. Amma wasn't fidgety like me, but she normally stayed on the move. This trip she habitually fell asleep in her chair. Whereas she used to pick up a book or go for a chat in the brightness of our sitting room, now she sought refuge in the darkest corners of the house. She used to like to fuss around the house, doing chores and keeping busy. Now she was visibly exhausted.

"I'm so tired," she would whisper as she drifted off.

And there were the nosebleeds. She brushed off the severity when I asked her to go to the doctor. She told me it was nothing and she would go soon. She didn't want the embarrassment of going to the doctor for something as minor as a nosebleed.

Amma's final note to me came four days later, on April 8:

Dear Katrin,

Face to the Sky. Keep your feet on the ground. And your heart in the right place. Remember, light up the day with the rays of appreciation.

Love you Always,

Grandma

I returned to Boston after a week in Iceland. I got back on a Friday and didn't talk to Amma at all that weekend. She had driven five hours to the other side of the country with Afi to attend his family reunion in a place called Akureyri. Despite her exhaustion, Afi told me she attended all the parties, socialized, and looked like a queen in her bright red suit.

But she knew her situation was serious. She made plans to go to the doctor when she returned on Monday. When I called her on Tuesday to check in, I was surprised when my mom answered the phone. She was fighting back sobs. My heart sank.

"It's leukemia, Katrin."

The words hit me like ice water.

I couldn't stop hyperventilating the rest of the morning. I was shaken to my core, and I couldn't speak without my eyes filling with tears. I told myself we would overcome this, that it was just another challenge, that Amma wasn't going to die. But I was scared.

Amma didn't want me to know. She thought it was best for me to focus on myself and not worry. It was a beautiful but useless sentiment. She was all I could think about.

"We can't come to Regionals" was the first thing Afi said when I called.

"Of course!" I said.

I had already taken this for granted. Nothing mattered more than Amma's care and recovery. My heart warmed inside my chest and I smiled at how great a man my grandfather was. He was trying to comfort me even though he was facing the most difficult time of his life.

"There are going to be some hard months," he went on. "We're just going to face this right now. We have a plan."

There was a regimen of chemotherapy that would take nearly a year. They would cycle different types for maximum effect. They knew the doses and when they would occur. It was even on the calendar.

Suddenly, Boston and Iceland felt like they were a million miles apart. I felt so helpless. I knew if I went home, Amma would feel like she was a burden. I resolved to wait until after Regionals to fly back to Iceland. I felt trapped in this no-man's-land, unable to be there for her and powerless over the outcome. Waves of emotion would wash over me sporadically, leaving me a panicked, hyperventilating heap. I was a mess—unable to eat or drink anything and crying rivers of tears without any warning. I couldn't even keep it together in public. When I went to CFNE, I burst into tears as soon as I crossed the threshold. At least there I was not lonely. The Bergerons are like family. I am comfortable being vulnerable with them.

My fragile emotional state was ever present, and anything could set me off. I would cry when I closed the bathroom stall. It was the feeling of being powerless more than it was actual sadness. I got into the habit of making a motivational poster for Amma every day. It was a small gesture, but it was the only way I could fathom helping. And it kept me focused on a positive outcome. I wrote them every morning and took pictures that I sent my mom so she could show my grandma.

April 13:

> *You are the strongest of anyone in the world, and together we are even stronger than that . . . can you even imagine?*

The only time I got to speak with Amma, the conversation was brief before she was whisked away for a meeting with the doctor. I did what I could to feel like I was there. At the time, I was working with Reebok to create my own shoe and asked Mom to show Amma the options so I could have her opinion.

Chemo was set to begin the following day and it would be difficult for everyone. The doctors had been clear that patients undergoing chemo often feel worse when the poison is introduced to their system long before they feel better. Amma needed her strength more than ever. In my heart, I believed we could overcome anything we put our minds to, and I tried to remind her of the same thing in another note:

> *The champion's walk is . . . one step at a time . . . all the focus on what's in front of you . . . and give 100 percent to whatever you're doing. Me, you, us.*

At 1 o'clock the next morning, I was jarred from my sleep. I had missed seven calls from my mom. It could only mean one thing.

"She's not going to make it, Katrin," my mom said.

Amma's body had been unable to handle the chemotherapy. Her body broke down, and she declined rapidly the moment it entered her body.

I felt numb.

There was no more sleep that night. I occupied my brain with the fastest ways I could get to Iceland. I frantically searched, considering any option to be a viable one. I would have connected in China if it meant I could leave right away. But it was useless. My only option was to wait until evening. It was 4 a.m. The thought of waiting a full day made me sick. None of my roommates were home. My loneliness and helplessness made the house feel like a prison. I was the fittest woman in the world and absolutely powerless. I sat on the floor, catatonic, for hours. I didn't know what to feel or think. I texted Ben to see if he could come over. I needed family and he was the closest I had.

He came over when he woke up at 6 a.m., and we sat in silence for hours. There was nothing that could be said, really. Life was dealing a harsh blow. After two hours, he forced me back into life.

"Stand up," he said gently. "We've got to go get you some breakfast."

In my head, my life was over. Ben was thinking about breakfast. I was shocked it was even a consideration but unable to verbalize my protest.

"Okay," I said, standing at his command.

His wife, Heather, met us at the restaurant. We remained silent for the whole meal. Afterward, I called the Icelandic airline

WOW. A representative told me to come to the airport later and they would figure out a way to get me on the evening's flight, even if it meant taking one of the stewardesses' seats.

I accompanied Ben to Blue Hills that day for the Competitor's Camp, not knowing what else to do. I concealed my heartache from the attendees, but I was dying inside. I wanted nothing more than to be home. Whitney Gelin and Ben were the only ones who knew my struggle, and her small act of kindness with the mud-sock is something that I will never forget. After the Blue Hills session, we went home to clean up, then headed to the airport.

When I arrived in Iceland, Afi picked me up. We cried. It was the first time I saw him emotional. His person was gone. It was gut-wrenching to see my grandfather by himself. Amma had been by his side since he was twenty. They had celebrated fifty-three years of marriage. During those years, they loved to dance. It was not uncommon for Afi to pick up Amma and dance in the kitchen if there was music on. Every once in a great while, he would try to teach me. At their last ambassador's ball, they were asked to dance the way only they could. Those are the memories I hold on to.

When Amma died, I bought two Icelandic protection angel charms. I put one on her necklace and one on mine. It was buried with her ashes. Having this physical totem I could hold gave me comfort. In moments of weakness or when I am feeling discon-nected, I will put on my necklace and feel Amma come into the room.

Amma died on Chocolate Day—fifty-four years to the day after she met my grandfather.

It haunts me that I didn't make it back in time to say goodbye. Amma died surrounded by her family, but *I* wasn't there. I know she didn't want to feel like a burden on me. She didn't even want me to come home. I guess neither of us really believed this could happen. This wasn't supposed to be the outcome.

The only coping mechanism I knew was to dive into training headfirst. And to train harder. I decided I was going to honor her with my efforts. From then on, it was all for Amma. While we waited for my aunts and uncles to return from various corners of the Earth, I buried myself in my training at CrossFit Reykjavik. My body was taking beatings, but I couldn't shake the dark cloud in my head.

There were a million details to sort out and decisions to make, but I had a hard time caring about any of them. The color of flowers, the songs we would play, those kinds of things. I felt like nothing in the world mattered anymore. When my family got upset with me for being late to the funeral, I was only partially remorseful.

Amma is gone, I thought. *Why does it even matter?*

The service was in the church where my grandparents were married. It was beautiful. The standing-room-only crowd that came to honor her dwarfed any service in the staff's collective memory. Amma had impacted so many people's lives. She had the ability to lift people up. It came easy to her. If she walked into an elevator, whoever was inside felt better about themselves when she left. She made everyone feel important.

Today, I feel her presence in everything I do. She loved candles, so I light some every morning over breakfast. She drank her coffee from one of her Finnish Moomin elf mugs, so I do the same—and think of her.

Amma is always with me. Our farewell tradition on the phone was to remind each other that we are always together, no matter the distance. That will never change. She always had more energy than anyone else. I try to tap into that energy to honor her. In life, I always felt her presence in the stands during competitions, whether she was physically present or not. In death, I would now feel her presence on the competition floor.

13

SEIZE THE DAY

AÐ GRÍPA DAGINN

The only cure for grief is action.
—GEORGE HENRY LEWES

An hour-and-a-half drive southeast of Natick, the world-famous Cape peels off Massachusetts into the Atlantic Ocean. At this time of year Cape Cod is in high-travel season. The beaches and towns are littered with tourists on vacation from all over the world. Our team is here to hunker down for the final month before the Games. We stay off the grid, block out the normal distractions of the outside world, and narrow our focus to a laser beam. This is the final push before competition. We are 100 percent focused on training, eating, and recovering.

This year of preparation had dwarfed any other in terms of training volume and difficulty. Training harder was the only thing that could console me. So I poured myself into it. More intensely than before. I could only escape the pain when I was buried in my work. Yet even the toughest workouts couldn't quell my heavy-hearted emotions. It felt impossible to mask my anguish. Everything I did was for Amma now. I was always pushing harder. I knew I couldn't have her back, but I believed that if I worked harder I could still make her proud.

I have arranged my life in a way that allows me to block distractions and keep my focus on training to be the best in the world 365 days a year. Still, it's different at the Cape. We can take that lifestyle and multiply it. This is our version of Rocky in Russia. It's an opportunity for Ben to tailor every hour of every day to tweaking areas of personal weakness that could help me succeed at the Games.

From sunup to sundown, we operate in a vacuum and immerse ourselves in training. Long-term this would be a formula for burnout. For a month, however, it's the main ingredient to our secret sauce. Members of our team push pause on their personal lives to focus on the holistic process that has led to our success over the course of the previous nine months.

We train all year with the intention of peaking at the Games. It's no use to peak during the Open or Regionals. The Games are where everything needs to come together. The ax has been sharpened. Now we want it to split a strand of hair.

Many of the improvements we see come in the form of work capacity. But the largest gains arguably come in mind-set. Here, digging into that pursuit of excellence is the difference maker. When we wake up in the morning, we contemplate reading selections that Ben has given us; they focus on the mind-set that lends itself to greatness. We put a lot of time into examining why we are working so hard, what's important to us as people, and what kind of changes we want to make in our lives. We focus on our core values and we share them in a very intimate and vulnerable way. We are constantly calibrating our True North: the guiding set of principles upon which we base all our decisions and actions.

Some exercises may seem gimmicky, but I believe they give me an edge in competition. If you know who you are and why you're doing what you're doing, you will have an easier time digging deep in the fourth round of a five-round workout. If you have ultimate belief in something, you have higher purpose. If you have higher purpose, you are able to accomplish amazing things. It's easy to quit something as hard as the CrossFit Games, especially without a firm grounding in why you are working so hard.

At the Cape, I shared a roof with Cole Sager and—for the first time in 2016—Brooke Wells. We are starkly different athletes but benefit from hearing the feedback Ben gives to each of us. Ben calls it "the overlapping effect," and it happens whether he's giving technique advice or critiquing a lapse in mind-set. What he tells one athlete can resonate with all of us.

Living in a small house with other world-class athletes under Ben's constant tutelage makes excellence the norm. When I'm at home, there are external pressures. Although I've done a good job of surrounding myself with people who are helping me work toward my goals, they can still be distracting. Even the mental pressure I put on myself to be present for a birthday party or participate in a get-together can steal time from training. On the Cape, there is no pressure to be anywhere else. The focus can be placed squarely on myself and what I need to work on. When living, breathing, and training like a champion is all you do, it becomes your version of normal.

Ben will tell you training is the easy part. Programming workouts to challenge our bodies is easy, but training us to recognize the thoughts that will make us successful is far more difficult. We spend a great deal of time there. We talk about what we are focusing on, what we want for ourselves. We do things I had never associated with training before in order to accomplish that.

Ben creates a binder that acts as a syllabus for our month. We focus on a vision and what it looks like, and we watch videos that solidify messages.

We will incorporate worksheets that pose deep and direct questions, then go spend an hour with ourselves to reflect on our answers. I thought about Amma often. Talking about it was the last thing I wanted to do at first. I was scared of my reaction, and I worried how others would react. It made me feel guilty for two reasons. The first was that I felt that by not talking about her, I ran the risk of forgetting her. The other was simply that she deserved to be recognized. I wanted to tell stories about her and share her light with the world. It took me a very long time, but eventually—*only recently*—I have started challenging myself to speak about her. I've started to find it therapeutic, and it makes me happy to think and speak more about her.

My grandmother's death is the single biggest adversity I have ever faced and I needed to wrestle with my feelings. I can find a positive takeaway in nearly anything else. But not this. I will never make sense of this loss. I felt an empty disregard for everything around me. I missed my best friend, as I'm sure I will continue to do every single day for the rest of my life.

Any time I wanted to quit, thoughts of how much Amma had supported my goals kept me going. I thought about her looking down on me, probably cheering her head off. I know she would want me to continue following my dreams. She would want me to do even better. Amma was a large part of my "Why?"

With a strong grounding in my purpose, I can suffer through almost anything. Our mental exercises at the Cape helped us understand our purpose. Self-knowledge allows instinct to take over in competition. When it gets hard—in the last thirty seconds of a workout, or in the middle of a ten-rounder—the answer for why you are working so hard will dictate what you do next. Stomp the gas, or hit the brake. Anyone who has trained hard for something knows what I mean.

Ben can help with this, but he can't take the field with me. Once you leave the warm-up area, you can't rely on your coach. The ability to dig deep has to be grounded inside of you.

Cementing these concepts was done in the gym, not just the classroom. As has been the case in my life, the most impactful lessons often came on the heels of failure. When those failures presented themselves, Ben was masterful at jumping on the opportunity to teach. The most dramatic example of this involved Cole Sager, overhead squats, and muscle-ups.

While the Cape is one of the most beautiful places I've ever been, the training environment is less refined than at CFNE. The bars aren't great and the rings are different. There's a degree of grit built into the training. I was already tired and not having a particularly great day to begin with and the workout of overhead squats and muscle-ups was not going well for me.

Cole was just crushing me, literally just cruising while I was hanging on for dear life. The rings felt slippery in my hands. It was all-around awful and I wanted no more of it. When it was clear that Cole was going to lap me, I gave up on my effort. I put it into cruise control and let him pull away. I furiously stomped outside. I was basically throwing a silent fit. I was so disappointed in myself. Not because I had lost—that would have been fine. I had given up and everyone knew it.

Ben followed me outside. I couldn't even make eye contact as he began to speak.

"Kat, this is gonna happen. It's not always gonna be a wheelhouse workout."

In moments like this, Ben's empathetic side shines through. You can tell he cares about his athletes. He wasn't trying to embarrass me. He was excited to help.

"Let's say I gave you hang power cleans, handstand walks, and running. I know the look in your eye when I give you that workout. You are going to crush that workout. You're going to be a tiger. You're going to give everything you want to that workout."

He was right. At the mention of my dream workout I perked up, hopeful we might actually do that next. But then he revealed his punch line.

"Then I'm going to give you a workout that's overhead squats and muscle-ups and you reel it in. You don't give it all you've got because you've convinced yourself that it's not a great workout for you. I don't care about the results. I know that's Cole's wheelhouse workout. I also know there will be workouts at the Games that you're not going to win, but I want you to bring that same mind-set to the workouts that aren't good for you."

He was right: This was going to happen, I knew that from my experiences in competition—both good and bad. There are countless times at the Games when you don't feel good. There are times when things don't line up as you want them to. Those are the times when champions pull away from the pack. The ability to work hard and give everything when the deck is stacked against you is what we call "going green." It's a champion's mind-set

Ben turned what could have been our worst training session into a lesson. We used it to our advantage, and in fact we still talk about that day. I realize there are no such things as wasted days, if you use them to your benefit. This day could have ruined me mentally going into the Games. Instead it became a practice scenario that benefited me. Your response is what dictates the outcome of your situation.

I learned that we always fight—regardless of if it's *our* favorite event or not. We always give it our best.

14

WARRIOR

BARDAGAKAPPI

Think gold and never settle for silver.
—JIM AFREMOW, *THE CHAMPION'S MIND*

Friday nights have long been celebrated at the CrossFit Games. But I love Mondays the most. For me, that's when it feels like everything really starts. We get our first chance to separate ourselves from the noise and distractions of fans, media, and coaches. We can catch up with old friends, meet fellow competitors, and get ready for the week to come.

Monday is also the night of the athlete dinner, which has evolved since my rookie season, though the outline is the same. Tradition now dictates a revelation about how and when to expect the start of competition. The mood always begins on a lighter note. But when Dave Castro starts talking, we listen. In the months leading up to the Games, organizers will leak tidbits of information insufficient to formulate a plan. On this Monday night at the start of the 2016 Games, we filed off a Greyhound bus and into a fancy restaurant at nearby Hermosa Beach. Dave entered the room like a shot, then shushed us like a stern father preparing to deliver punishment.

"This year is a special year for a number of reasons. Most notably we are celebrating the ten-year anniversary of the CrossFit Games," he began. "I don't always get excited for these announcements, but I am really, really excited for this one, and for what we have in store for you all this year."

With their quirky personalities, never-ending one-upmanship and surprises, the Games own a unique brand of pageantry. They ride the line between reality-show drama and science-class geeky. Announcements like this one can feel like a rose ceremony on *The Bachelor*. Events are kept secret—sometimes until the very last second—and announcements are drawn out and playful. At first, I thought the theatrics and secrecy were all gimmicks for the fans watching from home. But now I know they are tools Dave uses to test athletes' mettle.

In my fourth year as a Games athlete, I had finally stockpiled enough wisdom and experience to keep a cool head in the midst of Dave's mental assault. I believed him that this year would be different, and I was ready for the challenge. There were no jitters like the ones I had experienced in my first two seasons. Tonight, Dave set the tone more aggressively than in years past. His words were carefully chosen and he presented them more as a warning than a welcome.

"This is not a local competition," he continued. "This is not the Regionals. This is not even like any of the previous CrossFit Games. This will be the most challenging year—physically and mentally—that you all will encounter at the CrossFit Games. This ten-year anniversary will push you to limits where you never thought you could go, and that you have never taken yourself."

I was more than unafraid. I was glowing as the words left his mouth. Dave promised that the athletes who succeeded this year would have to be masters of their bodies and minds. In my first two years at the Games, this speech would have shattered my confidence and sent my mind reeling. Now I was chomping at the bit.

I had trained to thrive on adversity. The more brutal, torturous, and painful the weekend, the better my chances were of winning it all. Everything Dave said was music to my ears. I could hardly contain myself. I was smiling ear to ear. I want the Games to be as hard as possible. I want more adversity. I want more volume. I want the events to be more difficult. I thrive on that stuff. It's where I can set myself apart.

"There will be times this weekend when you're gonna get really scared," Dave continued, "where you're not gonna want to be doing the stuff that we're doing. You're going to question what we're doing and you're going to question why you're here."

Nothing makes me happier than hard work. It's almost as if the worse I feel, the better I feel. I literally love when the workout gets hard and starts to hurt. The cue that tells others to take their foot off the gas pedal is my cue to go faster.

"If at any point you feel unsafe or you're questioning what we're doing, please feel free to come up to me or one of my staff and say, 'I don't want to do this anymore.' And we will gladly pull you out and make you comfortable. We will take you back to the bus and your competition will be over."

This was about to get real. I felt bad for the rookies. I remembered how scared I was my first year when Dave had delivered a speech that didn't even compare to what we just heard.

"If you're not here to crush the people next to you and win the CrossFit Games," he said, "then you should leave now."

I surveyed the room to see who might be second-guessing themselves.

He went on to announce sparse details of the events we would face over the course of the week. There would be an ocean swim. This time, it was just a swim: 500 meters with the promise that there would be no surprises. I was hopeful my practice in open water at Cape Cod would be there on game day. Murph would make another appearance as well—this time partitioned into 5 rounds of 20 pull-ups, 40 push-ups, and 60 squats. We would also face a Squat Clean Pyramid that riffed on the snatch pyramid from Regionals earlier in the year.

The athletes around me giggled or gasped. Some were furiously mashing the keyboards on their phones to share the events with their social media followers—perhaps hoping for some external reassurance that they would thrive in these events.

When Dave was finished, he exited the building as fast as he had entered it. Dinner with Dave Castro is never dull, and we were all on edge after he had finished. We knew there was much more to come, and based on Dave's statements, we suspected surprises could be around any corner. The bulk of the action at the Games focuses on the weekend, but any veteran athlete worth their salt makes no assumptions about when, where, or how the competition will start or stop. In other words, we keep our shoes tied. Some athletes even came to dinner in their uniforms—just in case.

The real surprise came the following night at a reception for the teams in the Manhattan Beach Marriott courtyard.

After a brief outline of other challenges individuals and teams would face, Dave came through on his promise from Monday night.

"We are meeting in the lobby tomorrow at 3:30 a.m. If you are not there at that time, the bus is leaving without you and your CrossFit Games are over."

We were ushered over to a hotel meeting room, where we were given a note.

Athletes, Report to your assigned judges at 3:30 a.m. in the Marriott lobby. You must bring VALID PHOTO IDENTIFICATION.

It went on to list gear and equipment Reebok had assigned us upon check-in, all of which we were to bring with us.

"It's a great year to be a veteran," CrossFit analyst Pat Sherwood said. "Some of these rookies were walking around with saucer eyes, but the vets looked excited."

He was right. I was excited and relaxed. I knew I would perform well—as long as I could make it to the lobby on time. I'm not known for my punctuality, so Ben and O'Keefe were pounding on my door at 3:15 to make certain I was on time. When Dave greeted us in the hotel gym, I was still half asleep. I snapped out of it when he told us we would be getting on an airplane. We needed to make our bags ready for a flight. We wouldn't be able to take food and our coaches would not be following us where we were headed. From the lobby, we loaded onto buses that took us to LAX. There was immediately widespread speculation about where we were going and what we would be doing once we got there. Eighty athletes, forty judges, and a handful of medical and support staff shuffled through the airport in our brightly colored uniforms. To an outsider, it must have looked like a school for Spartan warriors was going on vacation.

The athlete liaison, Tim Chan, shouted our names one by one as he handed us boarding passes. When I received mine, I finally saw the destination: San Jose, California. I knew immediately we were headed to Aromas, the birthplace of the CrossFit Games. This was going to be unlike anything we had ever done. While other athletes stressed and speculated on what we would face, I settled into my seat and went to sleep. I was prepared, no matter what awaited us in Northern California.

When we got to Aromas, Dave announced that we were going to repeat the first two events of the 2009 Games: a 7K trail run through the surrounding hills followed immediately by a deadlift ladder. The finish order in the run would determine the starting order of the ladder—last place in the run would begin the deadlift ladder. The third event was a variation on what many of the most veteran athletes called the Games' most punishing event. It features a sprint straight up the most prominent hill on the property.

The town of Aromas is tiny: less than 5 square miles. As we drove from the airport along Highway 101 through California's North Central Valley, the landscape was familiar. I had never been there before, but I had watched countless videos of former Games events. The landscape was mostly barren, but abrupt hills dotted with ancient and wiry oak trees stretched out on the left side of the bus.

Aromas is 360 miles north of the StubHub Center, where competition would take place that weekend, and it couldn't be more different than the sprawling industrial suburb of Carson. Aromas is a typical Northern California agricultural town. Nearby Gilroy lays claim to the title "garlic capital of the world." The climate is dry and unforgiving, and I could already feel it from my seat on the bus. Especially in the height of the summer months like we were in at that moment, temperatures exceed 100 degrees. On that day, the sun was unforgiving. I'm familiar with heat, but there is a uniqueness to this area. It lowers your defenses with its proximity to balmy Monterey Bay, then shoves a hot, arid fist down your throat.

There is nothing attractive about mud in your teeth. I chewed on it as I fought along poison oak–lined single tracks with scraped, bloody knees and tore into the arroyo for the second time on the trail run. I had kept Sam Briggs and Anna Tobias in my sights the entire race, battling up and down the steep, dusty hills shoulder to shoulder with rookie Kristi Eramo. It was the craziest run I had ever done—treacherous boulders to navigate around, inclines so steep they required both arms and legs, and slippery descents that had me skiing in my Reebok shoes. I took fourth in the event and headed straight to the ice bath.

The trip to Aromas was the most unique experience I had seen at the CrossFit Games. The whole day was gritty and raw, just as I imagined it had been in 2009. At every turn it felt like there were opportunities to panic or lose my head. Before the run, people were offering poison oak preventative lotion. After the run, athletes cast chairs out of the way to warm up on the wet cement floor inside the barn at the Ranch. I kept my cool. I was proud of my ability to remain calm, even in the face of a thirty-eighth-place finish on the deadlift ladder.

"If I could design the worst event that I would ever face at the CrossFit Games, it would be a 1-rep-max deadlift. Now it's done, gone. I got it out of the way early in the competition, so now I can move on," I told CrossFit media cameras.

I did move on. Directly to the Ranch Mini Chipper, where the hill that had been made famous at the inaugural 2007 Games lived up to its reputation as a soul crusher. After wall ball shots and med-ball GHD sit-ups, I sprinted up the 1,200-foot vertical gain until the muscles in my legs locked up. It was a unique pain. I collapsed over the finish line into the dirt and straw that lined the path. I entered the event in thirteenth, which meant I was competing in the first of two heats. It was the first time I hadn't been in the final heat since the 2013 Games, which fired me up. I chased Brooke Wells through the entire event and my time stood up over the next heat, keeping me in the top five.

At CFNE, we talk about an individual's circle of influence. We identify what factors are potentially ours to control and put a great deal of focus on effecting change in those areas. We give nearly equal energy to identifying elements out of our control—the weather, another athlete's performance, someone else's reaction. With factors that are outside our control, we practice letting them go and focusing only inside our circle of influence. It's a critical skill that is indispensable at the Games where events are unknown and most athletes train in isolation from one another. It's also a critical skill to a healthy life and it came in handy on our way back to Los Angeles that night.

After the Mini Chipper event, we packed up and left the Ranch for the airport in San Jose early in the afternoon—well in advance of our flight, which was scheduled for 8 p.m. When we arrived, however, everything was upside down. Southwest Airlines was in the midst of a system-wide server outage that canceled thousands of flights. Many athletes took to their cell phones. They complained to their coaches, lamented what would happen and how this would affect their ocean swim the following day. I called Ben to make sure he knew what was going on. Then I put my bag down in the line so I knew it would be impossible to board the plane without waking me up, curled up in a hoodie, and got what little sleep I could.

We got back to LAX at almost 1 a.m. On the bus ride back to the hotel, some of the women were actually conspiring to boycott the swim event.

"What are they gonna do if we all don't show up? We need to sleep!"

I wondered if them not showing up for the event would change anything about the point standings. Probably not, I thought, as I dozed off again.

I was pleasantly surprised to see my mom and my grandfather waiting for me in the lobby, despite the hour. They had come to the Games to cheer me on and they weren't going to let a lack of sleep get in the way of a hug. I didn't talk a lot, but I loved that they were there. I gave them hugs and they walked me to my hotel room. It was just what I needed—for them to be there.

We met for breakfast the following morning in the hotel lobby. We have a rule at the breakfast table when we are at the Games: no talking about the competition. I just want them to be there as my family. I love to be surrounded by my people and we will talk about anything and everything else. But competition is off-limits. I count on my people to keep me grounded and sane in the midst of the insanity. On Thursday morning, we met early in the hotel lobby and drove ourselves to Manhattan Beach.

Thursday, Redondo Beach

The CrossFit Games are arguably the most egalitarian sport in the world. Women and men have earned equal amounts of prize money, promotion, screen time, and recognition since their inception. The sport has been called "wonderfully coed," and some events provide the opportunity to pit the men against the women head to head on the same course. We had not expected the ocean swim to be such an event. It was an unwelcome surprise.

Dave's announcement, twenty minutes before the start of the event, that all athletes—men and women—would compete together came as a shock. While I was not afraid to match myself against the swimming abilities of the men, a short sprint like this one was more like combat than sport. We would have to throw ourselves into the waves with eighty other bodies like a school of sardines. I set myself up in the back row at the start and devised a plan to swing wide of the crowd to keep myself safe.

I can actually swim really well, but you would never know it by watching me compete at the Games. In a pool, I can swim. But if you put me in open water, I panic as soon as I put my head under. I come up gasping for air as if I'm drowning. It's like I forget everything. I'll resign myself to a breaststroke or a doggy paddle, at least until I get a little bit of distance behind me.

During the swim at my first Games in 2013, my only goal was to survive. I was in zero rush whatsoever, and I had no sense of urgency. Racing was the last thing on my mind. When I finished the swim, I was still only a third of the way done but I took my time getting to my bike, just content to be on dry land. In 2015, I panicked again, despite how much I had worked on it. When this happens, I get disappointed and have an internal monologue about why I should be conducting myself differently.

Kat, you've practiced this. What are you doing? You can swim! Get a grip! Here we go again. Kat, are you really doing this?

I had convinced myself that this year would be different. But sure enough, when the mass of eighty bodies exploded into the surf around me, I choked up. I went into protection mode, not daring to put my head down for fear of the arms and legs kicking and splashing all around me. After we passed the breaking waves, I settled into more of a rhythm. In my defense, a mass start with the male athletes was no joke. Ben Smith, the 2015 male athlete, described it as "more of a fistfight and a run than a swim event." When we hit the waves, it was chaos.

After the first buoy, I forced myself to put my head in the water. My stroke continued to smooth out. By the time I reached the second buoy, I was fired up. I was becoming fearless in the water and it felt amazing. Some people know how to body surf, but I have no awareness whatsoever when I'm in the water. Likewise, I'm cautious on the return trip to the beach, anxious to anticipate when another wave will wash over me and potentially separate me from the little oxygen I was getting. This time I made the final turn for the beach and slammed on the proverbial accelerator. My body felt like I was in an all-out effort on the Assault Bike. Everything was burning. I was so lactic that my body went numb. I knew that if I got buried by a wave, I would probably need to be saved by the lifeguard. With my current state of oxygen deprivation, it would have been impossible to survive even a few seconds underwater. I threw caution to the wind and kept charging.

When I made it safely to the beach, I was thrilled. I bounded out of the surf and tried to sprint, but my legs weren't working. They were like noodles. I raced along the soft sand and over the finish line in eleventh place. It was my best swim event finish of my career on paper, but more important, in my mind, I had pushed my limits beyond what I thought I was capable of, and the result was tremendous. I was so happy with how hard I was able to push, but I was not surprised. Everything was falling into place as the result of hard work. Hard work that extended beyond the gym. To really excel at the CrossFit Games, athletes have to find little ways to positively impact their performance. This year, changes I had made in the kitchen, of all places, were paying huge dividends.

When I arrived at the Games in 2016 to defend my title, I was 8 pounds lighter than I had been the previous year. My body was visibly leaner, and seemingly more muscular than it had been the previous times I competed. My placements in the first three events spoke for themselves. After the swim event, people wanted to know how I had done it.

My secret weapon was my newly acquired nutrition coach,

Adee Cazayoux. Adee is now well-known for overseeing the performance nutrition of many top names in our sport with her company, Working Against Gravity (WAG). Adee was a competitive Olympic weightlifter herself, and her once modest business was born from what she calls a "jenky little blog" where she documented macronutrient tracking methods that she utilized to compete and make weight while pursuing qualification for the World Championship. Now WAG employs over fifty staff members and has affected tens of thousands of people.

I had never really known how to properly fuel my body for what I was asking of it. With my big days of training filled with grueling protocols I was definitely not eating correctly to recover. Coming out of gymnastics I was deathly afraid of carbs. I would eat very clean, but I didn't know much about timing or what the composition of my meals should look like. The biggest change that started immediately for me was that Adee had me lower my fat intake and up my carbs a lot! Coming from someone who at most ate maybe some fruit during the day, this terrified me. And not to mention that I relied heavily on fats as the majority of my caloric intake at the time. But Adee walked me through the process and explained why we were doing what we were doing.

I simply had no clue how extremely important it was for an athlete working at my level of exertion to eat carbs! All I was sure of was that it was going to make me gain weight. I had yet to learn about the role carbohydrates play during high-intensity workouts and also what our bodies need to recover after intense exercise. I started adding oatmeal with my eggs in the morning, eating a packet of raisins while I was training, having a banana with my protein shake after training, and adding rice or sweet potatoes to both my lunch and dinner.

I limited my fat intake by substituting whole eggs for a fifty-fifty combination of whole eggs and egg whites. I would limit my avocado intake to one half each day instead of a whole one, and my peanut butter intake had to take a big dip. It took a little time to get consistent and find my new norm, but I started to feel so much better when I did. I had more energy in training and I was recovering faster. My strength numbers, my times on the track, and my weight on the scale were all trending in the right direction. Adee was right! My body was thriving on this new mix of macronutrients. This balance is very personal to everyone, and what works for me most likely will not work for you unless you are training at a similar volume. Having a coach like Adee help you find the specific mix that works for your body is critical to success. There is no one-size-fits-all diet.

I was over the moon at how well I was performing, and honestly, I also felt good about the way I looked. What I didn't like was the way other people were voicing their opinions about my body. I had been in the spotlight a lot since becoming the Fittest Woman on Earth, which came with tons of perks. There were drawbacks as well, however. Most of all, I found it stressful to be under the magnifying glass of other people's scrutiny. There are external and self-imposed pressures to look and be a certain way when you are crowned the champion of the CrossFit Games, and that pressure feels compounded when photo shoots, videos, and social media posts are swirling around the internet.

Beauty and what people consider to be beautiful are subjective— a piece of art or a natural landscape. However, when it comes to defining beauty as it pertains to women, the majority of people tend to focus on what they see. Social pressures cause women to aspire to unhealthy aesthetics. Society still tells women that they need to be less. To be smaller. To be thinner. And honestly that is what I had aspired to be the majority of my life and growing up!

Competing with the fittest humans on the planet can make it challenging to be confident in your appearance. Many of the athletes in the CrossFit Games have a tiny amount of body fat covering abs on top of other abs. It's easy to feel like small imperfections set you apart in a bad way. It would be easy to let the outward appearance of these statuesque athletes make you self-conscious or uncomfortable. It seems easy for people to forget that professional athletes are people. We compete on a bigger stage than others, but we are not made out of wood. I'm a twenty-five-year-old woman who lives and breathes. I've created a championship mind-set and work capacity, but that doesn't make me immune to scrutiny of my body.

In gymnastics, a big focus was always put on being smaller, skinnier, and lighter—especially with the Romanian coaches. I never fit the mold the coaches were pressuring me into and I felt like I was constantly fighting two battles, one with them and one with myself. My body simply was not made for what they wanted. As a girl I relished beating the boys on the playground, but I was still self-conscious when I was bigger than them or had more muscles. When I was young it bothered me that I was bigger than most of the other girls.

Iceland certainly leads the world in women's rights, and our celebration of strong women shielded us in part from this way of thinking, but that does not mean the island is immune to the pressures and images that come from mainstream media. As social media became more popular, everything from fashion to fitness became more global. This has increased pressures on girls to meet a standard that is deemed beautiful in the mainstream, but it's not healthy. Iceland set me up for success when it came to loving myself, but CrossFit sealed the deal.

When I first stepped into CrossFit BC, I was amazed to find that I had to go into the bathroom to find a mirror. I was used to gyms that were hyperfocused on how you looked. The CrossFit community is hyperfocused on how you perform. CrossFitters think of our bodies as machines. The muscles and body types that others would mistakenly criticize are visual reminders to us of the hard work that we do daily in the gym and on the competition floor.

Our bodies and the muscles we carry are something we should and can be proud of. We have worked so hard for them. It is amazing what our bodies are capable of doing!

The CrossFit community celebrates strong women and powerful performances, helping to reinforce a new paradigm in which being a strong woman is inspiring and impressive. It's become popular to be capable in your own body. As a community we put far more value on physiology than on anatomy, and I want to pass that on to all women.

The skills we gain through training give women a new type of confidence. My hands may be rough, but that's because I can do amazing things with them. All my scars, bumps, and bruises represent hard work and accomplishment. The way I look represents the hurdles and struggles I've had to overcome. My confidence is grounded in my abilities; they are not based on a standard of how people think I should look.

None of this means that I don't like acting like a girl. You can still be girlie or feminine or whatever you want. The point is that you decide what that means to you. I still live by the motto "When in doubt, sparkle it out." I love to pamper myself and look my best, but this has nothing to do with beauty. Beauty and toughness are about confidence in who you are, whatever that means to you. That always shines through.

I see the shift toward this mind-set happening in women of all ages. When people first walk into CFNE they often want to look a certain way. Before long they are pulling me over to see their first pull-up. Instead of size 0 dresses, they want a rope climb. Where before they were concerned about getting bulky, now they are posting proud pictures on social media because they worked hard for their physical aesthetic.

I get contacted by young women who struggle with body image all the time, and I am thrilled at the opportunity to help reshape the goals, ambitions, and view of beauty for the next generation. I want to do my part to help them focus on what they can do and not how they look.

Being the best possible version of yourself is a highly personal thing. I want to help women of all ages embrace themselves and have confidence.

Ben and O'Keefe walked me back to the car. At the Games, I live in my own world. I'm so focused that I sometimes won't even hear people talking to me. In this moment, however, I was fully lucid. It was a beautiful sunny day and we stopped to take in the scenery. I was overwhelmed by a realization of just how important these two men are to my life and my success. They make sure that I'm fed and taken care of, they take care of all the little details and let me focus all my attention on being great, but that's really just the start. They are the linchpins for a team of people who surround me and challenge me daily to grow and improve myself. They have become family. They are indispensable.

Everything I do throughout the year culminates in one weekend. Everything is laser focused. I don't have my phone on me. I don't call or respond to texts. It's the one week out of the year where I focus on my thing and that's it. The Games require everything you've got, and they're what my life revolves around now.

After we returned from the beach I met up with the rest of my team back at the Marriott for a late breakfast. My mom, Heather and Ben and their daughter Maya, O'Keefe, and Afi all came by. Breakfast at the Games has become a tradition and whoever can make it will join us to sit and be with each other. The only rule is that we don't talk about the Games. There is no talk about my placement or things that are already in the past. We don't talk about events that are coming up. I don't want to talk about any of that. It's a time where I just want to appreciate them just being my mom or my friend. I treasure this time because it takes my mind off the competition. I can laugh and be myself.

On that beautiful morning, with two successful days already behind me, I took a minute to feel gratitude for the amazing people in my life. I am so incredibly lucky.

For Friday's final event at the 2015 Games, the fans had been given the power to choose our final workout. In a fan vote, they had selected Heavy DT over Double DT. What they didn't realize was that by selecting the heavy option, Castro had slotted Double DT for the following year, and we faced it now. The combination of moderate-weight barbell cycling fits squarely in my wheelhouse. I knew I could win the workout. And when you have an event that you know you can win at the Games, you go for it. The points system rewards home-run hitters and the rankings at week's end can be made or broken based on how many points you banked in earlier events. Ben saw the fire in my eyes and he encouraged me to show restraint in the early rounds so I could make the final push with no reservations.

"There are other times when we can back off. But this one is everything you've got. Show me you're smart, show me you're strong. Show me smart, show me strong."

I repeated the strategy back to Ben one last time. In regular DT, my bar would never leave my hands. Tonight I would break after the 12 deadlifts and intentionally drop it to the floor. This would be the only time my bar touched the ground, however. Once the movements went above my waist, the bar would stay in my hands. He didn't have to, but Ben reminded me that hang power cleans and shoulder to overhead are two of my favorite movements.

The first heat of women were already staged to take the floor. My heat was lined up in the corrals. We could hear the clamor of the official opening ceremonies inside the tennis stadium. For what felt like ten minutes, a rumble in the distance turned into a swirl of thunder as the largest airplane I've ever seen passed over our heads at the close of the U.S. national anthem. The C-17 known as the Globemaster III drowned out all other noise. The sound was so deafening, it vibrated my body. I looked around and could tell everyone was as fired up as I was.

The tribute held deeper meaning because DT and the Globemaster both served in the U.S. Air Force. Where Murph had honored U.S. Navy SEAL Lieutenant Michael Murphy, DT was dedicated to Staff Sergeant Timothy P. Davis, who had died in 2009. As in all Hero workouts, athletes felt a desire to go harder knowing they were honoring a real person who had made the ultimate sacrifice. The theatrics of the flyover and the cheering crowd took the excitement to another level. I had a good feeling this was going to go very well.

Before an event, when Athlete Control staff moves us to our second corral, I take my deep breath. It clears my head and keeps me grounded. By focusing on something I'm feeling but had not noticed before—like the cool steel of the corral barricade or my heavy breath in my chest—I get drawn back into the present moment. The sensation I usually go back to is that of my feet in contact with the floor. I also ground myself by thinking of Amma's second note: "Face to the Sky. Keep your feet on the ground."

I remind myself I'm not doing anything crazy or outrageous. It's nothing I haven't done before in training, and it's nothing that I can't handle. I remind myself to be here, right now. I exhale and

I feel like I'm back in control. I'm no less nervous, but I'm just here now. I have confidence in what I'm about to do. I have a strategy. I have a game plan. I just need to execute.

I repeatedly review the game plan in my head. I make sure I'm confident of what I'm about to do. I'm in my own world now. For an event in which I'm confident, I force myself to get aggressive. I slap my thighs right before my name is called, and I take the field.

On that night, the venue was pulsing with energy as I ran down the stairs to my lane. My spine tingled.

Before the event began, I took a deep breath on the starting mat. When I exhaled, my head emptied. The only conscious thought I allowed was a reminder to react quickly when the buzzer sounded. I perform best when I don't think. When I just let myself go, I can get into the zone. I know what to do and that now it's time to do it.

"It's double the reps. It's double the suffering. It's Double DT," said announcer Sean Woodland, sounding almost cheerful as he greeted the audience at home.

I followed my plan to the letter. I did not get flustered when Annie jumped out to an early lead. The first half of the workout was an Icelandic civil war. Annie, Sara, and I were virtually tied the entire way. Annie was directly next to me, and I could hear my name over the loudspeaker. All I was focused on, however, was my cadence. My grip felt fantastic and my hang power cleans were bouncing up to my shoulders. As we entered the final three rounds, the crowd got louder.

In the seventh round, my grip was slipping and I broke my cleans after 7 of the 9 reps. It was not my plan, but I didn't panic. I took one deep breath and forced myself to pick up the bar even though my body was screaming for rest. In my eighth round, I began to pull away and the momentum drove me harder. My pace was the same as it had been in my first round. I had sustained my effort. And as Sara made a last-ditch effort to catch me, I was able to throw my barbell overhead with the same ferocity as I had in Round 2.

The fans on the stadium floor are on eye level in the tennis stadium. Looking into the crowd, I felt as if all fifteen thousand people were lifting me up and pulling me toward the finish line. I don't live for these moments, but I sure do love them. An event win is the icing on the cake. The real feeling of pride comes from having a plan and executing it.

In the postgame interview I was asked how being the champion had affected the way I trained.

"I trained harder than ever. Every day I try to train like I compete so that every day I go as hard as I possibly can, knowing I'll leave nothing in the tank. That way I know I'll do the same thing out here on the floor."

The strategy was paying off. I left Friday feeling confident and happy.

When I was a gymnast, I would always come up short at meets. I was a beast in training but when it came time to perform in competition, I felt like a magnet for mistakes. I couldn't figure out what was going wrong. I didn't have performance anxiety. I was excited to compete. But I could never re-create my performances from training.

I was trying to exceed my capabilities. I was good on the beam in training, but I would get so nervous during competition, trying to do something better than what I had practiced. I would jump higher and run faster, forgetting everything I had done in training. When I mimicked my training, I had great success. At the time, I didn't understand why I was underperforming.

So, I always messed up. I never tried to do my best. Instead, I always tried to do something better, to no avail. Competition can give you a boost, but it's not a magic bullet.

With Ben's help, I had finally cracked the code in 2015. I had performed like a champion in competition by focusing on *my* best outcome—not my ideal one. Now, at the 2016 Games, I was offered another opportunity to overcome my battle with the rope.

I had overcome my fear and was no longer focused on others being faster than me. I was simply excited to give it my best. I knew I wouldn't win the event, but I was effectively cured of my rope-climb terror. Events that incorporated the StubHub Center's berm were typically my favorite. In general, they were longer—I had to grind them out. They required a lot more fitness.

The StubHub berm is eerily similar to the hill we run in the parking lot adjacent to CFNE. The distance and incline are virtually identical. The only real difference was the stairs, which wasn't enough to throw me off. The berm made me feel comfortable and at home. You get to the top and get a small rest before you give in to gravity and ride it back down.

In the warm-up area, I was slightly stressed about how to approach the odd object they were calling the Snail. The Snail was an enormous cylinder, turned on its side. It was half filled with sand, making it difficult and ungainly as you tried to push it.

Mat Fraser gave an impromptu tutorial: "To move something like that you should put as much force as you can into the middle. That's the only way you're gonna get it going."

Mat, who had just finished engineering school, analyzed all movements as if they were equations.

He clearly thought what he was telling me was common sense. I didn't let on any different, just bobbed my head and smiled. I had never touched the Snail, and would not be allowed to until I met it on the field, but Mat gave me insight on how to approach it.

Many of the women were trying for large pushes in hopes of making up more ground. They had varying degrees of success. I took Mat's advice and went a step further. With my arms locked at full extension, I pushed into that huge, annoying cylinder as if I were doing a handstand walk. I used short, choppy pushes to make it efficient and fast.

I was in my own world for that event. I didn't know where any of the other women were. Longer events into which I can settle in are my favorite. Two rounds in I started to feel too comfortable and increased my pace. Entering the final round, I pushed my pace to the limit. I was running fast now, and jumping up before I thought I could.

When I came off the rope climb, I realized I was in a tight race. Sara was right next to me; we were neck and neck. I barely beat her over the line. It was another win.

When I got back to the warm-up area, Ben congratulated me. He told me it was the best event he had ever watched me compete in. I had been smart and maximized every part of the event. I had not made silly errors by trying to be something I'm not, and I had pushed at exactly the right time. I was proud.

Gymnastics rings are difficult enough to hold yourself on top of normally. For the next event, Dave Castro asked us to turn ourselves upside down on them.

Earlier in the week, he had told us we would face ring handstand push-ups. Further details were absent.

It was the Monday prior to the Games in a small gym on top of a hill within range of Manhattan Beach. The space was tiny, and Mat, Michele Letendre, Cole Sager, and I were doing our best not to trample each other as Ben and O'Keefe looked on. The only rings in the building were set to hip height.

"Kick into a handstand," Ben instructed.

There's a misperception that gymnastics training should equate to success on the relatively modest movements that CrossFit incorporates on the rings. While this might be true for men, it fails to take into account that women are not trained on the rings. Even at the highest level of gymnastics, rings are reserved for men only. On my first approach, I didn't even make an attempt. I had to step back while I tried to wrap my head around the movement.

Michele flipped upside down as if she had been doing this her whole life. I was blown away. When I tried, I couldn't overcome the feeling I was going to fall through the front and face-plant in a heap under the rings. We put down a crash pad. I made countless attempts but couldn't commit. I would drop down as soon as I passed my comfort zone.

Mat and Michele seemed to have more bend in their arms when they inverted. Neither of them seemed to be breaking a sweat. They were going into a half press-up to assume their balance before pressing out. I, on the other hand, was having a hard time overcoming my formal gymnastics training. My instinct was to do a normal press-up, but the instability of the rings made the move nearly impossible. I would keep my arms straight and locked, which forced me to balance at the hinge point in my shoulder. It was farther away, making the challenge more difficult by a multiple of ten.

The good news was that I was watching them have success right in front of me. I knew that if they could figure it out, it was only a matter of time before I got it. The bad news was that the "matter of time" seemed to be a target that was moving in the wrong direction. After what seemed like an hour, I decided the only way I would succeed was to risk falling. I took a chance and threw myself forward. My shoulders traveled way farther in front of the rings than I was comfortable with. I sprawled my legs into a straddle and they caught the straps attaching the rings to the ceiling, saving me a split second before I toppled over. With one successful rep done, I knew I could do it again when it mattered.

When we saw the competition floor, I was excited that the rings were set to a similar height as they had been in practice.

The event was called The Separator. It was the second of the day and the ninth of the Games:

THE SEPARATOR

15 back squats (165 pounds)
20 burpees
6 ring handstand push-ups
18 front squats (145 pounds)
20 burpees
4 ring handstand push-ups
21 overhead squats (125 pounds)
20 burpees
2 ring handstand push-ups
Time cap: 16 minutes

In an event like this with so many unknown variables, there is really no way to guess what the outcome will be for you or the other athletes. I kicked up confidently into my first handstand and pressed it out.

"No rep!" my judge shouted.

I tried again and got another no-rep. I was successful on the third rep. The problem I now faced was that I had no idea what had distinguished the third rep from the first or second. I came down to take a rest. The frustrating part of no-reps is that I had performed 3 reps just to earn one. If that pattern continued, I would be in trouble. The judge reiterated the standard that had been briefed: The legs may not bend during the ascent. I truly had felt no difference between any of my reps. I did my best to ensure my legs stayed as straight as possible. I went slower than I thought I needed to, ensuring there was no wasted effort. I would go like hell to try and make up time on the squats and burpees.

Because of the difficulty of the ring handstand push-ups, there was forced rest. That meant a lot of standing around. And a lot of looking around. I noticed Sara had started hot and taken an early lead before accumulating several no-reps. It wasn't until the last round that I started to pull away. I went as hard as I could and I finished the last round.

I was the first to come off the rings on the final set of two. The moment my shoes hit the floor, I sprinted like I was being chased. I went so fast, I couldn't stop at the finish line without the help of the stadium wall. I hit it so hard, I bruised my palms. I didn't care. I was in a state of pure bliss.

"Yes!" I screamed at the top of my lungs.

In the post-event interview, I was asked if there were any movements or events I didn't want to see.

"No, I want to see everything," I replied. "That's why I train. I want to be challenged. And where else would you want to be challenged than here in the tennis stadium? This is where magic happens."

While I wasn't caught up in the leaderboard, I was obsessed with doing my best. Now I knew a lot more about how to play the game; I wanted to capture every single point I could. My worst nightmare was having to rehash the weekend after it was over and identify all the places I could have done better or where I gave away points.

Dave briefed the day's final workout—called 100%—twenty minutes before it began. It was a sprint: 40 box jump-overs at

24 inches for the women and 20 D-ball cleans at 100 pounds. I was nervous. This would be short and explosive. Longer is better for me—there's more room for adjustment, time for other athletes to make mistakes. This event had none of that. It was easily a sub-three-minute event full of opportunities to make costly mistakes.

When it started, I redlined almost immediately. Lateral jumping—a requirement in the event—is not among my strengths. My first mistake was doing too many reps on the box jump. I realized too late that I was on the wrong side of the box after my final rep. I lost time, but it wasn't the end of the world.

Just keep moving, I told myself. *Shake it off.*

By the time I got to the D-ball, I was behind the other top women by a handful of seconds—an eternity in an event like this. I started throwing the D-ball like my life depended on it. The floor layout was well suited to seeing where your competition was. I was on fire, turning around to pick up the ball before it had even hit the ground.

The rules dictated that the ball had to go over your shoulder before you could advance. D-ball over, turn, pick up, advance. I was in a hurry trying to use every split second to make up the time I had lost. My mind wasn't keeping up with my body. I got the ball to my shoulder on the fifteenth rep. I was facing the finish line and had pulled even with the leaders. I threw my ball into the next segment of the field prior to completing the rep.

As it was falling, I knew I had messed up. I locked eyes with my judge with the ball still in midair. "No rep!" he said loudly. One D-ball that late in the workout was so costly.

I finished the workout and jumped on the finish box. I was so angry with myself. I had lost points on a stupid mistake that had nothing to do with my capacity. I had handed off points. I could have forgiven myself for the box-overs, but the mistake with the ball was killing me.

It was late and it was dark outside already. I sat in the warm-up area and tried to stop fuming. When Ben came over, I vented.

"It's gonna happen," he said. "No one is going to have a flaw-less weekend. You made that mistake. How cool is it that you now have an opportunity to come back?"

I liked what I was hearing.

"You have an opportunity to fight and to make something good out of this."

It's way easier to stay on top and cruise through, but it's a challenge to make a comeback. I latched on to what he was saying. I went from being unhappy and disappointed to being excited for the challenge.

"When you win," he said, "it's gonna be that much sweeter."

Cole Sager found me as we were walking out. He had under-performed in the Squat Clean Pyramid the previous day. He had hoped for a top-ten placement in the event but finished last in his heat, toward the bottom of the overall standings. He could see I was down and relayed an experience of his own from the previous day.

"I could have felt sorry for myself and thrown in the towel," he told me. "But every time I cleaned a weight, the crowd went ab-solutely nuts."

He recounted the loss as if he were relishing it.

"I was alone on the field and everyone was cheering for me. It was electric."

He was smiling from ear to ear.

"It was one of the coolest moments in my competition career. I only experienced it because I wasn't doing as well as I wanted to. I made it into one of the best things that had ever happened to me."

Ben's pep talk in combination with Cole's interpretation of his experience snapped me out of the funk. I knew I could make something good out of my situation. I left the StubHub Center Saturday night fired up and ready to bring all my attention to bear on the final day of competition.

The days are long at the Games, typically ending around dinner time. Saturday, however, was a dramatic example of that. Ben and O'Keefe brought me food. This is almost an every-night ritual and the food is always the same: a mishmash of sweet potato, rice, chicken, and guacamole in large quantities. I would eat it on the way home.

Ben and I continued our conversation on the drive to the hotel. Car rides at the Games are critical. They are reserved for Ben and me only, and we can speak freely in the confines of the vehicle. We typically debrief the entire day. It's an indispensable part of my daily process that helps me move on. I need to talk about things—what was good, what was bad. We also talk about upcoming events and make a preliminary plan. I need a plan or I can't fall asleep. I need to know what events have been announced and briefly cover what they are. I also want the morning schedule: when and where breakfast is happening, and when we're leaving for the venue. We set ourselves up for success.

I even need to start planning the outfits that match the next day's events. Ben gets to escape this part of planning, but it's critical for me. Aside from ensuring I'm happy with the way I look, I also want to make sure I have the appropriate gear for the events themselves. Do I need long pants for cleans or rope climbs? Do I need my lifters or my runners?

As soon as we get back to the hotel, I'll have my bodywork therapist ready and waiting. Someone will always be in there with me. Oftentimes it's my mom or Heather, Ben's wife. Usually I don't even talk. Everyone has become accustomed to it. I love that they are there with me. It's comforting. However, I need to be silent and relax. Bodywork will usually take an hour. Then I'll immediately shower and do my best to get a good night's sleep. There was one final day before we crowned the Fittest on Earth.

"Katrin . . . To the right!"

I heard my name as clear as day, but the other words were a jumbled mess. I knew they were directed at me, but I couldn't decipher the message.

"Lane . . . Right. To the right!"

I was 50 yards into a 280-foot handstand-walking race. My shoulders and arms were burning and my head was filling with blood, causing my head to feel bloated and uncomfortable. My sight was impaired by red and black dots dancing in my field of vision as I reached the final stretch. Combined with the volume of the soccer stadium crowd, I might not have heard my judge if he were shouting in my ear. Calling to me from behind, there was no prayer. I had been inverted for 50 yards and I had momentum, so I decided to go until someone physically stopped me.

Then, *wham!*

I had collided with one of the tackling dummies placed carefully on the field demarcating the lanes. It wasn't enough to knock me over, but it did give me a jolt and knocked me farther off course. As I corrected and got back on track, the crowd raised their pitch to a roar. I could barely see now and it was all I could do to glimpse between my hands every other step. I was anticipating the ground changing colors from the natural green of the grass to the painted royal blue of the end zone, where I could kick down for the final run across the finish line. I stalled out 2 feet from the finish line. The moment felt like an eternity before I recovered. I still managed to edge out Kari Pearce by less than a second.

After the handstand walk, two events followed in quick succession: Suicide Sprint and the Plow.

EVENT 12: SUICIDE SPRINT

840-foot shuttle sprint for time

On the same 280-foot course as the handstand walk, athletes will run ⅓ of
the way down and back, then ⅔ of the way down and back, then sprint the full
length to the finish line.

EVENT 13: PLOW

560-foot plow drag for time (235/190 pounds)

The uniqueness of the Plow had made it nearly impossible to
warm up for. Ben tried to mimic the Plow by fashioning a har-
ness out of bands and making me pull him across the floor. It was
a strong effort, but I still had no idea what to expect when I finally got my hands on that thing. There was no way to judge the
pace from the previous heat, either. Some girls were devastated,
but the previous heat winner, Canada's Emily Abbott, was barely
breathing hard.

Keep going, I told myself.

I try to always frame my self-talk in the affirmative. Instead of
"Don't stop," I favor "Keep going." Halfway through the second
lap, I lost my pop but willed myself to keep moving. I felt like
every muscle in my body was infected with the flu. Unable to correct myself, I accidentally swerved into Sam Briggs's lane. I pictured myself at Blue Hills, and the fight I had crafted and honed
there. This felt strangely familiar. I dug in hard until I fell across
the finish line and collapsed.

I laid on the ground next to Sam and we congratulated each
other. When I tried to stand up, I was not surprised to discover
that I needed some help. I grabbed for the closest person to me,
who happened to be the filmmaker Ian Wittenber. With his camera in one hand and me in the other, he walked me over to the
medical team.

"When you're like Katrin and you can just flip the switch to be so in the game in the moment, sometimes your brain shuts off and your body takes over," 2009 Games champion and color analyst Tanya Wagner told the audience at home as I was carried off the field. "She wanted those points badly and she came out to get them. She won the handstand walk and the same thing with the Plow. She is on a mission. Maybe she pushed herself just a bit too hard."

With my team, "too hard" isn't a thing. We practice and face "too hard" all the time so that when opportunities like this arise, I can gamble on my ability to recover. Tanya was right about one thing: I can flip a switch in my head. But it's *not* for the points or the glory. It's for peace of mind.

The bright yellow bracelet I wore all those years ago to remind me of my goal to make the CrossFit Games was the first of many visual totems I have used to keep my goals and beliefs in the front of my mind. The bracelet on my wrist in 2015 was emerald green. It's a constant reminder that regret is more painful than any physical task.

Green represents our team's ethos of giving maximum effort no matter what. To know in your heart that your best effort was given. We call it "going green," but it usually feels more like "seeing red."

Ben brings the concept to life by comparing the controllable elements of competition—attitude, effort, reaction—to traffic lights. We avoid the cautious approach—yellow—and we will never, ever stop—red. The bracelet is a tangible reminder to cut the brake line whether the situation favors you or not. It's a reminder to cross the finish line with no regrets.

Externally it's only your results that are visible. Only you will know internally if your effort matched your potential. Pumping the brakes—or, worse yet, slamming down—invites the potential for regrets that could last a lifetime. Especially at the CrossFit Games, where each moment is a once-in-a-lifetime experience.

You might expect that Dave Castro would dislike the fact that only one woman completed a pegboard ascent in the final of the 2015 Games. You would be mistaken. Dave expected us to be excited for the opportunity to learn this skill over the course of the year between Games and show off the progress we had made. The event was appropriately called Redemption.

"These workouts are not designed to showcase the athletes, they are meant to test the athletes. The CrossFit Games are constantly redefining what is humanly possible," Dave said in a post–2015 Games interview. "A test that seeks to do that cannot afford to issue participation medals. People will fail, they have to. If they don't, the test isn't hard enough and we aren't moving forward."

His standards are interlaced with his background. In Dave's former profession as a SEAL, every test was an unforgiving pass-or-fail proposition. Unless there is a high fail rate, it's not hard enough. It's our job as athletes to rise to that challenge.

EVENT 15: REDEMPTION
For time:

3 pegboard ascents
21 thrusters (85–pounds)
2 pegboard ascents
15 thrusters (85–pounds)
1 pegboard ascent
9 thrusters (85–pounds)

Time cap: 10 minutes

To save my biceps, I focused our warm-up on mental preparation. I would stand on a mat and mimic the movement with my arms. Up two, down two. Over and over again.

There was one pegboard in the warm-up area. It was sunny and hot. Everyone was there with their person. We were all trying to read each other's energy and gauge their temperature. Is she nervous? Do they like pegboards or not? How are they gonna do? In those moments when I know the other girls are watching me, I stand up and I want to be confident. On the inside, I was terrified. I still couldn't do a pegboard ascent.

Ben and I had done a lot of work in training with pegboards, but never to completion. We would go up two pegs and come back down. We worked pegboards over and over and over again. The culmination of all that hard work was one solitary rep in the gym. I just could not figure it out. It had happened two weeks before the Games and it was a big win. At least I knew it was within the realm of possibility for me. It could be done.

I always travel with Amma's necklace in my competition bag. It's literally always with me and I guard it with my life. For the final event, I wore a high-neck sports bra. After considering the movements, I realized I could wear the necklace. Amma could take the floor with me for the final event. I felt her with me in all the events, and I tried to honor her by taking risks or adding an extra pound on the bar. I went a little faster and pushed a little harder just thinking about her. Now I would have a physical representation of her presence, too. I put the necklace on and tucked it in.

O'Keefe is good at reading the situation and giving me the input that I need. More often than not he will deliver a sarcastic "Don't fuck this up," in his signature deadpan style. Other times, he will just remind me to smile and it will cheer me up immediately.

He won't do that on the final just in case I actually do mess it up. I get my final pep talk from Ben, and in that situation he told me to do me.

"It's just you against you."

Everyone handles the jitters of competition differently. Some are chatty, some like to laugh. I turn inward. When we are in the corrals, I close my eyes and try to relax. I'll put my hands on either side of my lane and breathe deep while I wait for everyone to line up. I'll go through the event again in my head to make sure I'm calm and confident in what I'm about to do.

The Athlete Control team will tell us when it's time to move to the next staging area. This is when I'll put my game face on. I'm focused. We walk up the stairs and I get butterflies. We're crammed into the narrow hallway leading to the stadium. The sound reverberates under the bleachers. One by one our names are called and we step into the natural light pouring through the far end of the tunnel. This is the moment when I'm the most nervous. I feel overwhelmed.

Before I left the warm-up area, Ben drew an "A" on my arm. It reminded me why I was doing this and who I was pushing for— Amma. I put my hand out and felt like she was holding it. I could feel her there with me. When they called my name, my nervousness melted away, revealing my excitement. As I ran down the stairs, everyone was trying to grab me. I high fived as many as I could on the way down. I love this energy. I need it. I jogged to my lane. I felt calm and confident. This was what I'd been waiting for. Now I was in my element. From the floor, I couldn't make out individuals in the stands. I think there were Icelandic flags. Everything was a blur, like a huge ball of energy.

When the buzzer sounded, I dove in. I completed 2 pegboard ascents with relative ease.

I struggled on the third. My biceps were done and I got stretched out again. I went back to my scap retractions. I fought for it. Every time I descended I was sure my grip was going to fail.

The best girls in the heat were far ahead of me by then, but I did my best not to let it enter my mind. I made it and took my time with the thrusters, well aware I needed to rest before I could get back on the pegboard. Any time I reached for chalk, Amma's necklace would fall out. I felt like I was constantly being reminded she was with me.

I knew Tia was closing in on me. I knew she was going faster than me. She was ahead of me and closing the gap on my overall lead. But all I could do was wait until I was ready.

I found success again on the pegboard. Now I was certain Amma was there, squeezing my hand. It was a roller coaster of panic and relief. At the time cap, I had finished 5 pegboard ascents. It was a huge win for me.

Tia was on the finish line. She had completed the event. It was a really weird feeling. The Games were over. I wanted so bad for Amma, and I didn't know if I had done it. The women were huddled on one side of the floor. There was nothing more that I could do, but waiting to hear the result was torturous. Had it been enough? It was out of my hands. I walked to the red mats and sat down.

It felt like it took longer than usual to tabulate the scores. I took my necklace out and held it in my hand. It's the most that I've ever wanted anything. There was a camera in my face and I didn't know if they were there to capture my victory or my defeat. There was a camera on Tia as well. When Dave finally made his announcement, they would capture joy from one of us and devastation from the other.

"The Fittest on Earth is . . ." Dave said, pausing.

The tension was palpable.

"Once again," he started and I didn't hear anything else after that moment.

I had won again. A million feelings hit me at once.

Relief, excitement, and the feeling that I had done it with Amma. I could barely stand up—all I could do was mouth the words "Thank you" silently. Dave walked me to center court, holding my hand over my head.

Last year had been a surprise. Winning the Games had surpassed all my wildest dreams. It had seemingly come out of nowhere. It had meant so much to me because I wasn't chasing a result in 2015, I was chasing my dream. I was driven by pure love of the game. I didn't dare let myself believe the dream was reality until Dave said my name.

This second championship was different. In 2016, I was always chasing something because people thought 2015 was a fluke, and I wanted to show we had worked for it. But my drive had nothing to do with the expectations of others.

I had a new and stronger reason to fight: Amma. She had carried me through the weekend. She had helped me push to my absolute limits. This victory meant so much more because I felt like I had done it with her.

15

UNPREPARED

ÓUNDIRBÚIN

Your faith can move mountains and
your doubt can create them.
—ANONYMOUS

When the afterglow of the weekend finally dissipates, melancholy follows. Even in championship years. I'm told that even the fans feel it, too. The wind is taken out of our collective sails after blowing at hurricane force for months on end. Online, in life, and in the gym, everything has a stillness that I find uncomfortable.

I thrive on having a purpose. Leading up to the Games, it's at an all-time high as we work hard to bring everything together at the same time. My goals are on my mind constantly from the moment I wake up. Every second of every day is accounted for. I meet with my coaches and team and there is a high standard of expectation. I have goals and expectations for myself and I can feel physical improvement. In the approach to the 2016 competition I was so singularly focused that I didn't even buy a return flight home. The plan crescendos up and up and up. Then poof, it's gone.

I know I need the rest, but I don't like it. It's impossible to improve indefinitely, to always go up.

Training also drops to an uncomfortably low volume and I feel like I'm losing the improvements that were so hard-earned. It will only last for a few weeks. My team needs time off; we need to evaluate the year and then make a plan for moving forward.

After a championship year especially, sliding backward goes counter to my instinct. As the Fittest Woman on Earth, what I really want to do is hold on to my fitness for dear life. I get so scared that all my hard work will be lost.

Not to mention that I love working out. It was a passion and an outlet long before it was a competitive pursuit.

On Monday morning, the day after the Games, I had breakfast with my family. Ben, Heather, and Maya joined my mom, Afi, and me.

"I have a plan," Ben said.

Ben was just like me. The dust had hardly settled from the competition, we had won, and he was on to the next chapter already. If he didn't think it would lead to burnout, we would be training in the hotel gym right now instead of eating. I said nothing—just enjoyed my food and focused on his words.

"We're gonna get strong. We're gonna get so strong," he said with a look on his face that told me there was a lot of hard work on the horizon.

The Games ended on July 24. I stayed in L.A. for a week and then took the opportunity the downtime presented to visit Iceland. The month of August was difficult for me. No one held me accountable and by my standards I got relatively out of shape. I knew I would start training again in September, but that felt like a lifetime away. We would start with a modest workload and ramp it up slowly.

Being in Iceland post-Games made me feel more human, as strange as that may sound. My personal life is so dependent on my training that I tried to make up for lost time when I was home. I socialized with friends and family like a normal twenty-three-year-old. More normal, at least. During the heavy training season I felt like a hermit. Post-Games I was able to break free for a minute. I am actually a social butterfly when I give myself the opportunity.

The whole time, however, training was in the back of my mind. Winning the Games means nothing after it's done. The slate is wiped clean. It's not like you take a points advantage in the Open. If anything, being the champion, and especially a two-time champion, makes things harder. You have to learn how to carry the additional burden of the target on your back.

When we returned to CFNE, Ben had a plan in place to follow through on the prescription he had made at the breakfast table.

"We're gonna get so strong."

Fitness means proficiency in any athletic skill. But it's not enough to be good at everything—you have to be great, as your placement is most likely determined by your worst score, not your best. Athletes who want to excel rather than survive at the Games need to turn themselves into a Swiss Army knife of skills and abilities. Enhancing what you're already good at is part of the equation, but shoring up your weaknesses is critical.

Over four years of focused training with Chris Hinshaw, my endurance and recovery were fantastic. However, my top-end speed was not where it needed to be relative to my competitors'. I had finished tenth at the Games in the suicide sprint. However, it was sandwiched between the handstand walk and the Plow, and more of a testament to my recovery than my sprinting ability. I also had an engine that allowed me to cycle barbells for days and operate near my maximum exertion for longer than most athletes. The more grinding metabolic-conditioning-focused events favored me.

Strength and speed events are where I fell short of my goal to place top five in every event at the Games. We incorporated the help of a sprint coach, Eric Buscher, to inject some springiness and snap into my legs. We also wanted to sharpen my technique on the barbell, knowing it would aid in my explosiveness, speed, and power. For that, we brought in weightlifting coach Fred Calori.

I didn't know what a deep dive into Olympic weightlifting technique looked like. After my first heavy set of three, I walked around the bar and tried to set up for my next set. I wasn't even sweating yet.

"No ma'am," said Fred. "Take a seat."

He was serious. I had to sit down and rest between sets. I know there is logic to it, but I just couldn't get used to it. I didn't want to rest; it felt unnatural.

Work on the track was the same. We would smash the intensity for thirty seconds at a time and then stop. It was a large departure from how we had trained in the past. I trusted Ben and I believed it would work, but I was definitely in a strange landscape. The sled dog in me wanted to run.

December 2016

I went home for Christmas and was forced to face a looming fear. My friends make fun of me to this day, and, in retrospect, the stress I experienced from such a small obstacle is hilarious considering the real challenges I've faced. But it was terrifying to me. It had nothing to do with CrossFit *or* training: I needed to have my wisdom teeth pulled out.

I would always put it off in my mind, pushing back imaginary deadlines. *After the Games,* I would tell myself. Every time the day came, I would push it back further. *After the Open,* I told myself. *Post-Regionals?* Nope. I couldn't commit. This had been going on since I was eighteen, and now I had waited too long. They were presenting the danger of infection and I was told I was at risk for a flare-up that could possibly require emergency retraction.

"Maybe this could happen on the week of your competition," the doctor had said, knowing this would strike a major nerve. "What are they called? Regionals?"

I'm pretty sure they just wanted me to stop being a baby, but it was convincing. *What if it happens during the Games?* I thought. No time was a good time, but the fear of missing competition overrode my five-year-and-running aversion to the procedure. I called and booked an appointment for when I was in Iceland in December.

In the lead up to the procedure, I was freaking out. For years, it had given me anxiety. I hate the dentist. It's my worst nightmare to be looking up, watching them digging in my mouth and drilling into my teeth. I've never had broken bones or major surgeries, thank God. But I will cry at the sight of a hypodermic needle. I'm not a cool customer when it comes to any medical procedures. I don't know where it came from, but I freak out. Being in the dentist chair makes my top-ten scariest things I can imagine list. The lights, the thought of what they're doing for hours. It makes me so uneasy, I avoid it like the plague.

Despite my incredible, unbearable anxiety, I made it through the procedure with little drama.

I woke up with my chin down to my chest, and my cheeks looked like a hamster's stuffed with food. I looked like Jay Leno's little sister. Every time I looked in the mirror, my face surprised me. *That actually wasn't that bad,* I thought.

When the anesthesia wore off, I was in the most pain I've ever experienced. I returned to the dentist on multiple occasions to check in. Something had to be wrong. They assured me I was fine and that the pain was normal. I couldn't sleep, I couldn't eat. They were some of the hardest days I had ever experienced.

"You had surgery," they told me. "You're supposed to feel this way."

What kind of doctors are these people?! I wondered.

I had accounted for the surgery being difficult, but hadn't even considered that there would be a recovery period. I was out for five full days. My training suffered and it took me a while to break out of the fog. As far as training was concerned, December was more or less a wash.

February 2017

I had ramped my training intensity back up in January, intent on making up ground for any losses I had sustained after taking time off for the removal of my wisdom teeth. The focus was still on short, high-power-output sessions. My speed was certainly improving on the track and my lifts were all going in the right direction.

I felt physically strong, but the gains were accompanied by a fatigue that was more mental in nature. I felt tired all the time, and my recovery from our sessions was taking longer than I liked. You wouldn't know it from my performance in the Open. The five-week competition is typified by lung-burning, gas-tank-draining workouts, yet even with our training focus directed primarily at strength and speed, I had taken tenth place in the world. My fitness appeared to be on point. In addition to my overall placement, the performance was punctuated by a fourth-place finish in the squat snatch and chest-to-bar pull-up couplet of 17.3. My body was feeling strong and fit.

We went back to the track when the snow finally cleared. Instead of the three Hinshaw workouts per week to which I was accustomed, however, we were still focusing on my form; I was doing sprint work. I would only do one or two Hinshaw workouts, with the sprints taking up the bulk of my time on the track. Nothing lasted more than thirty seconds in those workouts.

The mental fatigue was due in part to my travel responsibilities that year. I love the opportunity to travel. It's fun to go see cool places and do fun things. But starting with the Open, it became too much. I visited Hinshaw in his new home in Cookeville, Tennessee, and participated in a few athlete camps, some for me and some for my sponsors. All those things are amazing, but a professional athlete, especially a two-time champion, needs to put training first. That had become nearly impossible. My headspace spiraled and I yearned for the routines I cherished in Boston.

I have my morning routine down to a science and I value every second of it. I am neurotic about having my food meticulously prepared and available at the gym. I am used to being coached in a certain way. I'm used to seeing my chiropractor and having access to my massage therapist. I like to sleep in my own bed. I was physically fit, but being away from all of it pulled me away from my game.

I had wrapped up the Open with a live announcement against Sara Sigmundsdóttir. I edged Sara out in the very last set of double-unders to take the win. The event itself was amazing to be a part of. I had won. The Open was over. I should have been celebrating, but when the lights were out and I went back to my hotel room, I felt like I had been hit by a train. I didn't want to do anything but sleep.

The months of travel had caught up with me and my headspace had deteriorated. Now that it was over I realized that I was in a bad place, possibly the worst I'd ever been in. It caught me off guard, because the shift had occurred gradually. By the time I recognized it, I was only a few months away from Regionals.

Ben was holding a training camp in Madison in conjunction with the Open Announcement. The whole team was in town, which never happens: O'Keefe, Mat Fraser, Cole Sager, and Brooke Wells. We visited local CrossFit affiliates and checked out the areas where we would be competing later that year. It should have been special. But I felt like I was sleepwalking.

During one of our sessions, I had a realization. I did not want to be there. I didn't want anything to do with it, actually. This really scared me. I had never felt that way before. I was with my team, whom I love as much as anything in this world. I had this amazing opportunity to train with them and get better. And all I wanted to do was leave. I was so tired I could have balled up on the floor and slept. In between workouts, I hid away in the back of the gym on the verge of tears. I was mentally exhausted. I felt so overwhelmed.

That was at the end of March, and it didn't go unnoticed. Ben and O'Keefe approached me separately. All I could express to them was that I was tired. Whatever is going on in your head, your body will follow. Soon I lost my zest for training altogether. I was not excited for the mental work, either. I lost the motivation to read and journal.

I started to hate the impersonal lens of the camera when the documentary team came to visit. I was annoyed when people asked me for pictures. Ever since I was a kid, I've loved the camera. My grandfather would follow me with a camcorder in my childhood years and you can see me light up every time I'm on center stage. When I started getting older, I would seek Afi out so I could address the camera.

"Hi, I'm Katrin Davidsdottir, and this is where I live . . ."

It's so funny to watch. In school it was the same. I was the first one to gravitate toward the camera. I couldn't understand why I was annoyed with it.

I felt like everything that wasn't making me a better athlete was just a distraction. I was tired of it. If someone asked me for a picture, I hated that they weren't asking for a conversation. They wanted the shallow and empty interaction of snapping me quickly for a social media post. It felt empty and draining when that happened. I love conversation. I like to hear stories and share mine. It was hard for me. I was depressed.

I didn't take off training completely, but I put in two very light weeks. I stopped traveling altogether. I focused on helping myself recover. I needed to plug back into my routine. I needed to feel better.

In April, I moved to a new apartment. There was a spare bedroom, which was a game changer. I could have guests now, and I loved having company. My dad came for a week and helped move me in. He did dad stuff, like building my furniture. It was fun to have him around. My mom came later in the month and Afi followed close behind her.

My best friend, Arnhildur Anna, came to stay with me in Boston. She is my best friend in the world—the peanut butter to my jelly, the macaroni to my cheese, and the social to my butterfly. She stayed for a week and it was like therapy. On my birthday, she and Heather covered my room with a hundred balloons. It was a great way to wake up and it made my heart sing. It had taken months, but I was beginning to bounce back.

2017 CrossFit Games East Regional

By Regionals, I had recouped some of my headspace. But I still had less fun than usual. I could feel the trade-off I had made in the prior year's work. My power was there on the low end, but I had lost an endurance gear that I was used to relying on. It was unfamiliar territory, and I was thrown off by it.

I noticed it right away on the first event. It was a long grind in a 14-pound weight vest that started with a 1,200-meter run and ended with twelve rounds of handstand pushups, chest-to-bar pull-ups and squats, all in the weight vest. I expected to win it, but crossed the finish line in third. The placement wasn't bad, but the way I felt, it came as an unpleasant surprise.

This was the first time I was forced to compete in CrossFit injured. Normally, I am just fearless. I don't have thoughts, I just perform. The final event on Saturday, however, injected a dose of fear. It featured heavy kettlebell deadlifts, and I tweaked my back in the first of four sets. It was nothing at first. But by the end of the event, it was all I could do to finish. I doubled over immediately after crossing the finish line and dug my fingers into my hip, trying to find relief.

I do my best to carry myself tall and not show any emotion, no matter what. Even if I'm hurting, I'll grit my teeth and hide it with a smile. I took my hands away from my back when I was on the competition floor, but had to pinch myself to deal with the pain.

"Something's wrong," I told Ben as soon as I came off the field.

Even a slight hyperextension would send pain shooting up my back. I couldn't bend down to pick anything up. I never considered dropping out of the competition. I can work with pain. It's not fun, I don't like it, and I probably won't have the best outcome, but I can do it. I was determined to push it through.

I spent hours that night trying to recover. I stopped thinking about event strategies and put all my focus into getting my back healthy, just trying to make it through. The next day, I was unable to warm up for the muscle-up event. I felt lucky that the first two movements were doable. I didn't warm up, I just had my PT take me through some movements.

The following day opened with a classic CrossFit couplet.

21-15-9 reps for time:
Muscle-ups
Single-arm overhead squats
Women use a 55-pound dumbbell
Time cap: 11 minutes

We had been working on muscle-ups since the 2015 Games. Every time I competed, whatever improvement I'd been feeling in training seemed to go out the window when I hit the competition floor. My judge was strict and I was forced to exaggerate my lockout. This made it hard for me to open up my hip and go down smoothly. I was reduced to singles by the end of the event. I was back to my old self and it disappointed me. I wanted to show my improvement. But my technique had deteriorated.

When you've put in so much work on a movement and even turned it from a weakness into something that you can drop the hammer on, you put a higher premium on excelling at it when it comes up in competition. When it falls apart, the disappointment is greater than if you hadn't worked on it at all. I want to show off my hard work. I want all that training time to pay off. It felt like I had stepped onto the floor having not put in a single second of work.

But I also had great events. Regionals were my first competition love, after all. I always get a kick out of seeing my family in the stands, holding the Icelandic flag.

Before the event, Ben encouraged me to be smart.

"Kat, I know you love competing and you love events like this. Our main goal is to make it to the Games. You have to make it through healthy. I want you to do what you can do, slow down if you need to. Just make it through this event healthy."

In the warm-up area, I put a belt on and tried a few reps. My back felt like it could give out at any moment. I wasn't able to warm up how I would've liked to. I was scared that I might do lasting damage. The last thing I felt was fierce. I realized how much of a blessing it was to compete healthy.

After Regionals, I had to take some time off to heal. It took a week before my back calmed down. Thankfully it wasn't anything major and it resolved itself. My back, however, is something that I'm constantly aware of.

I respect my fellow competitors and I know they are great athletes. I respect the competition itself. Second place was a necessary wake-up call. The silver medal made me work harder. I made a habit of carrying it in my training bag so that I would see it every session. It was a reminder that nothing was a given in this sport and I would have to earn my way when I got to Madison. The memory of underachieving makes me want to push myself harder. When I don't win, I see potential for improvement.

June 2017

My U.S. travel visa expired in June and I was forced to go back to Iceland. Ben and Heather wanted to take a vacation, so they came with me. In light of my mental fragility at the time, and the fact that I was always overextended when I went home, bringing them along wasn't the right decision. There is intense pressure to see people and be social when I've been away. It's a luxury problem, I get that, but this was during Games training, which is highly demanding. I tried to fit it all in, and my diet and rest suffered for it. Of course my relatives and friends weren't weighing and measuring and I didn't have my meal-prep company sending me food. At that point, it was stressful. The time difference affected me as well. There was too much to think about during those ten days.

After the Iceland trip, I returned to Boston. It was Games-training time. Traditionally, I love this time of year, when it's warm outside and sunny. I'm like a plant—the sun is medicine for my soul. Everything feels like it's working correctly and my joints feel better. I love sweating—it makes me feel like I get a better workout, even after the warm-up. The volume is also through the roof at this time. Ben coaches me every single day, even on weekends. There is so much running. There is so much fitness in general. The pressure and excitement are at an all-time high.

I was feeling so much more pressure than in years past, however. I was feeling threatened, if I'm being honest. If I got beaten in a workout, I would become defensive. I truly felt the weight of the target on my back for the first time since last year's Games. In the past I would thrive on people expecting big things of me, but everything about this was different. I felt unprepared. I wasn't where I wanted to be athletically, and it was eating at me. I had no confidence.

Brooke Wells took sixth place at the 2015 Reebok CrossFit Games. We had become friends and I really loved being around her. After the Games, I had connected her with both Ben and my nutrition coach, Adee. She became a member of the CompTrain team.

It was a little nerve-racking, opening up my resources and my team to another top-ten athlete, but I loved Brooke and wanted her to thrive. But pretty quickly I could tell it wasn't going to be easy for me. I was feeling insecure, and since we were going head to head, I was bringing Games-level intensity to every workout.

My relationship with Annie being the anomaly, I also don't know if it's possible for Games athletes of the same gender to train together full-time.

It's different with male competitors, too. In fact, one of my favorite training partners in the world is Mat Fraser. We can push each other so hard. Win, lose, or draw, it doesn't matter. We are not in direct competition. We spur each other on, but we are not contenders for the other's title. Brooke and I are, and I felt like we were trying to prove something every day.

And, if I'm being honest, I was feeling insecure. We were handing over the playbook to my championships.

Additionally I felt like I wasn't getting Ben's full attention. He now had a handful of athletes to assist and I felt like anyone else's gain was my loss. These thoughts run counter to everything I know, but I was having a really hard time. I'm not proud of this, but it was how I felt at the time.

Sometimes Ben would tell people just to watch *me* for instruction on what to do next.

"Watch how Katrin does it. See the way she does rope climbs?"

I didn't want to demonstrate. I needed coaching now more than ever. I felt like Brooke had everything to gain and I wasn't learning anything. She was doing my warm-ups and eating what I ate, which made sense because she was part of our team. But ultimately we would meet on the competition floor. It was an unhealthy training environment for me and it affected my relationship with Brooke. We both wanted to win the Games.

I finally broke in a training session and told Ben how I was feeling about the whole thing.

Normally, if I'm making progress, I'm good, and I can stay in my lane. It doesn't matter what anyone else thinks or does. If I can walk out there knowing I got better, then I'm happy with that.

In combination with the fact that I wasn't where I wanted to be, there was conflict in my heart and it raised my defenses. For the first time, I wanted to protect what I had. Suddenly, Brooke had the same nutritionist, agent, and coach. I didn't like it—it—she was in my space. I take full ownership of the fact that this is not the headspace of a confident champion.

Brooke left CFNE, but came back for Fight Camp in the final

run-up to the Games. Cole also came out and we headed to the Cape.

We were doing lots of personal-development work every morning and, as usual, digging into binders Ben had created for us. I was having a harder time investing myself.

"I want you to write a letter to yourselves from after the Games," he instructed. "What do you want to have accomplished? What are your hopes for your performance? Most important, who do you hope to be during the competition?"

Brooke, Cole, and I would write some of our core values, why we held them dear, and how we would live by them. It was great as a practice, but I take everything very seriously. I dug deep in those exercises and it required vulnerability. We would read our responses out loud, which was tough.

Living under one roof can be a party, but it can also be torture. It's hard to find an escape or get any alone time. Where I would typically thrive on this abundance of energy, I found myself yearning to be by myself. I found myself more tired than usual and even though the training was fun, I liked it far less than in past years.

Normally I'm sad when we leave the Cape. The arrival of the CrossFit Games signals the end of the best training we do. This year it was the opposite. I welcomed the start of the Games for the first time in my career—less because of how prepared I felt and more because I was ready for Games training to be over. It was a nuanced but highly meaningful difference.

In reality none of this was about Brooke. This was about me and my own headspace. Since then I've resolved my own feelings and Brooke has remained one of my closest friends in the sport. Now I can be so thankful to be taking this journey *with* her and not *against* her. Now I can see the push makes both of us better. In 2015, my love for training led me to victory. I was afraid that was in danger. Training was more of a challenge than a tool. All the pressure felt crushing. I had doubts about everything—my coaching, my preparation, and my abilities. Mostly, I was lonely. I missed Amma.

"Are you ready?" Heber Cannon asked point blank as we sat on the patio on the Cape.

Cannon is a highly talented filmmaker, formerly employed by CrossFit HQ Media. Along with Marston Sawyers and Mariah Moore, he is responsible for creating the CrossFit Games documentaries that have showcased the CrossFit Games in years past.

"No," I replied.

I was slightly detached from the conversation and was less worried than usual about what he would think.

"What do you mean?"

I caught him on his heels with my answer.

"I'm not ready, but I will be," I said casually.

"How can you be sure?"

He was prying now, trying to wrap his head around my curious answer.

"I always get there, Heber."

As the words left my mouth I wondered if I was lying. It was true that I had always been ready when the time came in years past. But I had huge looming doubts now. Normally I feel so fit at the Games. I get tired but I can just keep going. But at the Cape this year I had not felt that yet. I didn't have the extra gear. Everything was just a little bit off. I had fitness and my team was stronger than ever. But I was missing the spark. I didn't have "it." That feeling that I was about to take the stage and wow an audience. My swagger was gone.

16

THE TIGER AND THE DEER

DÁDÝRIÐ & TÍGURINN

*"Inside of me there are two dogs. One is evil—he is
anger, envy, sorrow, regret, greed, arrogance, self-pity, guilt,
resentment, inferiority, lies, false pride, superiority, and ego."
He continued, "The other is good—he is joy, peace, love,
hope, serenity, humility, kindness, benevolence, empathy,
generosity, truth, compassion, and faith. The same fight is going on
inside you—and inside every other person, too. When asked
which one wins I answer, the one I feed the most."*
—CHEROKEE STORY OF "TWO WOLVES"

Flying into Madison, Wisconsin, my plane passes directly over the
Alliant Energy Center on final approach. I know next to nothing
about this place and wonder what it will mean to the competition,
the events, and my ability to win. As I gaze out the airplane window at the venue, curiosity overcomes me. What will happen on
that competition floor? I had won the competition twice. I know
I'm fit enough to do it again. I feel a twinge of doubt. In Carson,
my confidence was bulletproof. I had felt prepared for anything.
Now my confidence is dwindling. The feelings are familiar. I had
last felt them in 2014.

When my plane lands, I consider the possibility that change
could be just what I need. I want to believe it's going to be good.

My optimism grows when I see how the city is embracing us. The Games have taken over Madison. Every restaurant, street corner, and park bench is adorned with CrossFit paraphernalia, advertisements, and fans of the sport. Uber drivers ask about the Games, and I walk by decals of myself and other Games athletes in the windows and on the walls of local establishments near the capitol building.

As soon as we arrive, we drive out of town in search of an obstacle course in one of Madison's neighboring towns. Ben is driving and it's another forty-five minutes to our destination. I sit shotgun, staring out my window at the expansive Wisconsin sky. On one side of road, I see ominous clouds in shades of gray and purple. On the other side, I see a clear blue sky and a beaming sun. The biggest rainbow I have ever seen spans the highway, connecting the fury and the peace.

"Amma is here," I say, recalling my beloved grandmother.

"I was thinking the same thing," Ben replies.

Still, I feel uncertainty nagging me.

August 1, 2017—CrossFit Games

"Turn here, go left, left, TURN!"

I was shouting and now the wheels of our rental car immediately screeched as we peeled onto a one-way street that hugs the waterfront of Lake Monona and continued to race along. I was in the passenger seat relaying the directions from my phone to Heather. According to Google Maps, we were nine minutes from the hotel. The bus for the individual athlete dinner would leave in ten.

Ever since my first Games in 2012, I've had a ritual of getting my nails done right after check-in on Monday. I was accustomed to Carson, where the salon was right next to the athlete hotel. It was a relaxing way to get my mind off the stress of the upcoming week. I could walk over, pick a color, and melt into the chair. In Madison, we had trouble finding a nail salon. Heather, her daughter Maya, and I walked around unsuccessfully and ended up having to drive across town, which we didn't realize would cut it close for a timely arrival for the athlete dinner. Showing up late would not be a good way to start the Games, but this is one pre-competition ritual that made me feel peaceful. We might have broken a traffic law or two, but Heather got me to the bus with a minute to spare. Most importantly, I was rocking the best nails in the field.

I sat with Annie at dinner. As comfortable as I now felt being a Games athlete, it blew my mind that this was Annie's eighth time competing. When Dave Castro arrived, the first thing we learned was that the schedule for the week would be different from years past. For the first time, we would not be competing early in the week. Events would run Thursday through Sunday. It was a small change, but a significant one for me personally. I wanted the test to be drawn out and difficult to suit my strengths. I was excited to see how Dave would match the wow factor that came from middle-of-the-night escapes to LAX, trips to military bases, and swims in the vast Pacific Ocean.

"I'm not big into welcomes and big kumbayas," he said. "Because at this stage, I view each and every one of you as subjects. Subjects that are gonna go through tests. Tests that lead to an event that finds the fittest man and fittest woman alive. And of those tests, some details are known, some details are not known. Some details will be found out literally moments before you take the floor this year."

Dave went on to release some of those details, starting with a ladder that would take us through bar muscle-ups paired with the heaviest cleans we had ever faced in competition.

"This is killing my OCD," joked competitor Patrick Vellner as Dave announced the event weights one at a time by scribbling them on poster board with a permanent maker, then passing them to the athletes nearest to him, who would hold them up for the rest of us to read. I was taking notes on my phone as he spoke. But when Dave announced the weights for female competitors, I was pulled back into the moment. The final two cleans would be 235 pounds—5 pounds over my 1-rep max. All I could do was hope for a dose of adrenaline.

Dave's Instagram had become an information portal for event details and advanced leaks. Over the month of July, he had posted some obvious clues and others that were nearly indecipherable. We knew we would face a custom-built obstacle course and a 1-rep-max snatch.

On July 12, he had posted a picture on his Instagram of an odd-looking bike. Most people had guessed we would be tackling a long distance on the road. Now Dave revealed that we would actually be trying our hands at the sport of Cyclocross. Madison is the home of Trek Bikes, and its team had put together a 1.5 mile course with obstacles, hairpin turns, and tight corners. On Wednesday we would perform a single-lap time trial on the course that would seed us for the race. Thursday was race day; heats of twenty athletes would fight through three laps for time.

"In Carson you had to worry about sharks." Dave smiled. "Here you have to worry about each other."

He went on to warn us that the event would be one of the more dangerous we would face. There was potential for injury, he noted, and we should be careful. I pictured chaos on the track as he spoke.

"There's a lot that can go wrong in this event on Wednesday

when you're doing the single-time trial. It's multiplied by twenty when you race on Thursday."

We spent most of our first day outside. There was still one un-known event that would christen our new venue later in the eve-ning, but before that we had two events that would pit us against the landscape of Madison as well as our fellow competitors.

The opening event was based on the physical tests Dave had been subjected to as a Navy SEAL, and the format was as simple as it gets. The sky was dark and ominous on the first day, and along with the other athletes, I was about to get my first introduction to the new brand of adversity we would face in Madison: rainstorms. In the Midwestern United States, those brought the potential hazard of lightning. Similar to the beach event in 2016, all eighty athletes—men and women—would be in one massive heat.

EVENT I: RUN SWIM RUN

Run 1.5 miles
Swim 500 meters
Run 1.5 miles

As I walked down the boat ramp at the start of the race, I could see the morning calm of Lake Monona thrashing with a flurry of athletes. At the moment of truth I did a shallow dive, put my face in the water, and came up gasping for air. *Really, Katrin?* I asked myself. I suffered through the swim and came out of the water in the middle of the women's pack.

My running was distressed from the swim, which I still didn't manage nearly as well as I'd hoped. Frustrated with the incongru-ence between my solid swimming ability in a pool and what hap-pens when I hit the open water in competition, I couldn't make up the ground I had lost. By the time I was running back into the Alliant Energy Center campus, the sky had opened up and I was dashing between sheets of rain. I crossed the finish line confused and disappointed with myself.

It wasn't time to panic. It was Friday and we still had everything left to do. Nonetheless, it was disappointing. Performing your best and missing out on points is one thing. Missing out on easy points early in the competition, however, will always come back to bite you at the end of the weekend. I was frustrated, but it was time to let it go. We had three hours before the next event. It was time to turn the page and move on.

The uniqueness of the Cyclocross event elevated it to my list of all-time favorites. Quann Park lies adjacent to the Alliant Energy Center. They call it a dog park, but they should call it a dog heaven. The 55 acres of low, rolling hills span farther than the eye can see. The Trek team had cut a track across it that looked like a giant maze emblazoned on the hillside.

The course was wet and slippery, making the obstacles more treacherous. Some women had survived serious crashes during the time trial. I was fearless in the face of all that. I was trying to take turns and cutting in on the other girls early in the race.

"Know yourself, know the course, and know how you fit within the scheme," commentator Chase Ingraham said. "And that's what Katrin Davidsdottir might do better than anyone else out here."

I had broken the course down into pieces in my mind, which made it really fun. I couldn't keep up with Sam Briggs and Kristin Holte, but I was very happy with my result. I finished in the top five, setting myself up to race in the second heat with the other top women.

After the Cyclocross event, I had a five-hour break. I used it to formulate a game plan for the evening event. When the Games had moved to Carson from the Ranch, the first event competitors faced in the tennis stadium was a couplet of muscle-ups and squat snatches. The workout was named Amanda in honor of Amanda Miller, a 2009 Games competitor who lost her life to melanoma just months after competing in Aromas. Since 2010, the event has been iconic. Dave had told us that morning that we would christen this new stadium with the same workout he had used to christen the StubHub Center.

The event had evolved, of course, to account for the increase in fitness since 2010. In addition to the rounds of 9, 7, and 5, Dave added two rounds on the front end of the event: 13 and 11. The event was called Amanda .45:

13-11-9-7-5 REPS FOR TIME:

Muscle-ups
Squat snatches (95 pounds)

Oh shit, I thought the moment that Dave had briefed it. This was not my jam.

Muscle-ups are like swimming, in that no matter how much focus and attention I give them in training, I often revert to old habits when I face them in competition. I kept my composure and went to talk to Ben. We devised a strategy. The only way this event would go terribly wrong was if I tried to compete with someone else. I was in the final heat, which meant that, at a glance, I could see women for whom this workout seemed custom-made. If I allowed myself to get caught up in the moment and took my muscle-ups to failure, my debut in the Coliseum would be a disaster. More than ever, it was imperative I put on blinders to the rest of the competition.

If you were to substitute overhead squats for snatches, this event was nearly identical to the workout that had induced my hysterics at the Cape when Cole Sager beat me. I pulled from that experience. For better or worse, I was going to give it everything I had.

Once the event began, I was pleasantly surprised that my muscle-ups were feeling decent for the first time in competition. I was able to string 8 reps together at the start of the event. They weren't the best reps, but they certainly weren't as disastrous as my swim had been.

I stuck to the plan, looking only straight ahead and ignoring the thundering noise that was swirling around the Coliseum. The weight was light for me, but I hit the snatches in singles and took a deep breath in between each one, trying to save my energy for the gymnastics work. From the outside looking in, I seemed composed. That also meant that I was going very slowly. The leaders of the event were long gone, but I had mentally let them go before the event even began. There were only two women left on the floor when I finished the event.

I put on a smile and tried to celebrate my small win: my muscle-ups had felt the same as they did in training. I had played smart and stuck with my game plan. In a way this was a "rope-climb workout." And while I had broken up my muscle-ups a little more than I would have liked, I had maximized my potential for that event.

Holding back had been the right thing to do. But I could have passed Kristin Holte in the final round if I had tried to hang on for a bigger set of muscle-ups. I stayed conservative and played it safe. The strategy made me uncomfortable. I felt like my 2013 self: playing it safe and simply trying to survive. This feeling was the only thing that disappointed me.

In Carson, I would have expected superhuman magic to wash over me, bestowing the power of endless muscle-ups. But I didn't feel any magic at all. It felt like business as usual. Among the Fittest on Earth, the finish was okay. But I didn't want it to be okay. I wanted to be me. I wanted to shine.

Friday

I woke up to another gloomy Midwestern day. It was not raining, but there was evidence of a big storm from the night before. It was wet outside and way colder than it had been on Thursday.

The first challenge we faced was the sprint obstacle course. When he announced it, Dave Castro had referenced the obstacle course at Camp Pendleton from my rookie years. My placement had been underwhelming, but I remembered it fondly as a cool event.

At the beginning of the week, my expectations for the Sprint O-Course were low. Upon arriving in Madison, I had driven with Ben, Mat, and Cole to a nearby town where they had an obstacle course to practice. I was proficient, but they were so fast.

One of the dangers of training with extremely fit athletes is that it can skew your barometer for what's normal. As a result, I don't think I'm athletic. Cole and Mat are to blame.

When I met Fraser for the first time in 2014, I didn't know who he was. He was a pretty good athlete, but nothing to write home about. We were training at a gym in Boston and the conversation somehow turned to backflips.

"Meh, I think I could probably do one," he said casually.

As a former gymnast I challenged him to put his money where his mouth was. He did a backflip on demand, with no experience to draw from. I was amazed. Later, back at CFNE, he figured out a roundoff back handspring backflip with a twist by watching a YouTube video. He had never done gymnastics. He just has a freakish sense of body awareness baked into his brain.

Cole is similar. If a challenge has obstacles like hurdles or jumping, he picks it up in seconds and makes it look so good. He is the most athletic human I've ever met. Both of them figure out odd objects in a heartbeat and do them so gracefully you would think they had learned the skills as babies. And then there's me. It takes me so much longer to figure out new challenges, which makes me crazy. Around these two, I feel like the least coordinated person to walk the Earth.

Our field trip to the obstacle course was basically an opportunity for them to laugh at me and tease me about not being athletic. They give me a hard time but it's all out of love. The benefit of chasing these two in training, especially with events like an obstacle course, is that I exceed my own expectations in competition. I'm far more athletic going head to head with the fittest women on Earth than when I line up against Cole and Mat.

The obstacle course had nine obstacles, with the most technical of them showing up at the very start. On Tuesday, Dave had given us the opportunity to practice the course. At the time, it was sunny and hot. But now the adversity I had been craving had arrived in the form of rain, wind, and cold. The remnants of the previous night's rainstorm had left the obstacles wet and slippery. It was 55 degrees Fahrenheit, but I felt like I had icicles on my nose. When we were sent to the field, we were only allowed to wear our uniforms—no warm-up clothes. Even the spectators were sparse and those who did make it were huddling under plastic ponchos. Many were bundled up like they were going snow skiing. My dad was the only one from my team who was willing to brave the elements to watch me compete.

I was fearless in my qualifying rounds. In the quarterfinals, the top two athletes from each heat automatically advanced. The athletes with the next four fastest times also moved on. I didn't make any mistakes on my first run. I accelerated over the back side of the course and edged out Emily Abbott on the last obstacle: the caving ladder.

In the semifinal round, only the heat winner would advance automatically. One non-winning wild card would also advance. So if you didn't win your heat, you had to stand by nervously, hoping your time was good enough to advance you into the final. I passed the first two obstacles without any drama, but a near slip on the balance beam made my heart jump out of my chest. I recovered and used the adrenaline to push harder. For the second time I arrived at the caving ladder second. The bottom swings freely and the ladder rungs are at awkward intervals. I fought the temptation to go faster and instead made focused, intentional steps that put me in the lead. My whole body was tingling standing on top of the platform. This win meant I advanced to the final with the top women.

I went straight to Ben, ecstatic, and said, "Ben, I *am* athletic!"

I had an automatic entry into the final, but the wild card athlete needed to be confirmed. After the last semifinal heat, we waited in the cold and the wind and tried our best to stay warm. I made my first mistake in the final on the monkey bars. I couldn't recover. Still, I was thrilled to feel like I had gotten a drop of my swagger back.

The next event was a 1-rep-max snatch. The snatch is my absolute favorite lift to perform in competition and I was riding the momentum of my finish on the O-Course. The feeling of taking a chance and diving under a heavy barbell is thrilling. The snatch is technical. That evens the playing field for me against women who can beat me in tests of brute strength. I also perform this movement better in competition. All my personal bests had come in front of a crowd.

We had hours to rest after the Sprint O-Course, and I was chomping at the bit by the time I started my warm-up. When we took the floor, we only had two opportunities to lift. The top ten women would advance to a bonus round for a shoot-out. The format forced us to make hard decisions. A typical strategy is to go for a safe weight on your first lift, then swing for the fences on your second.

Ben wanted me to go lower on my opener, but I was feeling great. I loaded the bar to 185. It felt like it flew overhead. It was a solid first lift, but I did some quick math to establish what I thought would keep me in the top ten and give me two more shots at the barbell. I opted for 195 pounds, which was the second heaviest weight I had ever lifted. I was in the last row of lifters and two athletes had already lifted 196. I glanced at the change plates and thought, *Why not? I'm never even gonna feel that anyhow.* I loaded the bar to 197. I would take a lead into the bonus round or I would crash and burn.

The weight flew up, but I caught it off-balance. Something was wrong. As I stood up with the weight, it shifted forward and my arm was contorted into a strange position as I adjusted to keep it overhead. There was a funny feeling in my elbow as I completed the lift. In my head, I was freaking out as I assessed the damage.

How bad is this? Can I straighten my elbow?

The lights and cameras were on me, though, so I smiled and celebrated. I was calm on the surface, but all I could think was, *Don't grab your elbow.* I didn't want to show weakness. I prayed that it was nothing serious.

I knew I would take the field with the top ten lifters, but I was brought over for an interview before I could leave the floor. Alarm bells were still going off in my head and all I wanted to do was debrief with Ben. I answered the interview questions but I could barely focus.

"What can we expect in this next round?" Amanda Krenz asked, wrapping up the interview.

How the hell was I supposed to answer that? I didn't even know if I would be able to come back to the floor.

"Bigger lifts," I said with a big smile.

It was all that I could come up with. And I was sure that I was right, I just didn't know if they would come from me. I only had a few minutes now, so I ran to the warm-up area.

"I hurt my elbow," I said matter-of-factly.

I knew Ben could see the emotion on my face.

We tested the range of motion and it seemed like it would be fine. Then Ben did his best to calm me down. His ability to be a nonemotional sounding board in times of high stress is one of the biggest advantages to having him as a coach. We had just over six minutes to talk and my interview had chewed into that. Now athletes were being summoned to line up for our return to the floor. Ben quickly formulated a plan.

"I want you to get back out there and snatch 135 pounds immediately," he said. "If that feels okay, go for it. If not, pull back. This is not the time in the competition to get injured."

At this point, I had no idea what was going on with my elbow. I wasn't sure if I had just tweaked it or if I was possibly facing a serious injury. The uncertainty scared me. On top of that, I had to approach the competition floor again and the only way to improve on my lift of 197 would require me to hit a lifetime best lift on an unstable elbow.

I got to my station and snatched 125 pounds. My elbow didn't explode. In fact, it felt fine. Still, a million thoughts raced through my head. Two months earlier I had been with Rachel Martinez at CFNE when she had dislocated her elbow on a snatch. It wasn't pretty and her recovery was arduous. I wondered how that would play on the broadcast. I fought the thoughts out of my head but they fought their way back in.

Katrin, this is the CrossFit Games, I told myself. *These are the moments you train for; these are the moments that count and these points matter. You better get yourself together and perform.*

I loaded the bar to 202 pounds. I was the final lifter in the rotation, so there were three minutes of lifting before me. The other girls were gunning for personal records (PRs), and the crowd was loving it. My plan was not profound: I was going to pull as hard as I could, no matter what, and let my instincts take over. When my name was called, I set up with a deep breath. The weight immediately felt heavy. To be successful in a snatch you have to be aggressive, and at that moment I was anything but. I bailed early, essentially performing a snatch pull.

We went back through the rotation again and I tried to fire myself up. I jumped up and down and slapped my thighs. In my final preparations, I extended my elbow, testing the range of motion and checking for problems. The elbow was fine, but my result was no different on the second lift. I pulled the bar to my chest before letting it drop. Multiple attempts were allowed in the twenty-second window and I instinctually lined up for another. I screamed at the bar from the top of my lungs and lined up for another attempt. I was angry and I fully intended on putting it over my head. But my body would not comply.

It was devastating. I love events where I'm on the big stage and achieving something superhuman. I wanted a Disney moment where the adrenaline picks me up and the crowd goes wild. Instead, I did two snatch pulls in front of a sold-out crowd. How embarrassing.

It would be silly to be disappointed with a 197-pound snatch. That's heavy. But I still hadn't found my magic. I was in search of that feeling. I was chasing the exhilaration that comes with a tremendous performance—the feeling of doing something I couldn't do before.

I sat with Ben after the event and we established that my elbow was fine to continue competing. I moved on, content to not be injured.

Where I had been thrilled with the start of the day, I felt the momentum shift in the wrong direction after the snatch. I wasn't performing poorly. I was doing okay. And that was exactly the problem. I didn't want to be just okay. I wanted to shine. In every event it seemed as if I was just outside of where I wanted to be. Through two more events on Friday—a chipper and a sprint that felt more like a street fight—I finished sixth or better. But that wasn't the point.

My standard criteria for measuring my effort has to cut both ways. If a poor placement on the leaderboard could still be considered a win if I performed my best or slayed a demon from the past, then the opposite had to hold true also. In 2017, my event finishes were good by most people's standards. However, I knew I was capable of more. I was consistently turning up finishes that were okay.

I was carrying myself like a champion in terms of how I was responding to these challenges, but it didn't change the fact that I was in a slump.

Saturday

Even an event win on Saturday morning in Strongman's Fear lacked the significance I so desperately desired. I was happy when I finished, of course, but the event had been tailor-made for me and I felt like I could have gone for five more rounds. The way the event played out made the victory feel less meaningful. I was still missing the magic. I didn't even feel like I had won. I hadn't done anything special or spectacular, I just did work. It was just another event.

On the emotional roller coaster of the Games, the Muscle-Up Clean Ladder event on Saturday was a low point.

The event called for eight rounds for time:

4 bar muscle-ups
2 cleans, ascending weight
F 145-160-175-190-205-215-225-235 pounds

This was the workout that had grabbed my attention when Dave had outlined it at the athlete dinner. On paper it did not suit my strengths, so I entered cautiously. I was trying to strategize my way to victory, and I was focused on all the wrong things. I tried to keep my heart rate down and make the early cleans feel light. I took more time so I could ensure the first cleans were easy to catch in a power position. I wanted to save my legs for the later rounds. I was trying to stay under control. I would walk to the barbell to make the cleans count.

When I got to the 225-pound bar, I immediately put away one successful rep. Then I failed for the first time. I didn't panic right away, but things started to unravel quickly. I took a chance, approaching the bar earlier than I thought I should. When I failed again, anxiety crept in. I still had a lot of work left and the weight would only continue to get heavier. Repeated failures on a heavy barbell can bury you in a pit of exhaustion. You have to walk the fine line that will allow your body to recover for a maximum effort. I didn't have time for this. There was a short time cap on the event and the clock was bleeding minutes. I successfully finished my second rep at 225, but my overall result was disappointing.

I went over the mistakes I had made and beat myself up for

them. I could have improved my tie-break time and I could have been more patient waiting for those cleans instead of failing.

When I've done great things in the past it's been because I took a chance. That's when I exceeded my expectations. If I could do it over again, I wouldn't change anything. I had to take chances.

The frustration of repeated mediocre performances was starting to mount. I couldn't hold it together. I returned to the warm-up area. When I saw Ben, I started crying.

"I'm so tired of 'okay,'" I told him. "'Okay' isn't good enough."

I wasn't performing terribly. I just couldn't put it all together. My plan wasn't panning out how it usually did. I wasn't on fire like I normally was. I expected excellence of myself, but instead the theme of the 2017 Games was "meh."

In 2015 and '16, I would go without thinking. I got out of my head and into the competition. I would take a chance in events and things would fall into place. I was constantly performing well and exceeding my expectations. I was in the zone. This year in Madison everything was just "okay." I wanted my spark back.

Ben was speechless. I was right and there was nothing to say.

THE TIGER EATS THE DEER

TÍGURINN BORÐAR DÁDÝRIÐ

*God, grant me the serenity to accept the things
I cannot change, courage to change the things I can,
and wisdom to know the difference.*
—"SERENITY PRAYER," OFTEN ATTRIBUTED
TO REINHOLD NIEBUHR

Waking up the day after the Games is like waking up in a silent, lonely room the day after your birthday party. The noise, the decorations, and the people are all gone. It's normal for me to feel lost and a little down during this time. Athletes can commiserate. The Games is such a focal point in our year and the week is so intense. And what goes up must, of course, come down.

This was different. I was in shock. Questions rattled around my brain, and I didn't have answers for them. I was as good this year as I had ever been. I had avoided huge mistakes. Why had I gone so slow? Where was the next gear? I was physically and mentally solid, yet I had proceeded cautiously on nearly every event. I overstrategized and overpaced. I tried to do everything so right instead of letting myself compete. I was less upset about my placement. That had something to do with it, of course, but the cracks that appeared in my mental foundation had been there before the competition even began. That was what was troubling me.

I went to Atlanta with my mom to visit family there. I took a full week off from everything: training, diet, even social media. The feelings of melancholy were ever present, but I still wasn't ready to admit to myself that I wasn't happy. I had learned a lot about myself, and I had been forced to face new challenges. I told myself this was reward enough, but I didn't believe it.

In September, I returned to Iceland. I tried to get my groove back with training. I wasn't doing anything too serious, just trying to reestablish a routine. The Games had ended more than a month earlier and I still wasn't feeling great. In years past, I could talk myself out of the post-Games blues. Even after my failure to qualify in 2014, I had been hungry to return to training. In these moments, the hunger was nowhere to be found. In fact, I was making excuses to draw out my absence from training even further. I went so far as to verbalize my distaste for training. I didn't recognize the person I was.

It wasn't just that I wasn't excited to train—it was way more than that. I would shudder at the thought of my programming when I saw it. It looked impossible and everything felt like a chore. I was tired, but not a sleepy tired—I felt like I was in a fog. I would wake up feeling tired. I also had physical symptoms—as if my body was fighting something off. I tried to have confidence that my systems would come back online, but it never happened. Instead, I continued to get more tired. When it persisted for another month, I became concerned.

Then I hit an athletic rock bottom of sorts. For the first time in my life, I quit a workout. It wasn't a Games event or Regional preparation, but rather a run-of-the mill 5-rounder. In the third round, I got nauseous and thought I was going to pass out. I stopped. This wasn't just abnormal, this was cause for major concern. Something might be seriously wrong here.

I searched my mind for answers, latching onto a remembered

tick bite I had gotten during the Games. *Is it possible I contracted Lyme disease? Maybe I have a thyroid problem?* Anything was on the table. I went to get a blood test and felt a strange desperation for a positive result. I wanted to have something that I could point to and say, "Aha, I knew it." I wanted something tangible to fight. I needed something I could fix.

At the time, I was staying with my mom, who knows me as well as anyone. She could tell I was unhappy. She tried to help.

"You know," she began, "you don't have to do this."

I was offended she would even speak the words.

"You can take this year off and come back stronger."

Another part of my brain considered what she was saying. I had always wanted to pursue other things. Maybe now was the time. Maybe a year off would be good for me. I had two championships and plenty of accolades I was proud of. Returning to school sounded nice, and I had aspirations to do public speaking. Whatever path I chose, I didn't want to feel like I did at that moment. I just wanted to take a break from being Katrin Davidsdottir for a second.

The blood results came back later that week. They were clear.

"You're fine," the doctor told me.

He was baffled at my disappointment. After all, this was good news. To me it signaled that the healing would have to happen between my ears. I decided that time away was not what I needed. I returned to New England to work myself back into full-time training.

When I got back to Boston, Matt O'Keefe took me out to dinner to catch up. O'Keefe is my agent, but above everything he is one of my best and closest friends. He is a mentor and a pillar of my support system and I wouldn't be where I am without him. His athletes affectionately refer to him as "Dad." O'Keefe is an actual father of two amazing children, and he brings his best qualities from that role into our relationship. He has held my hand through everything from the simple—like navigating basic contracts—to the slightly more complex—like forgetting to cash my check for the 2015 Games.

O'Keefe knows our whole team and he understands all the angles. He is my most valued sounding board. Because of my respect for him, our relationship is unique. He can be more direct than anyone else besides my father or grandfather, and his counsel always resonates with me. We talk almost daily and after some quick catching up, it was clear O'Keefe came prepared to slap me with a strong dose of tough love.

"Look, I know this year didn't go like you wanted it to," he started. "You can be upset and unhappy about it. That's your right. But it's done. You can't change it, so you have to accept it."

I was a little embarrassed. I didn't know where he was going with this.

"Let's change the things you can control and forget about what you can't. You need to remember that you are Katrin *Friggin'* Davidsdottir. If you want to be a champion, you've got to start acting like one!"

His voice was calm but stern. His eyes were intense. His words hit me like ice water. O'Keefe and I had shared many deep conversations over the course of our friendship, but I could feel his heart oozing out into the words he was telling me.

"Start acting like one."

I wasn't mad, because he was right. I had been wallowing in a pity party for months, moping as if Dave Castro would show up with a participation medal if I acted pitiful enough. There was no Lyme disease, nothing physically wrong. I just felt sorry for myself. I had forgotten what being a champion looked like.

Being a champion is not about holding your hand in the air and accepting a medal, it's about the way you carry yourself every second of every day. Where I stood on the leaderboard was a single measurement, from one competition. I was allowing my disappointment to negatively affect months of training and potentially the next competition if I didn't snap out of it.

I knew it wouldn't happen overnight, but after that conversation with O'Keefe, I committed to honoring myself with my actions. I focused on improving little things in all areas of my life by sheer force of will. I read and listened to more books on sports psychology. I sought out positive messaging and spent less time on social media. For a while, it felt like I was faking it. I started acting like I was happy and telling Ben I felt great when he asked me before training sessions. Sometimes I was lying through my teeth.

I've always relied heavily on my team. More than ever during this time, I recognized how much I depended on them. Each, in their own way, came to support me and lift me up.

At the suggestion of my nutrition coach, Adee, I added gratitude to my journaling. Adee is a guru at tweaking dietary intake to increase athletic output. Her work can be seen on the physiques and witnessed in the performances of her athletes. Adee's most impactful work, however, cannot be seen, because it's not about results between an athlete's clothes, but rather what's between their ears. She's as much my life coach, confidant, and close friend as she is my nutrition coach.

Adee has a degree in psychology and an incredibly empathetic nature. Her husband, Michael, is a highly intelligent and well-established athlete in his own right and a former addict. They inject the knowledge gained through their studies and collective experience to add a mindfulness and self-study complement to their programming and nutrition coaching. My weekly check-ins and phone calls start with nutrition talk, but often stretch into deep dives into my mind-set and performance in all areas of my life.

She sent me a book called *The Five-Minute Journal* to track my gratitude. In addition to three things I was grateful for, the journal tracked three things I wanted to accomplish, a lesson I had learned that day, and a few things that could have gone better. The journal was just one of her prescriptions that worked perfectly. I've always *tried* to focus on gratitude. By adding it to my daily routine, it became a habit. I had been fearful I wouldn't be able to think of three things. In reality, I have to battle myself mentally to prioritize and decide which three things I'm most grateful for. I was in a great place.

Afi would also take longer trips to keep me company when I was in Boston. We would spend mornings together and he would come to the gym to watch me train. His presence alone made me happy. The icing on the cake was when he decided to start training himself! He took great joy in showing me his progress and all the new party tricks he was learning. His enthusiasm and energy at seventy-six years old were contagious and invigorated my training.

O'Keefe kept me in check with tough love. He would call me out with brutal honesty when I was avoiding things I didn't want to do, but needed to. He would listen attentively when I needed to talk. He acted as a buffer to the world of contracts, obligations, and media that could potentially distract my attention.

The stage was nearly set for Ben and me to focus on what we do best: training our asses off. But first, we had to exorcise the demons of the previous year. We had difficult conversations. At CFNE it's taken for granted that obstacles are placed in your path for a reason. They force you to grow. Most people make the mistake of avoiding them at all costs. Facing them is the only way to improve and grow. We made notes of what we considered to be wins at the Games and dug in hard on the places we had been weak.

More than anything else in 2017, my performance lacked the ferocity that won me championships. We both blamed this on an overly cautious approach to the previous training year. We had decreased my workload in favor of staying healthy. It may sound insane to not follow that guideline, but I'm best when I don't.

Pulling back in training had created two major issues. The first was physical. I was simply missing a gear and the result was an inability to push further in critical scenarios. The CrossFit Games are more than a test of raw athleticism. They're a test of preparation and that's where we had come up short. In most of the 2017 events in which I had gambled and lost, I couldn't make a final push. In the worst-case scenarios, like Amanda .45 and the Madison Triplet, I was just fighting to stay alive. My physical shortcomings weren't products of the moment, but rather of the year.

The other issue was mental. I realized that the doubts I had flying into Madison would have been there in Los Angeles, too. Or any city, for that matter. I doubted myself because I knew in my heart that I was less prepared than in years past. Every champion knows what their edge is, and mine is outworking the competition. Knowing that I had trained harder and longer than the women on either side of my starting mat is like mental armor. It calms me down and lets me get out of my head. It allows me to stop thinking and start performing.

There were related problems as well. We had taken my endurance recovery for granted. If you took my top five finishes from the '16 Games (Ranch Trail Run, Double DT, etc.), it's an easy mistake to make. But it's still a mistake. As a result we deprioritized these assets in order to focus on power, strength, and speed. Two-hundred-meter dashes and 1-rep maxes replaced barbell cycling and Hinshaw's workouts. With the gift of hindsight, we now recognized that my proficiency was the result of training in borderline excessive quantities.

The most important part of the whole equation was my relationship with Ben. Ben has become the most highly sought-after coach in competitive CrossFit. His online training through CompTrain.co reaches thousands of athletes across the globe. Additionally, well-known athletes and up-and-comers will travel to Boston to train with him. I had felt like I had less access to him in 2017, and we agreed that I needed more attention and coaching directly from him. He assured me I wasn't expecting too much. He said that making a champion takes the focus of the whole team. We put a premium on my coaching.

It was time to look ahead. I asked Ben to make me work harder than he ever had. It's a funny thing because I wasn't even sure it was possible. He made sure I understood what I was asking. This made me nervous. I could see in Ben's eyes that we were going to go places we had never been. Of course, I knew exactly what I was asking for and we agreed that training from previous years was going to look pedestrian in comparison to what he had in store. It's a good thing I love hard work.

By the new year, I felt like myself again. My confidence was also returning, which was a direct result of our training. I had gained a different perspective on the 2017 Games. It wasn't the result I wanted, but in a strange way it was becoming my favorite Cross-Fit Games ever. The uphill battle had put everything I believe in to the test. I had to fight from behind when the deck was stacked against me. I had to find positivity when everything seemed to be going wrong.

I learned more that year than in either of the years that I won.

We talk about competitive excellence all the time. About giving your best effort regardless of the circumstances. The year 2017 was the first time I had not ended up on top of the leaderboard since I started training with Ben full-time. It's easy to stay positive when things are going your way. But 2017 showed me what it feels like when the going gets tough.

I no longer had regrets. Those had transformed into the drive to perform better. You can only regret something and truly call it a mistake if you don't learn and grow from it. I had learned hard lessons my first year in Madison and we were going to great lengths to address them. The feeling of hearing someone else's name at the end of the weekend still bothered me. All these feelings fueled my motivation. They made me train even harder.

The motivation was critical because Ben was delivering on his promise. To say that we took a different approach is the understatement of the century. I have never worked harder in my life. We did more of everything. There was so much to get done that I would get up extra early just to make sure I could fit it all in. Otherwise I would feel overwhelmed just looking at my programming for the day. The intensity was through the roof as well. I was trying things I couldn't have dreamed up myself. I would do whatever was assigned for the day, trusting fully that my coach knew what was best for me.

A few times a week I would look at my programming and think it was a typo. Or a bad joke. The weights seemed astronomical and the rep scheme Ben wanted me to keep within each minute seemed like science fiction. It was often like that with paces on the rower and bike, too.

After Ben reassured me that it was not a typo at all, I would let it sink in, and then I'd do it without a second thought. When I completed these seemingly impossible tasks, it was one of the best things ever. I would think, *Dang, I can do that?!*, and the bar would be raised in my mind. This is all money in the bank when I arrive at competition.

I even benefited when I came up short on these efforts. An EMOM is a workout where the tasks must be completed in a minute or less, with no rest between. Early in the year Ben assigned a twenty-minute EMOM of 18 calories on the Assault Bike and 18 GHD sit-ups. If you train with CrossFit, then just reading that might make you sick to your stomach. That was my reaction, anyway, and I thought there was no way I could pull it off. I hung in there and took it minute by minute. I eventually died, but not until I had made it way further than I thought I would. It recalibrated my mental framework again. I knew that if I was that close on my first try, then I could get there soon. I believed I could do it.

I pushed myself so hard on a few occasions that I was unsure whether I could recover. As I writhed on the floor in pain, Ben would often have to settle my fears and tell me that I was okay. It may sound crazy, but I needed to make sure that I felt that level of pain and discomfort. I tried to visit those feelings frequently.

"Uncomfortable isn't a choice in our sport, but where you experience it is," Ben would often say before asking, "Where do you want to experience it?"

I answered with my effort. I wanted to experience it here, in practice, where the stakes were low. It was a safe place to fail and learn. By throttling myself in training I become intimate with my capabilities. Then I could show up when it counts—under the lights at the Games.

I would spend the afternoons focused on recovery. Even after hours of stretching, rolling, and breathing I could still hardly pull myself together to drive home most nights. My muscles ached and cramped. I was sore all the time. At night I would fall onto my bed, exhausted. I couldn't even lift a finger. I loved it.

My progress was a testament to Ben and to Chris Hinshaw. Great coaches make you believe you can achieve things you previously thought were impossible. Both men have a gift for assessing an athlete's abilities and providing workouts that perfectly complement where they are in their progress. Having these two in my corner gave me true confidence. They made me feel like I was preparing myself as best I could. After the sessions, they wrote I would look at myself in the mirror and say, "We did everything we possibly could to be the best we can be at the CrossFit Games."

The East Regional in Albany, New York, was our first real opportunity to test my progress in 2018 against competition. The competition was one week away and we would be traveling soon. After our final day of training before we left to compete, Ben sat me down to talk.

"It's time to test this wall," he said. "Some days you may not feel your best. Some days you may not enjoy training. But you have still continued to show up. You have worked hard and given it everything you've got. Every day you have walked out of here fitter than you walked in. Every day you have laid one brick extremely well. Now we've built a solid wall, and it's time to test it out."

The last time I had competed in Albany, I was uncomfortable and battling injury. Now I was healthy and motivated. I could not wait to get on the competition floor and display the hard work I had been doing. I expected to do well, but the actual results left me at a loss for words. In order to qualify for the Games, athletes need to place in the top five at Regionals. I made history instead by winning all but one of the events and taking first place by a historic point margin. Two of my scores were the best in world. I was over the moon, and I could tell that Ben was pleased also.

More exciting than the results was how I felt throughout the weekend. When the other girls were running, I was sprinting. I was on attack the entire time; it felt like I was on another level. Performing six workouts in a weekend felt like a vacation compared to the work we had been doing in Natick.

I felt fitter than ever before. I was at an all-time high. I wanted to fly straight to the Games from Albany. I was ready for my rematch with Madison.

Before the Games, O'Keefe again invited me to dinner for a difficult conversation. He had been helping me secure a green card, and had run into some issues with the U.S. Department of Immigration. He left me a voice mail. He said it was urgent. We were on a timeline and this was kind of serious.

"Hey, Kat, call me ASAP. They said there was an issue with your birth certificate. It's weird, but I think they have you mixed up with someone else. No big deal, we will get this figured out. Just call me when you can."

O'Keefe sounded confused, but I knew exactly what was going on. I would need to shed light on a small fragment of my past in order to complete my business with the U.S. government. I felt a knot in my stomach. It's something that I don't talk about very much. But if there was anyone I could confide in, it was Matt O'Keefe. Besides, this was clearly going to extend beyond my confidants and friends if I wanted that green card.

The name on my birth certificate is Katrin Tanja Sigurgeirs-dottir.

David is my dad. But not my biological father.

My biological father was my mother's boyfriend when they were very young. Their relationship was short. My mom lived in England with her parents and only spent summers in Iceland.

Shortly after arriving home, however, she discovered that she was pregnant with me.

It was never any secret and I always knew of him. We had some contact when I was very young. Most of it was through my grandmother on that side—his mother. She loved being involved in my life and we would often send them home videos of me from London. Sadly she passed away when I was only about a year old. That kind of limited our contact. After all, he was a seventeen-year-old who had just lost his mom.

I'm still in frequent contact with his family—especially his mom's sister. She always invites me over for Christmas and other holidays. Birthday invitations are always extended as well.

He passed away when I was sixteen. I'm unclear on the details and don't really know what happened.

The funeral process was strange for me, and felt forced. My mom asked me to meet with the priest, who was trying to learn more about the person he'd be eulogizing. I didn't have much to offer at the time and it was hard for me to listen.

"You'll thank me for this later," my mom said.

She was right. I really do value the memories and stories from that experience. There was family and old friends. I felt like I got a glimpse into the person he had been. I didn't know him at all, so the stories I heard at the funeral were uplifting to me. They talked about him when he was a kid. He had platinum-blond hair and was witty and funny. He lived his life in the moment, never coveting things or time, and always eager to share with everyone.

I loved hearing what people had to say about him as a kid and as a teenager. I felt like I would have wanted to know him.

My bonds with his family are strong. Even though I only see them once or twice a year, I care for them very much. They are a really fun family. Most of the girls in the family are dancers, and it always cracks me up because they are so tiny. It makes me feel like I'm a complete Viking in comparison. They are amazing, and I feel lucky I am related to them.

My real dad, the one I've grown up calling Daddy, entered my life when I was just a few months old. He raised me and loved me. He did all the hard work of raising me and my siblings. He taught me how to interact with the world. He showed me the stars at night and taught me about the aurora borealis. I was never legally adopted, but in my heart and my mind I have always been Davidsdottir.

I don't need a piece of paper to tell me that.

EPILOGUE

KAIZEN

Failure shows us the way—by showing us what isn't the way.
—RYAN HOLIDAY, *THE OBSTACLE IS THE WAY*

I awake in another foreign bed in another foreign room. I get up, stretch, begin a general accounting of my sore body parts, then give up when I lose count. It's nothing new. This is my sixth Games. I'm accustomed to the physical assault that is the test of fitness. The similarities to last year end with my physical discomfort. This bed and hotel might be foreign to me, but I feel at home in my own skin. And my confidence is soaring. My mind belongs to me again.

I misjudged Madison on our first date. I blamed the new venue for my doubt and uncertainty. I was distressed about the move away from California, the place where I had built my career and won championships. I convinced myself that the magic of my past Games was trapped in the StubHub Center in Carson.

What a difference a year can make.

It took me until the end of last year's competition—during the 2223 Intervals event—to understand that my magic doesn't exist inside a venue. It's something I create for myself—on and off the competition floor. Through this lens, I see the same magic everywhere. I've felt it flow through friends gathered in gyms, parks, and garages, urging each other to push further than they want, then celebrating the results of their shared suffering.

The uncertainty, Ben and I realized, had come from a lack of preparation. Carson, Columbus, or Calcutta wouldn't have changed that. Preparation is my nuclear weapon. When I showed up without it last year, I felt like a superhero stripped of her powers.

Not this year.

I reinvented myself, yet again, with Ben's help. Regionals were proof. I didn't just win—I nearly swept the competition. I attacked with the ferocity I had longed for at last year's Games. I sprinted when others ran, attacked when others merely survived. My discomfort in the gym was rewarded under the lights.

As I braid my hair, a knock on the door signals Ben's arrival. Our ritual has become second nature. For the most part, things are falling into place. We're executing perfectly.

On the final day of this year's Games, I'm in it. Despite two events where I finished near the back of the pack, I've had some shining moments. I've won two events and been top five in at least four others. As usual, I don't know exactly where I'm sitting on the leaderboard, but I know I'm in the mix for the podium.

I also know enough to realize today is going to be a street fight. Getting back on the podium is going to require top finishes across the board, no matter what's thrown at me. I'm especially excited for this morning's event:

TWO-STROKE PULL
5 rounds:
300-mile run
15-calorie Assault Bike
44-foot sled pull

I see it as an opportunity to redeem my poor showing in last year's Madison Triplet. I plan to reclaim ownership of Sunday mornings at the Games.

"Stomp the gas and keep it there," announcer Sean Woodland booms over the television broadcast. "This one is all about engine!"

Sean's assessment is accurate. There's nothing fancy or strategic about this one—it's all gas, no brakes.

The 300-meter run course is virtually identical to last year's Madison Triplet.

Good, I think as I attack the first run.

I immediately establish myself as the leader in a heat of twenty women. I stay aggressive on the bike and pull like my life depends on it when I get my hands on the 153-pound sled. Afterward, I head out for the second run at a pace that borders on reckless. Annie and Brooke Wells are the only chasers I can see as I round the first corner.

I continue to extend my lead over the second and third rounds, pushing the pace on the run and bike, daring anyone to match my pace. I'm shocked to see Laura Horvath, the Hungarian rookie, appear next to me on the Assault Bike in Round 4. Laura is the new kid on the block at the Games, but I've competed against her at Regionals before. She catches me on the sled pull and rockets out of the stadium.

I try to catch her on the run but can't match her pace. When I return to the stadium, she has a 3-calorie lead on the bike. For a brief moment, I feel the urge to pull back and let her go. It's the little voice in the back of my head that plants doubt.

I glance at my forearm as I mount the Assault Bike and find motivation in the bracelet wrapped around it. This year the bracelet is white. White is a physical representation of an ethos we follow at CFNE: "Never whine, never complain, never make excuses." The reminder strengthens my resolve for one final charge. I grind on the pedals of the Assault Bike. I feel like I'm pulling with my soul. Alarm bells are sounding. I shut them down. I'm not thinking—just going.

The crowd erupts when I get off the bike first. My limbs feel like they're made of bricks, but I will myself to jog toward the sled. Laura sprints past me. I fight to stay alive, pulling my sled across the line before collapsing. I finish second in the heat and third in the event. I'm smiling inside. I didn't win, but I was proud of my effort. That was everything I had, physically and mentally.

As we debrief the event in the warm-up area, our whole team is smiling. In the midst of this physical battle, everyone is laughing and having fun. I realize we're a bunch of lunatics to love this so much. Not just the people in the room, either. There are fans camping outside the arena in tents and RVs, working out in their downtime and supporting us on the field whether we are first or last. They are completely insane, and I've never loved them more.

For my team, in particular, I'm happy we all enjoy this journey. It means everything to me that we embrace the preparation as much as the big show. I don't know what I would do without them. I am thankful I have this opportunity to do what I love most with the people I care about most. The time, effort, and love my coaches put into me every single day—along with the support that my family and friends show me throughout the whole year—is flooring. My heart wants to burst.

Next up is an event including heavy-rope double-unders and handstand walking through obstacles. I have an outstanding history with handstand walks in competition.

I cruise through the first two segments, sprinting through the slalom. I take my time up and down the stairs. The final obstacle is the trickiest: two ramps sandwiching a set of parallel bars. As I take a moment to recover, I see Kari Pearce shoot out ahead. I have competed with Kari for years at the East Regional. She's a strong gymnast and great on her hands. But her gamble doesn't pay off. She bobbles in the middle of the bars, loses her balance, and goes head over heels onto the far pad. I kick up to seize the moment and jump onto the finishing platform after successfully, albeit cautiously, navigating the bars.

I look down the line to see Brooke Wells smiling back at me! She won the event. This is unexpected. There were a few areas where I could have pushed, but that would have risked disaster. In addition to Brooke, three women from earlier heats also finished ahead of me. Still, I'm happy with my performance. I felt fresh for the big finale.

The 2018 Games' final event ushers in the return of the pegboard. How fitting. The last time pegboards were in the final event, it was also do or die.

I walk out onto the floor and can tell from my lane assignment that I'm either in third or fourth. There's no room for error.

I go unbroken on the pegboard. Last year we played it too safe, so I flirt with disaster. As soon as my feet hit the mat, I take off again up the board. I could hit the wall at any moment, but I don't. I'm prepared this year. I trust my training.

I'm third off the pegboard, behind Tia and Laura, who are already working on their thrusters. I close the gap, but they take first and second, respectively, and I cross the line third. I smile. Tia and Laura taking first and second guarantees that I've finished third overall.

Third.

Dave calls my name and I step back on the podium for the first time since being crowned champion in 2016. I high five and hug Laura and Tia as they ascend next to me.

As I stand there, Icelandic flag draped across my back, opposing emotions do battle in my head. I didn't come here for third place, and standing below two other women stings. But I feel proud. Unlike last year, this was my best effort. We walk away from this season with a heart full of incredible memories. There is no doubt that this was everything I had. I could not have been more prepared. This was the hardest I have ever worked in my entire life. I am really proud of that.

It occurs to me—not for the first time—how far I've come as an athlete and a person since that terrible day in 2014 when I sobbed on the competition floor. It also occurs to me that I never could have gotten here without that experience. Failure has been the key ingredient to my success in sports and in life. Had I not known failure, I would have continued to accept "good enough." I might be a mediocre lawyer or athlete. Instead, I'm a two-time CrossFit Games champion. Everything happens for a reason.

The community came first.

Before the Games, television shows and star athletes, there were all of you. Getting to share my journey with you is a gift, and I don't take that for granted. The amazing community built around this sport constantly inspires me. Ben founded CFNE five years before I picked up my first barbell, and the originals were practicing CrossFit before I could walk. I feel like my efforts are a representation and a tribute to the entire CrossFit community. The same way you all lift me up and support me, I find inspiration from all the people who reach out to tell me about their accomplishments I helped inspire. I find as much joy in your first pull-ups and Fran PRs as I do from standing on the podium. None of my success would be possible without the community.

Through it all, I get to inspire others to be better versions of themselves. That is the biggest blessing of all. If I learned anything from Amma, it's that every interaction is significant; it can leave a lasting impression on a person's heart.

My friend Dr. Sean Rockett is an orthopedic surgeon, a leader on the medical team at the CrossFit Games and one of CFNE's original members. Shortly after the 2017 Games, he sent me an email. The subject line simply read: "You are changing lives." Inside, I found a young lady's college essay that Sean's colleague had shared with him.

Anxiety and depression had plagued her young life. She was doing the bare minimum in all aspects of her life. She was in a bad place. After a lot of coaxing, her aunt dragged her into a CrossFit gym. She couldn't reject the enthusiasm and camaraderie of the community. Eventually she joined. She was motivated by *my* words in the documentary *Fittest on Earth* to become a better version of herself. She changed everything—not just in CrossFit, but in all aspects of her life. Her confidence soared and she was accomplishing things unimaginable to her just a few short years earlier. Sean signed the email with a note of encouragement:

> *What a story. Beautiful and congrats for being a role model to thousands of beautiful young girls and ladies who are finding their way in life. Sean*

I was moved to tears. And overwhelmed with gratitude. It's a huge privilege to be "Katrin Davidsdottir," and I will never take that lightly. It makes me want to be a better athlete. It makes me want to reach more people. I wish Amma could have seen this; it would have made her proud. Inspiring others is what I live for.

There is a Japanese word that Ben talks about sometimes. *Kaizen.* It doesn't have an English equivalent, but it translates loosely to "change for the better" or "continuous improvement." I love that. If I've learned anything from this journey, it's this: There is no destination that we can ever arrive at. There is no end point, just constant improvement. We work to become the best, and right now, it's time to get strong.

Here's to my team, which *you* are now part of! I am the luckiest girl in the world.

And we are just getting started.